Frontispiece Oliver (Richard Charles) Asking For More, Clive Donner (dir.), *Oliver Twist* (Trident Films, 1982).

Charles Dickens's
Oliver Twist

Charles Dickens's *Oliver Twist* (1837–9) is one of the most influential novels of the Victorian era. Since its publication, numerous adaptations of the novel, for both stage and screen, have ensured its continued impact in the cultural consciousness. Taking the form of a sourcebook, this guide to Dickens's novel offers:

- extensive introductory comment on the contexts, critical history, adaptations and interpretations of the text, from publication to the present
- annotated extracts from key contextual documents, reviews, critical works and the text itself
- cross-references between documents and sections of the guide, in order to suggest links between texts, contexts and criticism
- suggestions for further reading.

Part of the *Routledge Guides to Literature* series, this volume is essential reading for all those beginning detailed study of *Oliver Twist* and seeking not only a guide to the novel, but a way through the wealth of contextual and critical material that surrounds Dickens's text.

Juliet John is a Senior Lecturer in English at the University of Liverpool and Director of the Gladstone Centre for Victorian Studies in Wales and the North West of England.

Routledge Guides to Literature*

Editorial Advisory Board: Richard Bradford (University of Ulster at Coleraine), Jan Jedrzejewski (University of Ulster at Coleraine), Duncan Wu (St Catherine's College, University of Oxford)

Routledge Guides to Literature offer clear introductions to the most widely studied authors and literary texts.

Each book engages with texts, contexts and criticism, highlighting the range of critical views and contextual factors that need to be taken into consideration in advanced studies of literary works. The series encourages informed but independent readings of texts by ranging as widely as possible across the contextual and critical issues relevant to the works examined and highlighting areas of debate as well as those of critical consensus. Alongside general guides to texts and authors, the series includes 'source-books', which allow access to reprinted contextual and critical materials as well as annotated extracts of primary text.

Available in this series:

Geoffrey Chaucer by Gillian Rudd
Ben Jonson by James Loxley
William Shakespeare's The Merchant of Venice: A Sourcebook edited by S. P. Cerasano
William Shakespeare's King Lear: A Sourcebook edited by Grace Ioppolo
William Shakespeare's Othello: A Sourcebook edited by Andrew Hadfield
John Milton by Richard Bradford
John Milton's Paradise Lost: A Sourcebook edited by Margaret Kean
Alexander Pope by Paul Baines
Mary Wollstonecraft's A Vindication of the Rights of Woman: A Sourcebook edited by Adriana Craciun
Jane Austen by Robert P. Irvine
Jane Austen's Emma: A Sourcebook edited by Paula Byrne
Jane Austen's Pride and Prejudice: A Sourcebook edited by Robert Morrison
Mary Shelley's Frankenstein: A Sourcebook edited by Timothy Morton
The Poems of John Keats: A Sourcebook edited by John Strachan
Charles Dickens's David Copperfield: A Sourcebook edited by Richard J. Dunn
Charles Dickens's Bleak House: A Sourcebook edited by Janice M. Allan
Herman Melville's Moby-Dick: A Sourcebook edited by Michael J. Davey
Harriet Beecher Stowe's Uncle Tom's Cabin: A Sourcebook edited by Debra J. Rosenthal
Walt Whitman's Song of Myself: A Sourcebook and Critical Edition edited by Ezra Greenspan
Robert Browning by Stefan Hawlin
Henrik Ibsen's Hedda Gabler: A Sourcebook edited by Christopher Innes

* Some books in this series were originally published in the Routledge Literary Sourcebooks series, edited by Duncan Wu, or the Complete Critical Guide to English Literature series, edited by Richard Bradford and Jan Jedrzejewski.

Thomas Hardy by Geoffrey Harvey
Thomas Hardy's Tess of the d'Urbervilles edited by Scott McEathron
Charlotte Perkins Gilman's The Yellow Wallpaper: A Sourcebook and Critical Edition edited by Catherine J. Golden
Kate Chopin's The Awakening: A Sourcebook edited by Janet Beer and Elizabeth Nolan
D. H. Lawrence by Fiona Becket
The Poems of W. B. Yeats: A Sourcebook edited by Michael O'Neill
E. M. Forster's A Passage to India: A Sourcebook edited by Peter Childs
Samuel Beckett by David Pattie

Charles Dickens's
Oliver Twist
A Sourcebook

Edited by Juliet John

Routledge
Taylor & Francis Group

LONDON AND NEW YORK

First published 2006 by Routledge
2 Park Square, Milton Park, Abingdon, Oxon, OX14 4RN

Simultaneously published in the USA and Canada
by Routledge
711 Third Ave, New York, NY 10017

Routledge is an imprint of the Taylor & Francis Group

© 2006 Juliet John

Typeset in Sabon and Gill Sans by RefineCatch Limited, Bungay, Suffolk

British Library Cataloguing in Publication Data
A catalogue record for this book is available from the British Library

Library of Congress Cataloging-in-Publication Data
John, Juliet, 1967–
    Charles Dickens's Oliver Twist : a sourcebook / Juliet John.—1st ed.
        p. cm.—(Routledge guides to literature)
    Includes bibliographical references and index.
    ISBN 0–415–25529–5 (hardback : alk. paper)
    ISBN 0–415–25530–9 (pbk. alk. paper)
    1. Dickens, Charles, 1812–1870. Oliver Twist.   I. Title.   II. Series.
    PR4567.J64 2005
    823'.8—dc22

                                                        2005014270

Library of Congress Cataloging in Publication Data
ISBN 13: 9–78–0–415–25529–5 (hbk)
ISBN 13: 9–78–0–415–25530–1 (pbk)

To Hamish, who also asked for more

Contents

List of Illustrations   xv
Annotation and Footnotes   xvi
Acknowledgements   xvii

Introduction   1

1 : Contexts   5

Contextual Overview   7

Literary and Biographical Background   7
Social, Historical and Cultural Background   11
  The Poor Law Amendment Act   11
  Utilitarianism   13
  The Civilization of Everyday Life?   14

Chronology   19

Contemporary Documents   24

From the Poor Law Commission, *Second Annual Report*   24
From 'The Poor Law Debate', *The Annual Register, 1834*   24
From letter to Thomas Beard (17 May 1837)   27
From letter to Thomas Haines (3 June 1837)   27
From letter to Richard Bentley (16 September 1837)   28
From letter to Mrs George Hogarth (26 October 1837)   28
From letter to Richard Bentley (?early January 1838)   29
From letter to G. H. Lewes (?9 June 1838)   29
From letter to George Cruikshank (?6 October 1838)   30
From letter to John Forster (6 or 13 October 1838)   30
From letter to John Forster (21 January 1839)   31

[An Appeal to Fallen Women]. (28 October 1847)   31
From letter to Mrs [Eliza] Davis (10 July 1863)   33
From letter to Mrs [Eliza] Davis (16 November 1864)   34
From John Forster, *The Life of Charles Dickens*   34
From George Cruikshank, 'The Origin of *Oliver Twist*' (1871)   35
From Queen Victoria, *The Girlhood of Queen Victoria*   37
From Edward Bulwer Lytton, Preface (1840) to *Paul Clifford* (1830)   38
From Edward Bulwer Lytton, 'A Word to the Public' (1846)   38

2: Interpretations   41

Critical History   43

Early Critical Reception   51

From [Charles Buller], 'The Works of Dickens' (1837)   51
From [John Forster], review in the *Examiner* (1837)   52
From [G. H. Lewes?], review of *Sketches, Pickwick* and *Oliver Twist* (1837)   53
From [Thomas Henry Lister], review of *Sketches, Pickwick, Nickleby* and *Oliver Twist* (1838)   54
From anonymous review of *Oliver Twist, The Spectator* (1838)   55
From unsigned review of *Oliver Twist, Literary Gazette* (1838)   56
From William Makepeace Thackeray, 'Horæ Catnachianæ' (1839)   57
From [Richard Ford] 'Oliver Twist; or the Parish Boy's Progress' (1839)   57
From William Makepeace Thackeray, *Catherine* (1839–40)   60
From [Anonymous], 'Charles Dickens and His Works' (1840)   60
From [Anonymous], 'Literary Recipes' (1841)   61
From George Gissing, '*Oliver Twist*' (c. 1898–1900)   62

Modern Criticism   63

From G. K. Chesterton, '*Oliver Twist*' (1911)   63
From Edmund Wilson, 'Dickens: The Two Scrooges' (1941)   64
From George Orwell, 'Charles Dickens' (1946)   65
From Humphry House, 'The Macabre Dickens' (1947)   66
From Humphry House, Introduction to *The Adventures of Oliver Twist* (1949)   67
From Graham Greene, 'The Young Dickens' (1951)   67
From Harry Stone, 'Dickens and the Jews' (1959)   68
From John Bayley, '*Oliver Twist*: Things as They Really Are' (1962)   70
From Steven Marcus, 'Who is Fagin?' (1985)   71
From John Lucas, *The Melancholy Man* (1970)   72
From J. Hillis Miller, 'The Fiction of Realism' (1971)   73
From Dennis Walder, *Dickens and Religion* (1981)   75
From Helena Michie, *The Flesh Made Word* (1987)   77
From D. A. Miller, *The Novel and the Police* (1988)   77
From John O. Jordan, 'The Purloined Handkerchief' (1989)   79
From Deborah Heller, 'The Outcast as Villain and Victim' (1990)   82

From Patricia Ingham, *Dickens, Women and Language* (1992)   84
From John Bowen, *Other Dickens* (2000)   87
From Juliet John, *Dickens's Villains* (2001)   89

3: The Work in Performance   93

Introduction   95

From letter to Frederick Yates (?29 November 1838)   102
From George Almar, *Oliver Twist* (1838)   103
From John Forster, *The Life of Charles Dickens*   105
From the reading text of Dickens's 'Sikes and Nancy'   105
From pressbook, William Cowen (dir.), *Oliver Twist* (1933)   106
From pressbook, David Lean (dir.), *Oliver Twist* (1948)   107

Reviews of Screen Adaptations   108
From [Anonymous], 'Berlin Cinema Fight', *Guardian* (21 February 1949)   109
From [Anonymous], 'Baton Charge on Berlin *Oliver Twist* Objectors', *Daily Telegraph*
    (22 February 1949)   110
From Rhoda Koenig review, *Evening Standard* (7 July 1999)   111
From James Rampton, *Independent Review* (1 December 1999)   111

4: Key Passages   115

Introduction   117

Key Passages   119

The Author's Preface to the Third Edition of *Oliver Twist* (1841)   119
Preface to the Cheap Edition of *Oliver Twist* (1850)   124
The Opening   127
Oliver Asks for More   129
Oliver at Mr Sowerberry the Undertaker's; Noah Claypole   134
Oliver's First Experience of the Artful Dodger, London and Fagin and his Gang   137
Oliver 'Between Sleeping and Waking'; Oliver is Given a Lesson in Pickpocketing 143
Bill Sikes   145
Oliver, Mr Brownlow and Books; Mr Grimwig   147
Nancy Argues with Fagin   149
The Narrator on the Novel: The 'Streaky Bacon' Passage   151
Oliver's Education in the Thieves' Den   153
Oliver Reads a Book Resembling the *Newgate Calendar*   155
Mr Bumble and Mrs Corney   156
Rose Maylie   158
Blathers and Duff; Conkey Chickweed   159

A Rural Idyll; Oliver Half Asleep   161
Nancy's Interview with Rose   163
Fagin Consoles Charley Bates over the Capture of the Artful Dodger; The Trial of the
   Artful Dodger   164
Sikes's Murder of Nancy   168
The Flight of Sikes   170
The Pursuit of Sikes at Jacob's Island and his Death   173
Fagin's Trial and Fagin in the Condemned Cell   177
The Happy Ending   182

5: Further Reading   185

Recommended Editions   187
Recommended Critical Works   187
Reference Works   189

Index   190

Illustrations

Frontispiece: Oliver (Richard Charles) Asking for More, Clive Donner
(dir.), *Oliver Twist* (Trident Films, 1982).   i

Figure 1: 'Food, Glorious Food!', from Carol Reed (dir.), *Oliver!*
(Warwick-Romulus, 1968).   26

Figure 2: Alma Taylor as Nancy, in Thomas Bentley (dir.), *Oliver Twist*
(Hepworth, 1912).   88

Figure 3: Photo-strip from Frank Lloyd (dir.), *Oliver Twist* (Jackie
Coogan Productions, 1922).   94

Figure 4: Manuscript of a version of *Oliver Twist* submitted to the Lord
Chancellor in 1855.   98

Figure 5: Alec Guinness as Fagin from David Lean (dir.), *Oliver Twist*
(Cineguild, 1948).   101

Figure 6: George Cruikshank, 'Oliver Asking for More', Dickens House
Museum.   135

Figure 7: George Cruikshank, 'Oliver introduced to the Respectable Old
Gentleman', Dickens House Museum.   142

Figure 8: Fagin (Ron Moody) and Sikes (Oliver Reed) from Carol Reed
(dir.), *Oliver!* (Warwick-Romulus, 1968).   146

Figure 9: George Cruikshank, 'Fagin in the Condemned Cell', Dickens
House Museum.   181

Annotation and Footnotes

Annotation is a key feature of the sourcebooks within this series. Both the original notes from reprinted texts and new annotations by the volume editor appear at the bottom of the relevant page. The reprinted notes are prefaced by the author's name in square brackets, e.g. [Robinson's note].

Acknowledgements

I am very grateful to Duncan Wu for approaching me to edit a sourcebook, and to all the editorial staff at Routledge – Liz Thompson, Fiona Cairns, Kate Parker, Julene Knox, Polly Dodson, and Katherine Sheppard – who have shown admirable patience with me. I am grateful as ever to Alice Jenkins for suggesting me as an editor in the first place and for providing unstinting personal and academic support throughout the book's gestation. My debt to Paul Schlicke and Robert L. Patten is enormous, to their Dickensian scholarship and their Dickensian generosity. Without David Paroissien's indispensable *Companion to Oliver Twist* (Edinburgh University Press, 1992), the present volume would have been significantly weaker and longer in the making. The scholarship of Kathleen Tillotson, Philip Collins, Madeleine House, Graham Storey, and Stephen Gill has also been invaluable to me in the compilation of this volume. Janice Allan's meticulous editorial comments were conscientious above and beyond the call of duty, and she has tried to ensure that the book will be user-friendly – if it is not, the fault is all my own. Richard J. Dunn has been extremely generous in allowing me to reprint the 'Chronology' from his excellent *David Copperfield* Routledge Sourcebook. Several other colleagues and friends have helped me in various ways both personally and professionally: Paul Baines, Carson Bergstrom, Dinah Birch, John Bowen, Rachel Connor, Andrew Cooper, Philip Davis, Nicki Hitchcott, Avril Horner, Frank and Helen Maslen, Jane McMillan, Brian Maidment, David Mills, Gail Marshall and Andy Todd, Francis O'Gorman, Sue Powell, Dominic Rainsford, Susan Rowland, Jill Rudd, and Vera Tolz. The librarians at the British Film Institute and the Dickens House Museum have been particularly helpful to me, and I am also grateful to the librarians at the British Library, the John Rylands University of Manchester Library, the Sidney Jones University of Liverpool Library, the University of Salford Library, and St. Deiniol's Library, Hawarden. Completion of this book has been a team effort: without Calum, my mother Jackie, Ceri Bourne, and Sharon Goodwin, I would not be able to function at all. My father introduced me to *Oliver Twist* (in fact *Oliver!*) and my sister read Dickens before I did. My son Hamish is currently no fan of Oliver Twist and has done his best to supplant him in my affections since his arrival; in this he has succeeded. My daughter Iona has just watched her first screen adaptation of the novel and wants to know why it contains 'so many baddies who aren't good like Oliver': I hope this book provides some answers.

My contributions to this book in places draw on work already published: 'Twisting the Newgate Tale: Dickens, Popular Culture and the Politics of Genre', in *Rethinking Victorian Culture*, ed. by Alice Jenkins and Juliet John (Palgrave Macmillan, 2000), pp. 126–45; Juliet John, *Dickens's Villains: Melodrama, Character, Popular Culture* (Oxford University Press, 2001); Introduction to Juliet John (ed.), *Cult Criminals: The Newgate Novels*, 6 vols (London: Routledge, 1998), Vol. I, pp. v–lxxi.

The publisher and volume editor wish to thank the following for permission to reprint material under copyright.

Excerpts from 'Twisting the Newgate Tale', by Juliet John from *Dicken's Villains: Melodrama, Character and Popular Culture*, 2001. Reproduced by permission of Oxford University Press.

Excerpts from the introduction of *The Adventures of Oliver Twist*, 1949, Charles Dickens, edited by Humphrey House. Reproduced by permission of Oxford University Press.

Excerpts from *Other Dickens: Pickwick to Chuzzlewit*, by John Bowen, 2000. Reproduced by permission of Oxford University Press.

Excerpts from *Letters of Charles Dickens*, edited by Humphry House and Graham Storey, 1965. Reproduced by permission of Oxford University Press.

Excerpts from 'Sikes and Nancy' in *Charles Dickens: The Public Readings*, 1975, edited by Philip Collins. Reproduced by permission of Oxford University Press.

Excerpts from CRITICISMS AND APPRECIATIONS OF THE WORKS OF CHARLES DICKENS by G. K. Chesterton. Reproduced by permission of A. P. Watt Ltd on behalf of The Royal Literary Fund.

Excerpt from THE WOUND AND THE BOW by Edmund Wilson. Copyright © 1978 by Edmund Wilson. Reprinted by permission of Farrar, Straus and Giroux, LLC.

Excerpts from 'Charles Dickens' in DICKENS, DALI & OTHERS: STUDIES IN POPULAR CULTURE by George Orwell. Copyright © 1946 by the Estate of Sonia B. Orwell. Reprinted by permission of Harcourt, Inc.

Excerpts from *Charles Dickens* by George Orwell (Copyright © George Orwell, 1940). Reproduced by permission of Bill Hamilton as Literary Executor of the Estate of the Late Sonia Brownwell Orwell, Martin Secker & Warburg Ltd.

Excerpt from THE LOST CHILDHOOD AND OTHER ESSAYS by Graham Greene. Reproduced by permission of David Higham Associates.

Excerpts from Harry Stone 'Dickens and the Jews', in *Victorian Studies* 2(3) 1959, Indiana University Press. Reproduced by permission of the publisher.

Excerpts from by John Bayley, 'Oliver Twist: Things as they really are', in John Gross and Gabriel Pearson eds *Dickens and the Twentieth Century*, 1962, Routledge & Kegan Paul. Reproduced by permission of the publisher.

Excerpts from John Lucas, *The Melancholy Man: A Study of Dickens's Novels*, 1970 (current edition Harvester Press, 1980). Reproduced by kind permission of the author.

From J. Hillis Miller, 'The Fiction of Realism: *Sketches by Boz, Oliver Twist*, and Cruikshank's Illustrations', in *Dickens Centennial Essays*, Ada Nisbet and Blake Nevius, eds. Copyright © 1971 The Regents of the University of California. Reproduced by permission of the University of California Press.

Excerpt from Dennis Walder, *Dickens and Religion*, Allen and Unwin, 1981. Reproduced by kind permission of the author.

From THE FLESH MADE WORD: FEMALE FIGURES AND WOMEN'S BODIES by Helena Michie. Copyright © 1990 by Oxford University Press, Inc. Used by permission of Oxford University Press, Inc. and the author.

Excerpts from D. A. Miller, *The Novel and the Police*, University of California Press. Copyright © 1988 The Regents of the University of California. Reproduced by permission of the publisher.

Excerpts from John O. Jordan, 'The Purloined Handkerchief', *Dickens Studies Annual*, 18 (1989). Reproduced by permission of AMS Press, Inc.

Excerpts from Deborah Heller, 'The Outcast as Villain and Victim: Jews in Dickens's *Oliver Twist* and *Our Mutual Friend*', in *Jewish Presences in English Literature*, Derek Cohen and Deborah Heller eds, McGill-Queen's University Press, 1990. Reproduced by permission of the publisher.

Excerpts from Patricia Ingham, *Dickens, Women and Language*, 1992. Reproduced by permission of University of Toronto Press and Pearson Education Ltd.

Excerpts from [Anon.], 'Berlin Cinema Fight', *Guardian* (21 February 1949). Copyright © The Guardian. Reproduced with permission.

Excerpts from [Anon.], 'Baton Charge on Berlin *Oliver Twist* Objectors', *Daily Telegraph* (22 February 1949) © Telegraph Group Limited 1949. Reproduced with permission.

Excerpts from Rhoda Koenig on political correctness and Bleasdale's *Oliver Twist* (1999), *Evening Standard* (7 July 1999), p. 13. Reproduced by permission of the Evening Standard.

Excerpts from James Rampton, 'Keep your nose out of it', *Independent Review* (1 December 1999), Copyright © 1999 The Independent. Reproduced by permission.

Figures 1, 2, 5, 8 and Frontispiece provided by The British Film Institute.
Figures 3, 6, 7 and 9 provided by The Dickens House Museum.
Figure 4 courtesy of The British Library.

Every effort has been made to trace and contact copyright holders. The publishers would be pleased to hear from any copyright holders not acknowledged here, so that this acknowledgement page may be amended at the earliest opportunity.

Introduction

'Please, sir, I want some more.' Oliver Twist's simple request for more food must be one of the most well known of all literary quotations in the English language. Orphan Oliver's words, like his story, have assumed a cultural significance far greater than a writer of even Dickens's self-confidence can have foreseen. The very bareness of Oliver's demand for more (is it a request or a demand?) has ironically seemed to invite interpretation and re-interpretation. This is not just a boy stating that he wants more food. To many, it is a symbolic moment, symbolic of rebellion, aspiration, entrepreneurship, democracy, capitalism, the quest for identity, desire, appetite – or all of the aforementioned. There is no denying that Oliver's stated desire for more is of a piece with some of the dominant ideological myths of the past two centuries, in Western culture at least. Oliver asks for more and he eventually gets more – he presages the American dream.

But the symbolic implications of Dickens's original text are perhaps less familiar to many than the songs of Lionel Bart's musical, *Oliver!* (1960), or the words and images of other theatrical adaptations. Many students of Dickens's novel find themselves in the strange situation of believing that they know the novel when in fact they have never read it. Apart from *A Christmas Carol* (1843), *Oliver Twist* (1837–9) is the most frequently adapted of Dickens's works. Indeed, Dickens's favourite and most spectacular public reading of his own works was the violent murder of Nancy by Sikes, which he insisted on performing despite the adverse effects his doctor observed it to have on his health. Stage adaptations began before the original tale had concluded; when Dickens attended George Almar's 1838 adaptation (see **pp. 103–5**), he threw himself on the floor rather than suffer its indignities. The early American film industry loved Oliver, silent-movie makers exploiting the visual symbolism of the novel as well as the commercial spin-offs that could be associated with Oliver asking for more. In 1948, David Lean's classic adaptation of the novel caused violent riots for days on end on its release in Berlin, from Jewish protestors objecting to its alleged anti-Semitism. The film was banned for a period from cinemas in the USA and withdrawn in Germany. The disturbing undercurrents of both Lean's adaptation and Dickens's text come as quite a surprise to students weaned on the carnivalesque levity of Lionel Bart's musical.

Oliver Twist is a novel that has become, in Paul Davis's phrase, a 'culture-text' – a literary text whose impact on the cultural consciousness goes beyond the literary.[1] Its cultural prominence arguably owes as much to mass dissemination via theatrical and screen adaptations as it does to the power of the original novel, though the two are no doubt related. Indeed, the idea that *Oliver Twist* ever existed as a separate literary entity or 'original novel' is itself highly problematic. Dickens's 'novel' started as a series rather than a novel at a time when novels were not categorized by reviewers as 'Literature'. *Oliver Twist* was not originally a discrete text and it would have been read alongside other articles, stories and adverts in the magazine in which it first appeared, *Bentley's Miscellany*. It was also 'extracted' in newspapers as soon as it was published, without Dickens receiving a penny. For many modern readers, screen culture is as much a reality as the journalistic and theatrical context was to the readers of Dickens's day. *Oliver Twist* always has been, and always will be, an illegitimate text of mixed and impure origins. Thus, while this sourcebook is aimed at readers studying Dickens's 'novel', prioritizing an appreciation of 'the text' in its own right, it also encourages reflection on the larger cultural life of the text and on the processes that occur in the making of a popular classic.

Any talk of 'the text' is as problematic as talk of 'the novel', as a brief textual history will confirm. The first edition of the story in book form was published in November 1838 in three volumes, before the serial had run its course in *Bentley's Miscellany*. This edition revised material from the serialized version. The novel was further revised by Dickens in 1846, 1850, 1858, and 1867; the passages included in this volume are taken from the 1846 edition, which forms the basis of the definitive Clarendon edition of the novel. Dickens wrote three Prefaces to the novel, the first and most interesting in 1841, the second in 1850 and the third – an amended version of the first Preface – in 1867. *Oliver Twist* was the only Dickens novel illustrated by George Cruikshank, and the relationship between the text and the illustrations in *Oliver Twist* has been the subject of speculation ever since Cruikshank, Dickens's more established illustrator, claimed that Oliver's story had been his idea and not Dickens's (see **pp. 24–39**). For a detailed publishing history and a meticulous account of the changes Dickens made in different editions, Kathleen Tillotson's 1966 Clarendon Press edition of the novel is the authoritative text. The most memorable changes made by Dickens are perhaps in the 1867 version where, in response to charges of anti-Semitism, Dickens changed many of the original references to 'the Jew' to 'Fagin' (see **pp. 33–4** and Stone and Heller, **pp. 68–70, 82–4**). But the most significant point to be gleaned from the history of the disseminaton of *Oliver Twist* is arguably less about detail than about overview: if the history of *Oliver Twist* is examined, then it problematizes any purist idea that literature functions in a privileged and separate space.

This sourcebook is designed to aid further understanding of the written text and of the importance of various contexts in shaping different readings of *Oliver Twist*. The 'Contexts' section includes an Introduction to relevant socio-historical, literary, cultural and biographical factors that influenced the life of the novel in the nineteenth century. This is followed by a Chronology, which situates Dickens's life and career in the context of larger developments in the period. The

---

1   Paul Davis on *A Christmas Carol*, in *The Lives and Times of Ebenezer Scrooge* (New Haven, Conn.: Yale University Press, 1990).

main feature of the 'Contexts' section, however, is the selection of extracts from nineteenth-century writings on, or relevant to, the novel. The 'Interpretations' section combines an outline of the critical history of the novel with extracts from early reviews as well as many brief extracts from a wide variety of modern critics. Extracting is no substitute for reading the original, however, and the sourcebook is designed to point students to critical works in their entirety – to both works sampled here and to those highlighted in bibliographies.

The 'Work in Performance' section contains an original essay (**pp. 95–102**) on the rich performance history of *Oliver Twist*, asking why the novel has been so widely adapted and what the notion of a 'culture-text' tells us about the relationship between literature and popular culture. The extracts reproduced in this section vary from nineteenth-century adaptations and Dickens's own readings, to stills, advertising and pressbook material from screen adaptations throughout the twentieth century. This section matters, even if readers are not primarily interested in adaptations: the passions roused show the union between text and performance at its best, troubling and exciting audiences as Dickens's text did on first publication. The issues raised so heatedly give us a fresh sense of what is at stake in the novel and to whom. The 'Key Passages' section (**pp. 115–83**) contains annotated key passages from the novel prefaced by introductory headnotes. Headnotes are not designed to confine readers to a particular reading but to offer explanation along with suggested links with the critical ideas and arguments put forward elsewhere in the sourcebook. This section, like the 'Further Reading' list (**pp. 185–9**), aims to stimulate the student's own interpretations of the extracts included here and of the novel in its entirety.

1

Contexts

Contextual Overview

Literary and Biographical Background

In retrospect, *Oliver Twist* could be remembered as the first Victorian novel. Though its first appearance in print in 1837 coincided with the year of Queen Victoria's accession to the throne, Oliver's entrance was significantly more muddled than that of the young queen. When *Oliver Twist* first appeared in print, Dickens was fulfilling an obligation to his publisher to supply 'an original article' each month for the new journal which he was also to edit, *Bentley's Miscellany*. *Oliver Twist* was not first contracted as a novel: Dickens's first 'original article' for the *Miscellany* was a farcical tale, 'The Public Life of Mr Tulrumble, Once Mayor of Mudfog'. When Dickens started Oliver's tale, in the next issue of the journal, Mudfog was its setting – but this connection to his first article for *Bentley's* was soon dropped and did not appear when *Oliver Twist* appeared in book form (see **pp. 127–8**).

The serial publication of *Oliver Twist* between 1837 and 1839 was fraught with conflict: Dickens fell out with his publisher, relations with his illustrator were at times strained, and he was intensely, perhaps excessively, affected by the death of his sister-in-law, Mary Hogarth (see **pp. 27–9**). At the root of all this conflict was Dickens's changing idea of himself. His rise to prominence as a literary colossus must be one of the most remarkable and surprising in literary history. When Dickens was born in 1812, his father was a clerk in the Royal Navy Pay Office. His family moved house often, disrupting the children's education until 1824 when, at the age of twelve, Dickens was sent to work full-time in a blacking factory.[1] His father had been arrested for debt and his family lived in the prison (the imprisonment of debtors was the norm at this time, though families were not themselves prisoners). Dickens became a lodger with family friends and worked long days for poor money at the factory – an experience that was to affect him deeply (see Wilson, House and Marcus, **pp. 64–7, 71–2**). He was particularly sensitive about the humiliating loss of social status that factory labour implied and the lack of concern for his education, which he imputed to his parents,

---

1   A factory that manufactured blacking, which was used to clean boots and shoes (shoe polish); sometimes lead blacking was used to clean stoves.

particularly his mother. Though his family was released from jail the same year under the Insolvent Debtors' Act, and Dickens had returned to school the following year, by the age of fifteen, he had left school to become a clerk at a solicitors' firm. By the time Dickens began *Oliver Twist* ten years later, he had become – at the age of twenty-five – a literary sensation.

His celebrity resulted from the phenomenal success of his first 'novel' – also conceived as a serial – *The Pickwick Papers*. Published monthly from 1836 to 1837, *The Pickwick Papers* catapulted Dickens to fame. 'He has risen like a rocket', as Abraham Hayward put it in the *Quarterly Review*.[2] Meteoric as his rise to fame had been, however, it was not necessarily expected to last – he would, in Howard's words, 'come down like the stick'[3]. Considering his background, however, Dickens had shown considerable force of personality and some talent to establish a successful journalistic career by his mid-twenties. He had learned shorthand to become a freelance legal reporter in his late teens, shifting to parliamentary reporting for the *Mirror of Parliament* and then the *Sun*. By the time he met his wife in 1834, he had moved to the *Morning Chronicle* and the first of the creative sketches that were to become *Sketches by Boz* had been published. When he began work on the *Pickwick Papers*, however, he was not established enough to be the first-choice author for its publishers, Chapman and Hall, yet Dickens ensured that *Pickwick* became, in Paul Schlicke's words, 'the publishing sensation of the century'.[4]

When Dickens began *Oliver Twist* in 1837, he was famous but comparatively unestablished. It was this uncertain status that contributed greatly to tension between himself and both his publisher, Richard Bentley, and his more established illustrator, George Cruikshank. Dickens was still writing *The Pickwick Papers* when he started *Oliver Twist*, yet flushed with the inexperience of first success, he had heavily committed himself to an implausible number of other ventures, including a three-volume novel for the publisher John Macrone and two more novels of equal length for Bentley. From the start then, he was over-confident and over-burdened, and before long, Dickens was venting his feelings of frustration at his workload and lack of control over his situation at his publisher, Richard Bentley (see **pp. 28–31**). There were several issues that contributed to the falling out between Dickens and his publisher. One was Dickens's discovery, in May 1838, that Bentley was docking his pay whenever he wrote fewer pages of *Oliver Twist* than his contract stipulated. Previously, Bentley had objected to Dickens's suggestion that the serialized *Oliver* count as one of the two novels he owed him, on the grounds that this would mean that Dickens would be paid twice for the same work. Dickens understandably felt that his value had risen since the initial contract was agreed, but legally, Bentley was in the right. Dickens's resentment at what he felt was Bentley's exploitation of his talent simmered very near the surface until he eventually resigned as editor of *Bentley's Miscellany* in

2   [Abraham Hayward?], review of *Pickwick Papers*, Nos. I–VII, and *Sketches by Boz*, *Quarterly Review*, 59 (October 1837), pp. 484–518 (p. 518).
3   ibid.
4   Paul Schlicke (ed.), *The Oxford Reader's Companion to Dickens* (Oxford: Oxford University Press, 1999), p. 451.

January 1839 (see **p. 31**), despite a new agreement having been signed between the two men.

The rights and wrongs of Dickens's relationship with Bentley are complex, as Robert Patten makes clear in his definitive study, *Charles Dickens and his Publishers*.[5] Limitations on space mean that only two of Dickens's letters on the topic are reproduced here, his threat to resign from the editorship of the *Miscellany* (**p. 28**) and his letter to Forster (**p. 31**) on his actual resignation. However, both letters make clear the fundamental issues for Dickens: the relative status, authority and monetary worth of the artist in relation to the publisher. Dickens deserves more money and autonomy, in his view, because of his popularity and fame. Dickens's ego is clearly alive and well here, but there is also something far more important evident in his power battle with his publisher. By using fame and popularity as his main criteria for establishing the 'worth' of the author, Dickens is redefining authorship and artistry in a modern world. Moving away from the Romantic idea of the artist as 'unacknowledged legislator of the world' (Percy Bysshe Shelley, in *A Defence of Poetry* (1821; 1840)), Dickens argues that material wealth and contractual power should be the lot of the author whose worth is judged not by a small circle of intellectual peers but by the public. The author to Dickens is not only a creative artist but also a businessman and an entrepreneur in a literary marketplace; the publisher is an exploitative disseminator.

Dickens's redefinition of the role and worth of the artist did not extend equally to his valuation of collaborations with visual artists, including the illustrator of *Oliver Twist*, George Cruikshank. Cruikshank was famous in his own right when the two began *Oliver Twist*, yet Dickens adopted the role of the senior partner in their relationship. Like Dickens, Cruikshank employed caricature, techniques from the popular theatre and social satire in the tradition of the eighteenth-century artist, William Hogarth (1697–1764). Whereas Dickens was initially employed on *Pickwick* to supply text to accompany Robert Seymour's illustrations, Cruikshank was employed by Bentley to provide a plate (illustration) for each number of the *Miscellany*. Dickens soon decided (perhaps a little patronisingly) that *Oliver Twist* would 'bring Cruikshank out' and pledged to supply a copy of his text by the fifth of each month.[6] Dickens was often extremely late with text, however, forcing Cruikshank to produce some illustrations before he had received the text. This cannot have simplified working relations between the two men, yet Cruikshank supplied twenty-four plates for the novel and acted as a go-between in the dispute between Dickens and Bentley, apparently trusted by both. There was no serious falling out between Dickens and Cruikshank at the time of the novel's publication, though Dickens may have irritated Cruikshank by disliking (according to Forster's note to Bentley) six of the plates for the last volume.[7] Forster must have exaggerated because only the intended final plate, *Rose Maylie and Oliver* (the 'Fireside' plate) was withdrawn. Though there was no open rift

5   Robert Patten, *Charles Dickens and his Publishers* (Oxford: Clarendon Press, 1978).
6   Letter to Richard Bentley [?18 January 1837], in *The Letters of Charles Dickens*, Pilgrim edn, edited by Madeleine House and Graham Storey, 12 vols (Oxford: Oxford University Press), Vol. I, pp. 223–4 (p. 224).
7   Charles Dickens, *Oliver Twist*, edited by Kathleen Tillotson, Clarendon edn (Oxford: Clarendon Press, 1966), p. 393.

between the men, Cruikshank may have been surprised by Dickens's determination to impose his own will and vision. In Stephen Gill's words: 'An artist of Cruikshank's stature did not expect to be enslaved to the words; Dickens, though still a novice, did not expect to be upstaged by images.'[8] The two did not work together again.

There is, however, critical consensus that the words and images in *Oliver Twist* function interdependently. Henry James was surely right when he wrote of the inescapable power of Cruikshank's images to fix characters and ideas in the mind.[9] There is critical disagreement, however, about the relative roles of Dickens and Cruikshank in the conception of *Oliver Twist*. Controversy was sparked by Cruikshank retrospectively when he claimed first to a journalist (1847) and then in a letter to *The Times* and an essay published after Dickens's death that, 'I am the originator of *Oliver Twist*, and that all the principal characters are mine' (see **p. 35**). For many years, critics followed the line taken by Kathleen Tillotson that this claim was 'preposterous',[10] but subsequently material has been discovered that confirms that Cruikshank had conceived of a series about the life of a London thief years before *Oliver Twist*, and that he may have influenced the plot's focus on London low life, the interest in the scandal of baby-farming and the creation of Fagin.[11]

What makes it particularly difficult to establish a clear sense of the origins of *Oliver Twist* is, first, that Dickens wrote notoriously little about his own methods of composition – as he goaded G. H. Lewes, 'Draw your own conclusion and hug the theory closely' (see **p. 29**) – and, second, that when Dickens did write about himself and his writing, his accounts could smack of the fictional. In her Introduction to the Clarendon edition of the novel, Kathleen Tillotson claims that Dickens had conceived of *Oliver Twist* as early as 1833, but in an influential essay, 'The Text and Plan of Oliver Twist',[12] Burton M. Wheeler argues that it began as a short serial, only becoming a novel in Dickens's mind four instalments later; the plot, according to Wheeler, did not take shape 'even in general form' until seven instalments had been published. The truth, it seems, is somewhere in between.

Biographical accounts of the novel's origins have been extremely prominent in Dickens studies. Influenced by Edmund Wilson's essay, 'Dickens: The Two Scrooges',[13] Humphry House's Introduction to the (New) Illustrated edition of the novel and his essay, 'The Macabre Dickens' argues that 'the intimate understanding of morbid and near-morbid psychology' revealed in novels like *Oliver Twist* originated from the feelings of alienation and unhappiness Dickens

8 'Appendix 1: Dickens and Cruikshank', in Stephen Gill (ed.), *Oliver Twist*, World's Classics (Oxford: Oxford University Press, 1999), p. 443.
9 *A Small Boy and Others* (New York: Macmillan, 1913), pp. 125–6, 322.
10 Dickens, Clarendon, *Oliver Twist*, p. 394.
11 Richard A. Vogler, 'Cruikshank and Dickens: A Reassessment of the Role of the Artist and the Author', in *George Cruikshank: A Revaluation*, edited by Robert L. Patten (Princeton, NJ: Princeton University Press, 1974), pp. 61–91. See **pp. 000–0**, 'Oliver Asks for More', n. 3, for an explanation of baby-farming.
12 Burton M. Wheeler, 'The Text and Plan of *Oliver Twist*', *Dickens Studies Annual*, 12 (1983), pp. 41–61.
13 Edmund Wilson, 'Dickens: The Two Scrooges', in *The Wound and the Bow: Seven Studies in Literature* (New York: Oxford University Press, 1965), pp. 51–2. See **pp. 64–5**.

experienced in the blacking factory (see **p. 66**). Such theories are interesting but problematic, not least because they read Dickens's own version of his life too uncritically. The fact that Dickens revealed his past only to Forster and only when he was fully established creatively, socially and financially shows the degree of control – today we may say 'spin' – that Dickens was capable of. A certain mythologizing, for example, begun by Dickens and perpetuated by his critics, has gathered around Dickens's response to the death of his sister-in-law, Mary Hogarth, during the writing of *Oliver Twist*. There is no doubt that Dickens was sincerely devastated by Mary's death; he was uncharacteristically unable to write and interrupted the serialisation of *Oliver Twist* the month after her death on 7 May 1837. He wore her ring for the rest of his life (see **pp. 28–9**), dreamt of her night after night, kept her clothes, a lock of her hair, and wanted to be buried with her. His obsession with Mary informed the character of Rose Maylie in *Oliver Twist* and a string of other idealized (young) female characters in subsequent novels. Even his memory of Mary was not free from the fictionalizing that was second nature to him. The two letters about the death of Mary included in this volume (**pp. 27–9**), for example, are just two of many Dickens wrote on the subject and it is notable, if the letters are analysed closely, that they become steadily more dramatic as time goes on, reminding us that Dickensian truth is often a hybrid of the factual and the fictional.

What we do know is that when Dickens started writing *Oliver Twist*, he was a jobbing author, novels were not considered 'Literature', and 'Literature' was for the elite. By the end of the 1830s, this, like so much else in Victorian Britain, was clearly changing.

Social, Historical and Cultural Background

The Poor Law Amendment Act

Dickens uses *Oliver Twist* to protest against the 'Poor Law' and the workhouse system. His satire on the system for poor relief is bold enough to be intelligible on its own terms, but the nuances and repercussions of Dickens's critique can be more fully appreciated with some knowledge of its topical concerns (see also **pp. 127–35**). Though accounts of the Poor Law debate are available in most self-respecting modern editions of the novel, not all of these accounts are as precise as they might be, perhaps assuming too much knowledge in students new to the period. My summary is necessarily a collage of the work of others, and I am particularly indebted to the informative summaries in Stephen Gill's 1999 Appendix and Kathleen Tillotson's 1982 Introduction to Oxford World's Classics editions of the novel, as well as to Peter Fairclough's Appendix to the Penguin Classics edition of *Oliver Twist* (Harmondsworth: Penguin, 1966).

The Poor Law Amendment Act was passed in 1834 and this 'New Poor Law' brought into effect widespread changes to the way in which poor people were treated. However, before we can properly understand the New Poor Law and the controversy it provoked, it is helpful to have a sense of the old system that it replaced. According to Gill, the main features of English Poor Law policy before 1834 date back to the reign of Elizabeth I (1533–1603), when it became the duty of each parish to appoint overseers responsible for relieving the needy: the poor, sick and destitute.[14] (The 'parish' was the term given to the unit of local government). Funds for the poor were raised by a rate levied on property, and these were distributed to the needy who could reside either in workhouses or in their own homes; the latter was known as 'outdoor relief'. This system basically remained in force until 1782, when a new law allowed parishes to merge into larger units (called 'Unions') in order to provide larger and more economically efficient workhouses. Three years later, magistrates in Speenhamland in Berkshire decided to link relief – or benefits, as we say now – to the price of bread and to supplement wages accordingly, a measure that was widely adopted. This benevolent allowance system, whereby labourers' wages were topped up to subsistence levels by money from the Poor Rate, was obviously expensive for parishes and could act as a disincentive to employers from paying decent wages. The question of who was entitled to relief was also, as it is today, a vexed one, and parishes did not want to pay out more than they had to, commonly moving on those they did not want to support. After the end of the Napoleonic wars in 1815, a number of developments – increasing deprivation in agricultural areas, social unrest, a population increase, and the spiralling cost of poor relief – made reform of the Poor Law essential.

The main aim of the Poor Law Amendment Act was to make dependence on poor relief so unattractive an option that those who could would be forced to earn their own keep. The Act implemented the principles of a Commission established in 1832 to examine the current situation. Its report had two main principles: the first was the 'workhouse test' for the able-bodied pauper, which proposed that if genuinely destitute, the pauper should enter the workhouse and work there for the parish. He was found not genuinely destitute if for any reason he declined to enter the workhouse. The second principle was that of 'less eligibility', a shorthand phrase that meant that conditions in the workhouse should be made less 'eligible' or attractive than those of the 'independent labourer', however needy. The 1834 New Poor Law also meant that the poor-relief system became – at least in theory – centralized and consistent. Poor Law Commissioners in London headed a pyramid organization; under them worked first Assistant Commissioners and then elected Boards of Guardians in Unions of parishes. The Commissioners issued guidance to local Boards on everything and gave progress reports to parliament. Even details such as diet were centrally prescribed: in recommendations issued by the Poor Law Commissioners in 1836, gruel and bread are standard, there is no fruit, and very little meat, vegetables or fat.[15] See the 'Dietry for Able-Bodied Men and Women' issued by the Poor Law Commission (**p. 25**).

Apart from the inadequate diet, the Act imposed other punitive measures. Most controversially, married couples were separated on entering the workhouse. Astonishingly, women were held solely responsible for the care of illegitimate children (see the *Annual Register* extract, **p. 24**), in an attempt to discourage promiscuity and over-population for which women were primarily blamed.

---

14 Dickens, Oxford World Classics, *Oliver Twist*, p. 451.
15 David Paroissien, *The Companion to Oliver Twist* (Edinburgh: Edinburgh University Press, 1992), pp. 298–303.

How they produced children without some promiscuity on the part of men was obviously a moot point. It is also difficult to understand the rationale behind freeing men from any responsibility for their offspring and entrusting women alone with the financial upkeep of children they also had to rear alone. From a modern perspective, the Law seems not only harsh but deeply gendered, condemning women who could not work and raise a child simultaneously to workhouse life for themselves and their children. Inside the workhouse, there was little chance of exercise and the work undertaken was unremitting and degrading. Under such conditions, ill health was obviously rife, and as Dickens mentions in passing (see **p. 128, n. 2**), medical arrangements were inadequate (doctors were cheap rather than good). Discipline was strict, there was no privacy and paupers were not permitted to worship in a public church. The Act stigmatized poverty.

Utilitarianism

Dickens's objections to the punitive operations of the New Poor Law are writ large in *Oliver Twist*. What may be less obvious to the student reading the novel for the first time, however, is that Dickens's critique of the Act and its consequences is informed by a philosophical and theoretical opposition to its grounds, as well as by a human concern for those it victimized. The architects of the 1834 Poor Law Amendment Act were the authors of the original Royal Commission report: Nassau Senior, the political economist, and Edwin Chadwick, friend and disciple of Jeremy Bentham, the founding father of the social theory of Utilitarianism. Utilitarianism has become associated with the social theory that 'the greatest happiness of the greatest number' of people should prevail. The 1834 Amendment Act was steeped in its teachings, as well as in those of the political economist Thomas Malthus, whose *Essay on the Principle of Population* (1798; rev. edn. 1803) posited that population growth necessarily tends to exceed the means of existence. Dickens despised political economy in general and Utilitarianism in particular: in his view, both reduced people to statistics, taking no account of feelings, imagination, creativity, or individuality. He particularly loathed the denial of altruism and goodness that underpinned the Benthamite assumption that self-interest underlies human behaviour. He did not value Utilitarian faith in human reason; according to Utilitarian theory, reason would lead people to appreciate that it was in their interests to do the right thing as surely as, from Dickens's standpoint, good would come from instinct and natural benevolence. Dickens's most famous and thoroughgoing attack on Utilitarianism comes in *Hard Times* (1854), but *Oliver Twist* is steeped in anti-Utilitarian feeling.

In *Oliver Twist*, Dickens simplifies the actual organisation of poor relief, combining into one body the Central Board of Commissioners with the local Board of Guardians; he calls these composite representatives of the system 'philosophers' in a dig at Utilitarianism, obvious only if the reader knows the context. Likewise, those who openly flaunt the philosophy of self-interest are the criminal Fagin and his gang who believe in looking after 'number one' and those such as the beadle Mr Bumble, entrusted with upholding a system designed for the social good. Oliver's goodness, like that of the Maylie circle and indeed Nancy – the 'soul of goodness in things evil'[16] – acts as a riposte to Utilitarian philosophy, just as the philosophical context enlivens the famously one-dimensional goodness of *Oliver Twist*.

Dickens has been accused of unfairness and a lack of understanding of the Poor Laws and the ideas informing them (see, for example, early reviews in the *Examiner* and *Quarterly Review*, pp. 52, 57–60). The latter judgement almost certainly underestimates Dickens's familiarity with utilitarian ideas; the *Morning Chronicle* and the *True Sun*, for which Dickens wrote as a journalist, both had radical and Utilitarian sympathies. There are inconsistencies in his satire on poor relief: the practice of baby-farming,[17] the parish apprentice scheme and the settlement dispute, among other aspects. Kathleen Tillotson defends Dickens against charges of historical inaccuracy by arguing that the New Poor Law was not as uniformly applied as its architects had intended it to be.[18] Though this is no doubt true, it is also true that Dickens is not known for his respect for historical fact, as his historical novels *Barnaby Rudge* (1841) and *A Tale of Two Cities* (1859) make plain. 'Facts' were always less important to an anti-Utilitarian such as Dickens than were spirit and feeling. It was the perceived lack of spirit and feeling that bothered Dickens about the New Poor Law (see 'The Opening', **p. 127**, and 'Oliver Asks for More', **p. 129**).

The Civilization of Everyday Life?

Robin Gilmour has argued that: 'The civilisation of everyday life was a Victorian achievement as remarkable and far-reaching as the democratic and industrial developments of the period.'[19] The 1830s was crucial in this process. It was a period of intense social reform, which appeared to be a dramatic step forward to the Britain that we know today. The Poor Law Amendment Act was just one piece of legislation that seemed to its authors, if not to everybody, to make Britain a fairer, more regulated and better place. Of all the new Bills, the Great Reform Act of 1832 must surely be the most important and fiercely contested Act passed that century, signalling as it did the symbolic beginning of a democratic society. It widened the political franchise by extending the right to vote to include the rich middle classes, as well as by redistributing members of parliament to correspond with the great centres of population. The Bill was symbolic of drastic changes underway and to come: by the end of the century, all males over twenty-one years of age had the right to vote. Obviously, the widening of the political franchise, along with the radical social changes wrought by industrialization and urbanization, meant a complete change in the power structure of British society. Though it may seem difficult now to see the link between the Reform Bill and the New Poor Law, the Poor Law also aimed to promote independence and self-reliance through the imposition of measures that were the same for all those affected. Both Acts,

---

16 This descriptive headline was added to the last section of Chapter 16 in 1867, when Nancy confronts Fagin shortly after recapturing him.
17 Paroissien, *Companion*, p. 41.
18 Dickens, Clarendon, *Oliver Twist*, p. ix.
19 Robin Gilmour, *The Victorian Period: The Intellectual and Cultural Context of English Literature, 1830–1890* (London: Longman, 1993), p. 9.

like the Factory Act of 1833 and the Municipal Reform Act of 1835, aimed to civilize the lives of ordinary people. When Lord Melbourne voiced his objections to the 'low' subject matter of *Oliver Twist* to Queen Victoria (see **pp. 37–8**) he was objecting to the democratizing current of the period.

Dramatic changes in the legal system appeared in keeping with the new spirit of the age: Robert Peel's Acts (1827, 1828 and 1830), as well as his establishment of the Metropolitan Police in 1829, helped to shift the law away from the use of violence as a central weapon.[20] Lord Grey's government, which came to power in November 1830, effected dramatic, visible change in the legal system, and by 1841, there were only eight offences still punishable by death (as opposed to around 200); in actuality executions were only being carried out for murder. Prison replaced hanging as the main instrument of discipline. It would be wrong to assume, however, that these 'civilizing' measures led to an immediate reduction in crime. The collection of national crime statistics for England and Wales, began in 1810 and improved in the 1830s, tells us that for the first half of the nineteenth century, crime increased. The figures for theft show a significant increase, though they also suggest that most theft was petty, involving theft of clothing from washing lines, for example, or property such as crockery from landlords; most stolen property was sold or pawned. Violent crime, like the murder of Nancy, usually involved people who knew each other; the novel's bungled burglary involving firearms would have been more uncommon.

Dickens was fascinated by crime and, in addition to his daily walks around the streets of London, he explored the slums in company with police officers. His novels thus pick up on contemporary anxieties about crime, and *Oliver Twist* is no exception. Fagin is thought to have been based on the notorious East End receiver of stolen goods Ikey Solomons, who was transported to Van Dieman's Land in 1827. In the second quarter of the century, there were many stories, Solomons's apart, about 'kidsmen' training children in the 'work' of pickpocketing in return for board and lodging. Juvenile crime was perceived as a problem and *Oliver Twist*, like other 'Newgate' novels, is acutely aware of this (see John, **pp. 89–91**). Though crime was largely perceived to be a masculine activity, prostitution was rife. Many prostitutes, like Nancy, began to exchange sex for money as children forced to survive without an income on the city streets.

Like other contemporary commentators, Dickens saw the city and poverty as the seeds of crime. Dickens is one of the great writers on the city, at the same time stimulated and disturbed by the extremes of life created by the rapid urbanization of the nineteenth century. (In 1812, the year of Dickens's birth, the population of London was nearly a million; by the time of his death in 1870, it was 3,200,000.) In his description of Jacob's Island, for example (see **pp. 173–7**), he makes clear the relationship between overcrowding, poor housing and sanitation, poverty, disease and crime in slum areas. In his massive survey of the urban poor, *London Labour and the London Poor* (1851), Henry Mayhew tends to reflect the attitudes towards criminals held by the Utilitarian reformer Chadwick in the 1830s: criminals were lazy working-class people who wanted to avoid working hard for

---

20 Robert Peel (1788–1850) was Home Secretary in 1822 and dominated parliament between 1830 and 1850, becoming prime minister in 1834–5 and 1841–6.

a living. Dickens includes a multiplicity of criminal characters in his fiction, but of the working-class criminals, those who freely choose a life of crime as an easier way to make a living are in the minority. In *Oliver Twist*, even those who appear to do so – such as the Artful Dodger and Charley Bates – have been indoctrinated from childhood into a life of crime (from which Bates eventually escapes; see John, **pp. 89–91**).

The fear of crime among the working classes was accompanied by anxieties about the consequences of giving the lower order of society access to books and education. Books and newspapers were expanding their readership and were moving further down the social ladder in the early Victorian period than ever before. In *The Victorian Novel Before Victoria*, Engel and King argue that 'Forces outside the court in 1830 [...] were radically reforming the dissemination of fiction so that it began to reach the same class which the Reform Bill enfranchised'.[21] Until 1830, the cheap fiction market had largely been left to small and disreputable publishers such as the Minerva Press, but in June 1829 when Tom Cadell issued the Author's Edition of the *Waverley* novels in 5-shilling volumes, 'he inaugurated the vogue of inexpensive recent fiction imprints'.[22] In 1831, Colburn and Bentley's Standard Novels were published at 6 shillings each. These developments began a trend of sharply falling book prices, leading to a broader readership, a trend that continued until 1850. The positive side of what was nothing less than a revolution in publishing in the 1820s and 30s was the access gained by a growing number of people to the written word. Chittick argues that 'the democratization of politics was not only reported but reflected in the press'.[23] Dickens's career was obviously influenced by, and a significant influence on, this democratization and the growth in literacy in the period – despite his fierce protectiveness of his works as capital. Important in this process was the dramatic proliferation in the number of literary journals in circulation, the increasing tendency to serialize novels in periodical form and the increasing readership for newspapers. Arguably, the Victorians were witnessing the beginnings of the mass media. Moreover, as 'the people' seemed to be gaining access to more power, they felt they wanted more. The working-class Chartist movement, for example, founded the same year as *Oliver Twist* was published, demanded the following: universal suffrage, vote by ballot, annually elected parliaments, payment for members of parliament, abolition of the property qualification and equal electoral districts.

In this context, it is perhaps not surprising that *Oliver Twist*, like other 'Newgate' novels, aroused anxiety because of its focus on low-life characters and its alleged glamorization of criminal characters (see **pp. 38–9, 43–4, 57, 60–2, 119–24, 137–42, 153–6, 159–60, 164–8; John, pp. 89–91**). Newgate fiction appeared to be part and parcel of the democratizing – some would say civilizing – forces of the 1830s and, as such, a threat to the status quo. Lord Melbourne is not, however, a lone voice of discontent about the forces of change.

21 Elliott Engel and Margaret F. King, *The Victorian Novel Before Victoria: British Fiction during the Reign of William IV, 1830–37* (London: Macmillan, 1984), p. 5.
22 ibid.
23 Kathryn Chittick, *Dickens and the 1830s* (Cambridge: Cambridge University Press, 1990), p. 24.

To the influential theorist Michel Foucault, for example, the huge increase in bureaucracy, 'surveillance' and regulation that this supposed 'civilizing' involved has imprisoned rather than liberated individuals.[24] In *Discipline and Punish*, Foucault depicts the change in the law at this time as symbolic of a change in society as a whole – not, as the traditional narrative goes, from a primitive to a civilized society, but from a society in which freedom and individuality are real, to a (capitalist) society in which 'surveillance' and 'discipline' are used to normalize human behaviour and limit individual freedom. In Foucault's view, the prison is the archetype for other repressive Victorian institutions and for modern society at large: schools and police, for example, control and dehumanize by monitoring and recording. Even the expansion in the literary marketplace, for Foucault, can oppress the disempowered: the literature of crime, for example, which emerged during and after penal reform, for Foucault, was a tool of the establishment rather than a threat to it.[25]

Dickens also detected the 'surveillance' that underpinned bureaucracy and institutions: his attack on the workhouse in *Oliver Twist* is just one example. At the same time, however, he showed an optimism about social change and individual agency that Foucault does not possess and was passionate about aspects of social justice throughout his career. His disagreement with Edwin Chadwick about the Poor Law, for example, did not stop him from agreeing with the Benthamite about the necessity of improvements in sanitation. Dickens makes clear his concerns for public health in the urban landscapes of his novels – most memorably perhaps in the description of Jacob's Island – as well as in public pronouncements such as the 1850 Preface to the Cheap Edition of *Oliver Twist* (see **pp. 124–7**). Dickens wanted dramatic social change in many areas, but he disliked the legislation which was its necessary precursor. The notorious lack of theoretical consistency in Dickens's political views, looked at from this perspective, may well spring from his abhorrence of 'regulation'.

Though the mass distribution of a book such as *Oliver Twist* may have seemed threatening to some, the claims the novel makes for the downtrodden are as inconsistent as they are heartfelt. Its potential radicalism is undermined by the fact that goodness is largely associated with the middle classes – even Oliver speaks in received pronunciation and is rewarded by discovering his genteel origins. The egalitarian tendencies of the novel are further problematized by the treatment of Fagin, which many from Dickens's day onwards have found anti-Semitic. Dickens defended himself against intentional racism in his exchange of letters with Eliza Davis (see **pp. 33–4**), but the fact that he amended many mentions of 'the Jew' to 'Fagin' in the 1867 edition of the novel suggests that he partly accepted the charge. It is true that Dickens's anti-Semitism reflected that of his time, as Harry Stone has argued (see **pp. 68–70**) – Jews were second-class citizens before the law and unambiguously excluded from the democratizing and civilizing tendencies of the day – but perhaps more sensitivity to injustice could be expected of a writer with a reputation as a social reformer. A similar point can be made about Dickens's notoriously patriarchal treatment of women; Dickens's

---

24 See Michel Foucault's *Discipline and Punish: The Birth of the Prison*, trans. by Alan Sheridan (London: Penguin, 1991).
25 ibid., pp. 68–9.

society denied women the vote and his novels reinforce the gendered status quo. But *Oliver Twist*'s representation of Nancy shows Dickens's questioning of social norms, as does his involvement with Urania Cottage, a home for fallen women (see **pp. 31–3**). Though the radicalism of the character of Nancy is frequently overestimated, her characterization at least reflects an attempt to understand the politics of social alienation (see Michie, Ingham and Bowen, **pp. 77, 84–9**). The representation of Fagin does not. 'The civilization of everyday life' is thus a patchy affair in both *Oliver Twist* and Victorian Britain.

Chronology

I am extremely grateful to Richard J. Dunn for allowing me to reprint the chronology from his *Charles Dickens's David Copperfield: A Sourcebook* (Routledge, 2004). Bullet points are used to denote events in Dickens's life, and asterisks to denote historical and literary events.

For an exhaustive list of Dickens's publications, both major and minor, the reader is referred to Paul Schlicke's *Oxford Reader's Companion to Dickens* (Oxford: Oxford University Press, 2000). Those interested in Dickens's life can consult John Forster's original biography, *The Life of Charles Dickens*, ed. J. W. T. Ley (London: Cecil Palmer, 1928), Edgar Johnson, *Charles Dickens: His Tragedy and His Triumph*, 2 vols (London: Gollancz, 1953), and/or Peter Ackroyd, *Dickens* (London: Sinclair-Stevenson, 1990).

1812
- Charles Dickens (CD) born (7 February) in Portsmouth
* England at war with America; Prince of Wales serving as Regent

1815
* Wellington defeats Napoleon at Waterloo; Jane Austen, *Emma*

1817
- Dickens family moves to Chatham, near Rochester, site of CD's happiest earliest years and near Gadshill, his principal residence 1860–70
* Sir Walter Scott, *Rob Roy*

1820
* Death of George III; Regent Prince becomes George IV

1822
- Dickens family moves to London

1824
- CD leaves school and works for about six months at Warren's blacking factory; his father imprisoned for debt

1825
- CD attends Wellington House Academy
* First passenger railway

1827
- CD leaves school and works as solicitor's clerk

1829
- CD self-taught shorthand, becomes reporter and works as clerk at Doctor's Commons

1830
- CD in love with Maria Beadnell, a prototype for Dora Spenlow in *David Copperfield*
* George IV succeeded by William IV

1831
- CD employed as parliamentary reporter

1832
* First Reform Bill

1833
- Relationship with Maria Beadnell ends; CD publishes first sketch, 'A Dinner at Poplar Walk', later collected in *Sketches by Boz*

1834
- CD becomes reporter for *The Morning Chronicle*, meets Catherine Hogarth
* New Poor Law; Thomas Carlyle, *Sartor Resartus*

1836
- CD marries Catherine Hogarth; *Sketches by Boz, First Series*; begins monthly parts of *Pickwick Papers; Sketches by Boz, Second Series*; meets John Forster (attorney and man of letters, later first biographer of CD)

1837
- Begins monthly parts of *Oliver Twist* (in *Bentley's Miscellany*); Mary Hogarth dies, 7 May; concludes *Pickwick Papers*
* William IV succeeded by Victoria; Thomas Carlyle, *The French Revolution*

1838
- Begins monthly parts of *Nicholas Nickleby*; finishes writing *Oliver Twist*, the first edition of which is published in three volumes
* Publication of the People's Charter and National Petition, a workers' effort persisting in the 1840s, to require annual parliaments, universal male suffrage, equal electoral districts, secret ballot, removal of property qualification but payment for members of parliament

1839
* Concludes *Nicholas Nickleby*; serialization of *Oliver Twist* ends

1840
* Weekly numbers of *The Old Curiosity Shop* (in CD's magazine, *Master Humphrey's Clock*)

1841
* Preface to *Oliver Twist* published with third edition defending the novel against charges of coarseness and immorality; weekly numbers of *Barnaby Rudge* (in CD's magazine, *Master Humphrey's Clock*)
* Thomas Carlyle's *On Heroes, Hero-Worship, and the Heroic in History*

1842
* CD and wife visit America, where he was criticized for speaking in favour of an international copyright law. *American Notes*; begins monthly parts of *Martin Chuzzlewit* (which would later draw on his American experiences)

1843
* *A Christmas Carol*
* Thomas Carlyle, *Past and Present*

1844
* CD and family live in Italy for a year (July 1844–June 1845); concludes *Martin Chuzzlewit*; *The Chimes* (second Christmas book)

1845
* *The Cricket on the Hearth* (third Christmas book); leads amateur theatrical company, begins autobiography (surviving fragment published in John Forster's 1872 CD biography) that he draws on directly for early parts of *David Copperfield*

1846
* *The Battle of Life* (fourth Christmas book), *Pictures from Italy* (appearing first in *Daily News*, edited briefly by CD); begins monthly parts of *Dombey and Son*
* Irish famine

1847
* CD works with Angela Burdett Coutts to establish and help manage home for fallen women, writes 'An Appeal' to prospective residents
* William Makepeace Thackeray, *Vanity Fair* (concludes serially in 1848), Charlotte Brontë, *Jane Eyre*; Emily Brontë, *Wuthering Heights*

1848
* Concludes *Dombey and Son*; publishes *The Haunted Man* (fifth Chrismas Book)
* Revolutions in Europe

1849
- Begins monthly parts of *David Copperfield* in May

1850
- 1850 Preface to Cheap Edition of *Oliver Twist*; establishes weekly magazine *Household Words*; concludes *David Copperfield* in November; attends unauthorized stage adaptation of *David Copperfield*
* Australian Colonies Act; William Wordsworth (posthumously), *The Prelude*; Alfred Lord Tennyson, *In Memoriam*

1851
- Begins *A Child's History of England* (to run occasionally in *Household Words* until 1853); deaths of father, John Dickens (prototype for *David Copperfield*'s Mr Micawber), and infant daughter, Dora (born during the novel's serialization, she shared the name of David's first wife)
* Great Exhibition (Crystal Palace) in London

1852
- Begins monthly parts of *Bleak House*
* Death of the Duke of Wellington, hero of Waterloo and later Prime Minister

1853
- First public reading (for charity) of *A Christmas Carol*; concludes *Bleak House*

1854
- Weekly parts of *Hard Times* (in *Household Words*)
* Crimean War begins

1855
- Begins monthly parts of *Little Dorrit*

1856
* End of Crimean War

1857
- Completes *Little Dorrit*
* Thomas Hughes, *Tom Brown's Schooldays*

1858
- CD performs public readings from his works for profit; separates from wife

1859
- Weekly parts of *A Tale of Two Cities* (in CD's *All the Year Round*, which succeeded *Household Words*)
* Charles Darwin, *On the Origin of Species by Means of Natural Selection*; George Eliot, *Adam Bede*; Samuel Smiles, *Self-Help*

1860
* After rereading *David Copperfield* to avoid repetition, CD begins monthly parts of *Great Expectations* in his magazine *All the Year Round*

1861
* Concludes *Great Expectations*; first public reading from *David Copperfield*
* Death of Prince Albert; beginning of American Civil War

1864
* Begins monthly parts of *Our Mutual Friend*

1865
* Completes *Our Mutual Friend*; survives train derailment when returning from France with actress Ellen Ternan
* End of American Civil War

1867
* New edition of *Oliver Twist* contains editorial changes that attempt to redress tendencies in the text that had been criticised at anti-Semitic; triumphant reading tour of America (November–May 1868); adds preface to *David Copperfield* for collected edition of works
* Second Reform Bill further extends voting franchise but, like the 1832 Reform Bill, was a political compromise

1870
* Farewell reading tour in England; begins but completes only six of projected twelve monthly parts of *The Mystery of Edwin Drood*; dies 9 June, buried in Westminster Abbey

1872
* First disclosure of Dickens's childhood labour and father's imprisonment for debt in John Forster's *The Life of Charles Dickens*. Subsequent volumes of this biography in 1873, 1874

Contemporary Documents

From **The Poor Law Commission,** *Second Annual Report,* Appendix A, No. 7

The diet outlined on the table opposite is one of six 'dietaries' issued by the Poor Law commissioners in 1836 in order to not only ensure some kind of economic standard diet for paupers but also to enable flexibility. Local authorities could choose the dietary they deemed most appropriate. The diets had been tested and were deemed 'sufficient in quantity'.[1] While Dickens savagely satirizes what he sees as the meagre rations when Oliver famously asks for more, David Paroissien points out that 'comparatively, the dietaries of 1836 were not excessively severe'; the urban poor generally had a 'monotonous and inadequate' diet, and undernourishment was common.[2]

From **'The Poor Law Debate',** *The Annual Register: The History of Europe, 1834* (London, 1835), pp. 222–33

The Annual Register is an annual record of British and international events started by Edmund Burke in 1758. Its record of the parliamentary debate about the Poor Law gives an outline of the principles of the Law and some objections to it, including the relief of fathers from any obligations towards illegitimate children (see **pp. 11–13**).

The great principles of the proposed plan, then, went to this, to stop the allowance system – to deprive the magistracy of the power of ordering out-door relief—to alter in certain cases the constitution of parochial vestries[1]—to give large

1 Poor Law Commission, *Second Annual Report*, p. 63.
2 Paroissien, *Companion* to *Oliver Twist*, p. 294.

1 Meetings of a body of parishioners in the vestries, or side-buildings of churches.

From The Poor Law Commission, *Second Annual Report*, Appendix A, No. 7

No. I. *Dietary for Able-Bodied Men and Women*

		BREAKFAST		DINNER				SUPPER		
		Bread	Gruel	Cooked meat	Potatoes	Soup	Suet or rice pudding	Bread	Cheese	Broth
		oz	pints	oz	lb	pints	oz	oz	oz	pints
Sunday	Men	6	1½	5	½	–	–	6	–	1½
	Women	5	1½	5	½	–	–	5	–	1½
Monday	Men	6	1½	–	–	1½	–	6	2	–
	Women	5	1½	–	–	1½	–	5	2	–
Tuesday	Men	6	1½	5	½	–	–	6	–	1½
	Women	5	1½	5	½	–	–	5	–	1½
Wednesday	Men	6	1½	–	–	1½	–	6	2	–
	Women	5	1½	–	–	1½	–	5	2	–
Thursday	Men	6	1½	5	½	–	–	6	–	1½
	Women	5	1½	5	½	–	–	5	–	1½
Friday	Men	6	1½	–	–	–	14	6	2	–
	Women	5	1½	–	–	–	12	5	2	–
Saturday	Men	6	1½	–	–	1½	–	6	2	–
	Women	5	1½	–	–	1½	–	5	2	–

Old people of 60 years of age and upwards may be allowed one ounce of tea, five ounces of butter and seven ounces of sugar per week, in lieu of gruel for breakfast, if deemed expedient to make this change.

Children under nine years of age to be dieted at discretion; above nine, to be allowed the same quantities as women.

Sick to be dieted by the medical officer.

Figure 1 'Food, Glorious Food!', from Carol Reed (dir.), *Oliver!*
(Warwick-Romulus, 1968).

discretionary powers to the central commissioners—to simplify the law of settlement and removal—to render the mother of an illegitimate child liable to support it, and save from imprisonment for its aliment the putative father, to whom she might swear it.

[. . .]

By the proposed clause, if a labouring man fell sick, or was deprived by other causes of his ability to support his family, and required a little temporary relief, he would be driven, with perhaps a large family, into the workhouse, from which it would be impossible to say when he would return. This would be a very great hardship, and would be attended with the most injurious consequences. The same observation applied to widows, to orphans, illegitimate children, and others, who, from want of a little temporary relief, which could be administered at the discretion of persons on the spot, might be confined to the workhouse for the rest of their days. The clause was bad, too, in point of economy, for by forcing a whole family to seek protection in the workhouse, expenses to a much greater extent must be necessarily incurred to the parish, than if they were relieved at their own home. In many instances the aged poor were content to receive half-a-crown a-week from the parish funds in aid of their maintenance out of the work-house; whereas, if they were compelled to reside within the workhouse, a much larger sum of money must be expended in their support. The temporary relief required would be small; but, by being confined to the workhouse, they would be prevented from obtaining employment, and consequently would remain for a much longer period a burthen upon the parish. Besides, in many instances the members of the same family might be separated and placed in different work-houses, by which means the amount would be greatly augmented. In large manu-facturing towns, where it was impossible to find employment for the poor, the operation of this clause would be peculiarly injurious. Before the men went to the workhouse, they would be compelled to sell all their furniture, hand-looms, &c; and having disposed of every thing they possessed and gone to the work-house, they had no prospect of ever returning to their work, as the most they would be allowed was a penny a-day from the workhouse. [. . .] All this evil might be averted by a temporary relief out of the workhouse.

The clauses which relieved the fathers of illegitimate children from all legal obligation to maintain them, and laid that burden on the mother as if she had been a widow, occasioned a good deal of discussion. [. . .]

From **letter to Thomas Beard (17 May 1837),** Pilgrim edn, Vol. I, p. 259[1]

This letter to Dickens's friend, the journalist Thomas Beard (1807–91), about the premature death of Dickens's sister-in-law, Mary Hogarth, was written ten days after Mary's death and embellishes earlier accounts when it claims that 'the very last words she whispered were of me'. See **p. 11** for an account of Dickens's response to Mary's death and its effect on the writing of *Oliver Twist*. Mary was an influence on the character of Rose Maylie and other sub-sequent angelic young women in Dickens. See also **pp. 158–9**.

[. . .] Thank God she died in my arms, and the very last words she whispered were of me.

Of our sufferings at the time, and all through the dreary week that ensued, I will say nothing—no one can imagine what they were. You have seen a good deal of her, and can feel for us, and imagine what a blank she has left behind. The first burst of my grief has passed, and I can think and speak of her, calmly and dispas-sionately. I solemnly believe that so perfect a creature never breathed. I knew her inmost heart, and her real worth and value. She had not a fault.

[. . .]

From **letter to Thomas Haines (3 June 1837),** Pilgrim edn, Vol. I, p. 267

Thomas Haines was a long-serving and respected reporter at the Mansion House police office. Allan Stewart Laing (1788–1862) was the infamously severe Hatton Garden police magistrate on whom Dickens based the appropriately named character of Mr Fang in *Oliver Twist* (Chapter 11).

---

1   All letters are taken from *The Letters of Charles Dickens* edited by Madeleine House and Grahame Storey, The Pilgrim edition, 12 vols (Oxford: Oxford University Press, 1965–2002). Page numbers are indicated in the headings to the individual letters.

[. . .]

In my next number of Oliver Twist, I must have a magistrate; and casting about for a magistrate whose harshness and insolence would render him a fit subject to be 'shewn up' I have, as a necessary consequence, stumbled upon Mr. Laing of Hatton Garden celebrity. I know the man's character perfectly well, but as it would be necessary to describe his appearance also, I ought to have seen him, which (fortunately or unfortunately as the case may be) I have never done.

In this dilemma it occurred to me that perhaps I might under your auspices be smuggled into the Hatton Garden office for a few moments some morning. If you can further my object, I shall be really very greatly obliged to you.

[. . .]

From **letter to Richard Bentley (16 September 1837),** Pilgrim edn, Vol. I, p. 308

Richard Bentley (1794–1871) was one of the leading Victorian publishers, whose journal, *Bentley's Miscellany*, was edited by Dickens at the time that *Oliver Twist* was published in it. Relations became strained because Dickens felt tied to a contract he signed before he became so successful. The resignation contained in this letter was temporary as Dickens subsequently managed to negotiate better terms until he finally resigned in 1839 (see **pp. 8–9**).

Sir.

When I left town, I placed a number of accepted articles in the Printer's hands, with directions to set them up in sheets, beginning at the commencement of the number, and to send proofs to me. The whole of this arrangement has been altered by you; proofs of articles which I never saw in Manuscript have been forwarded to me; and notwithstanding my written notice to the Printer that I would revise no such papers, this course has been persisted in, and a second sheet sent.

By these proceedings I have been actually superseded in my office as Editor of the Miscellany; they are in direct violation of my agreement with you, and a gross insult to me. I therefore beg to inform you that henceforth I decline conducting the Miscellany or contributing to it in any way; but in order that you may suffer no inconvenience or embarrassment from the shortness of this notice, I will write a paper this month, and edit the Magazine this month—no longer.

[. . .]

From **letter to Mrs George Hogarth (26 October 1837),** Pilgrim edn, Vol. I, p. 323

In this letter, Dickens claims that he has not taken Mary Hogarth's ring off his finger since she died. The fact that he writes to his mother-in-law in such terms implies that he was confident that she would not see his behaviour as inappropriate. See **p. 11** and **p. 27** for an analysis of Mary's relevance to *Oliver Twist* and Dickens's subsequent fiction.

My Dear Mrs. Hogarth.

[. . .]

I have never had her ring off my finger by day or night, except for an instant at a time to wash my hands, since she died. I have never had her sweetness and excellence absent from my mind so long. I can solemnly say that waking or sleeping I have never once lost the recollection of our hard trial and sorrow, and I feel that I never shall.

[. . .]

From **letter to Richard Bentley (?early January 1838),** Pilgrim edn, Vol. I, p. 350

In this letter, Dickens shows the irritation with plagiarized adaptations of his works, which only intensified as his career progressed. At the time of *Oliver Twist*'s publication, Dickens had very little defence from copyright law and earned nothing from adaptations or pirated editions. He became involved with a campaign to strengthen copyright law in favour of authors, and in 1842 the Copyright Amendment Act strengthened the author's rights domestically, though the lack of protection against plagiarism abroad always irked him.

My Dear Sir

I inclose you the commencing number of *two* imitations of Oliver 'by different hands'. The vagabonds have stuck placards on the walls—each to say that *theirs* is the only true Edition. They will follow us through the book, of course.

[. . .]

From **letter to G. H. Lewes (?9 June 1838),** Pilgrim edn, Vol. I, pp. 403–4

George Henry Lewes (1817–78) was a writer and critic as well as the partner of George Eliot. Lewes was interested in the emerging science of psychology and Dickens's reply is likely to be a reply to a question from Lewes about the source of the passage describing Oliver's mental state in Chapter 34, when, semi-conscious, he becomes aware of the presence of Monks and Fagin (see **pp. 161–3**). Dickens's response can be seen either as illustrating his lack of reflection on his own methods, or as an inverted mystification of the art of authorship, or (more probably) as an example of his principled belief that literature should be readily accessible and explicable. Dickens's mention of Mr. Weller refers to Tony Weller, the father of Sam Weller, the likeable manservant in Dickens's *The Pickwick Papers*.

[. . .]

With reference to that question of yours concerning Oliver Twist I scarcely know what answer I can give you. I suppose like most authors I look over what I write with exceeding pleasure and think (to use the words of the elder Mr. Weller) 'in my innocence that it's all wery capital'. I thought that passage a good one *when* I wrote it, certainly, and I felt it strongly (as I do almost every word I put on paper) *while* I wrote it, but how it came I can't tell. It came like all my other ideas, such as they are, ready made to the point of the pen—and down it went. Draw your own conclusion and hug the theory closely.

I strongly object to printing anything in italics but a word here and there which requires particular emphasis, and that not often. It is framing and glazing an idea and desiring the ladies and gentleman to walk up and admire it. The truth is, that I am a very modest man, and furthermore that if readers cannot detect the point of a passage without having their attention called to it by the writer, I would much rather they lost it and looked out for something else.

Faithfully Yours
CHARLES DICKENS

From **letter to George Cruikshank (?6 October 1838),** Pilgrim edn, Vol. I, p. 440

George Cruikshank (1792–1878), the artist and caricaturist, was the most popular illustrator of his day by the mid-1830s. Cruikshank was the illustrator of *Oliver Twist*; some of his illustrations to the novel are reprinted in this source-book (**pp. 135, 142, 181**). Cruikshank claimed to have given Dickens the idea for the novel (see **pp. 9–10** and his letter to the *Times* below). This letter shows the thought that went into the interdependent relationship between text and illustration (see Hillis Miller, **pp. 73–5**). Cruikshank did in fact illustrate part of this scene.[1]

My dear Cruikshank
    I find on writing it, that the scene of Sikes's escape will not do for illustration. It is so very complicated, with such a multitude of figures, such violent action, and torch-light to boot, that a small plate could not take in the slightest idea of it.
    [. . .]

From **letter to John Forster (6 or 13 October 1838),** Pilgrim edn, Vol. I, p. 441

John Forster (1812–76) was Dickens's friend and first biographer. Dickens's description of Fagin as an 'out and outer' suggests that Dickens was convinced of his unambiguously evil nature. As his comments in the 1841 Preface to the novel illustrate, he was less clear in the case of Bill Sikes.

[. . .]

---

1   See 'The Last Chance', Dickens, *Oliver Twist*, Chapter 50.

I dreamt last night—strange to say—of the books you have sent home. I don't ride till tomorrow, not having yet disposed of the Jew who is such an out and outer that I don't know what to make of him.

[. . .]

From **letter to John Forster (21 January 1839),** Pilgrim edn, Vol. I, pp. 493–4

> In this letter, Dickens is explaining to Forster why he has asked the publisher Bentley for a postponement of six months after the completion of *Oliver Twist* and before the commencement of *Barnaby Rudge*. The quarrel with Bentley that ensued over Dickens's demand signalled the end of his editorship of *Bentley's Miscellany*. The terms in which he expresses himself in this letter show his very modern sense of the commercial possibilities of authorship. See also **pp. 8–9**.

[. . .] I know you will not endeavour to dissuade me from sending it. Go it MUST. It is no fiction to say that at present I *cannot* write this tale. The immense profits which *Oliver* has realised to its publisher, and is still realising; the paltry, wretched, miserable sum it brought to me (not equal to what is every day paid for a novel that sells fifteen hundred copies at most); the recollection of this, and the consciousness that I have still the slavery and drudgery of another work on the same journeyman-terms; the consciousness that my books are enriching everybody connected with them but myself, and that I, with such a popularity as I have acquired, am struggling in old toils, and wasting my energies in the very height and freshness of my fame, and the best part of my life, to fill the pockets of others, while for those who are nearest and dearest to me I can realise little more than a genteel subsistence: all this puts me out of heart and spirits: and I cannot—cannot and will not—under such circumstances that keep me down with an iron hand, distress myself by beginning this tale until I have had time to breathe [. . .].

[An Appeal to Fallen Women] (28 October 1847), Pilgrim edn, Vol. V, pp. 698–9

> Dickens acted as executive manager of Urania Cottage, a home for prostitutes and women in difficulties founded jointly by himself, in a supervisory role, and his friend, the philanthropist Angela Burdett Coutts (1814–1906), who provided the money. This letter was distributed to possible applicants. The home hoped to rehabilitate the women, retraining them in manners and morals and enabling them to start new lives abroad. It demonstrates, as does the character of Nancy, that Dickens's attitudes to women (particularly deviant women) were more complex than is sometimes appreciated, though the letter also assumes somewhat conventionally that prostitutes lead doomed lives and are in need of rescue. See also **pp. 149–51, 163–4**.

You will see, on beginning to read this letter, that it is not addressed to you by name. But I address it to a woman—a very young woman still—who was born to be happy, and has lived miserably; who has no prospect before her but sorrow, or behind her but a wasted youth; who, if she has ever been a mother, has felt shame, instead of pride, in her own unhappy child.

You are such a person, or this letter would not be put into your hands. If you have ever wished (I know you must have done so, sometimes) for a chance of rising out of your sad life, and having friends, a quiet home, means of being useful to yourself and others, peace of mind, self-respect, everything you have lost, pray read it attentively, and reflect upon it afterwards. I am going to offer you, not the chance but the certainty of all these blessings, if you will exert yourself to deserve them. And do not think that I write to you as if I felt myself very much above you, or wished to hurt your feelings by reminding you of the situation in which you are placed. GOD forbid! I mean nothing but kindness to you, and I write as if you were my sister.

Think, for a moment, what your present situation is. Think how impossible it is that it ever can be better if you continue to live as you have lived, and how certain it is that it must be worse. You know what the streets are; you know how cruel the companions that you find there, are; you know the vices practised there, and to what wretched consequences they bring you, even while you are young. Shunned by decent people, marked out for all other kinds of women as you walk along, avoided by the very children, hunted by the police, imprisoned, and only set free to be imprisoned over and over again—reading this very letter in a common jail—you have, already, dismal experience of the truth. But, to grow old in such a way of life, and among such company—to escape an early death from terrible disease, or your own maddened hand, and arrive at old age in such a course—will be an aggravation of every misery that you know now, which words cannot describe. Imagine for yourself the bed on which you, then an object terrible to look at, will lie down to die. Imagine all the long, long years of shame, want, crime, and ruin, that will rise before you. And by that dreadful day, and by the Judgment that will follow it, and by the recollection you are certain to have then, when it is too late, of the offer that is made to you now, when it is NOT too late, I implore you to think of it, and weigh it well!

There is a lady in this town, who, from the windows of her house, has seen such as you going past at night, and has felt her heart bleed at the sight. She is what is called a great lady; but she has looked after you with compassion, as being of her own sex and nature; and the thought of such fallen women has troubled her in her bed. She has resolved to open, at her own expense, a place of refuge very near London, for a small number of females, who, without such help, are lost for ever: and to make it A HOME for them. In this Home they will be taught all household work that would be useful to them in a home of their own, and enable them to make it comfortable and happy. In this Home, which stands in a pleasant country lane, and where each may have her little flower-garden, if she pleases, they will be treated with the greatest kindness; will lead an active, cheerful, healthy life; will learn many things it is profitable and good to know; and, being entirely removed from all who have any knowledge of their past career, will begin life afresh, and be able to win a good name and character. And because it is not the lady's wish that these young women should be shut out from the world, after they have repented and have learned how to do their duty there, and because it *is* her wish and object that they may be restored to society – a comfort to themselves and it – they will be supplied with every means, when some time shall have elapsed, and their conduct shall have fully proved their earnestness and reformation, to go abroad, where, in a distant country, they may become the faithful wives of honest men, and live and die in peace.

I have been told that those who see you daily in this place, believe that there are virtuous inclinations lingering within you, and that you may be reclaimed. I offer the Home I have described in these few words, to you.

[. . .]

Believe me that I am, indeed,
YOUR FRIEND

From **letter to Mrs [Eliza] Davis (10 July 1863),** Pilgrim edn, Vol. X, pp. 269–70

Eliza Davis was the wife of P. J. Davis, a solicitor who had bought the lease of Tavistock House from Dickens in August 1860. Mrs Davis had complained that Dickens's anti-Semitic treatment of Fagin had done Jewish people a 'great wrong'. Dickens's response in the two letters below suggests that the anti-Semitism was unthinking, though his claim that he always 'speaks well' of Jewish people is not borne out by all his writings and correspondence. He obviously tried to make amends, however, as he changed many references to 'the Jew' to Fagin in *Oliver Twist*, and he changed the character of Riah in the novel *Our Mutual Friend* (1864–5), from a miser to a persecuted, benevolent employee of a Christian who pays him to pretend to be a stereotypical Jewish moneylender. The 'error' he refers to in the second letter included here probably refers to the representation of Riah. See also Stone and Heller, **pp. 68–70** and **pp. 82–4, 108–13**.

[. . .] I must take leave to say, that if there be any general feeling on the part of the intelligent Jewish people, that I have done them what you describe as 'a great wrong,' they are a far less sensible, a far less just, and a far less good-tempered people than I have always supposed them to be. Fagin, in Oliver Twist, is a Jew, because it unfortunately was true of the time to which that story refers, that that class of criminal almost invariably was a Jew. But surely no sensible man or woman of your persuasion can fail to observe—firstly, that all the rest of the wicked *dramatis personae*[1] are Christians; and secondly, that he is called a 'Jew', not because of his religion, but because of his race. If I were to write a story, in which I described a Frenchman or a Spaniard as 'the Roman Catholic,' I should do a very indecent and unjustifiable thing; but I make mention of Fagin as the Jew, because he is one of the Jewish people, and because it conveys that kind of idea of him which I should give my readers of a Chinaman, by calling him a Chinese.

The enclosed is quite a nominal subscription towards the good object in which

---

1   (Dramatic) characters.

you are interested; but I hope it may serve to show you that I have no feeling towards the Jewish people but a friendly one. I always speak well of them, whether in public or in private, and bear my testimony (as I ought to do) to their perfect good faith in such transactions as I have ever had with them; and in my Child's History of England,[2] I have lost no opportunity of setting forth their cruel persecution in old times. [. . .]

From **letter to Mrs [Eliza] Davis (16 November 1864),** Pilgrim edn, Vol. X, p. 454

Dear Madam,—I have received your letter with great pleasure, and hope to be (as I've always been in my heart) the best of friends with the Jewish people. The error you point out to me had occurred to me [. . .] when it was too late to correct it. But it will do no harm. The peculiarities of dress and manners are fixed together for the sake of picturesqueness.

Dear Madam—Yours.

CHARLES DICKENS

From **John Forster, *The Life of Charles Dickens*,** edited by J. W. T. Ley (London: Cecil Palmer, [1928?]), p. 26

In this mid-1840s extract from John Forster's classic biography, Dickens recalls his unhappiness at the blacking factory he was forced to work at as a child and his acquaintance with Bob Fagin, a colleague at the factory. Dickens kept this part of his life a secret even from Forster until he was established professionally and socially (see **pp. 7–8**). Many writers have speculated about the relationship between these early experiences and Dickens's writing (most notably, Edmund Wilson and Humphry House, **pp. 64–7**) and Steven Marcus (see **pp. 71–2**) hypothesizes that Bob Fagin's name is transferred to the villain of *Oliver Twist* because of Dickens's feelings of resentment at his life in the factory.[1]

It was not long, before Bob Fagin and I, and another boy whose name was Paul Green, but who was currently believed to have been christened Poll (a belief which I transferred, long afterwards again, to Mr. Sweedlepipe[1], in *Martin Chuzzlewit*, worked generally, side by side. Bob Fagin was an orphan, and lived with his brother-in-law, a waterman. [. . .]

'No words can express the secret agony of my soul as I sunk into this companionship; compared these every day associates with those of my happier childhood; and felt my early hopes of growing up to be a learned and distinguished man, crushed in my breast. The deep remembrance of the sense I had of being utterly neglected and hopeless; of the shame I felt in my position; of the misery it was to my young heart to believe that, day by day, what I had learned, and thought, and

---

2   Serialized between 1851 and 1853.

1   Poll Sweedlepipe is a barber in Dickens's novel *Martin Chuzzlewit* (1843–44).

delighted in, and raised my fancy and my emulation up by, was passing away from me, never to be brought back any more; cannot be written. My whole nature was so penetrated with the grief and humiliation of such considerations, that even now, famous and caressed and happy, I often forget in my dreams that I have a dear wife and children; even that I am a man; and wander desolately back to that time in my life. [. . .]'

From **George Cruikshank, 'The Origin of *Oliver Twist*',** *The Times* (30 December 1871)

George Cruikshank's claim that he was the originator of the idea for *Oliver Twist*, first voiced in 1847 to a journalist, was labelled 'preposterous' by Kathleen Tillotson, but subsequent research has found some grounds for the claim (see **p. 10.**) Cruikshank' s mention of sketching Newgate prison is interesting because in Chapter 25 of *Oliver Twist*, the Artful Dodger sketches 'a groundplan of Newgate on the table'.[1] See **pp. 43–4** for more on Newgate, and Cruikshank's illustration, 'Fagin in the Condemned Cell', **p. 181**. See also Hillis Miller, **pp. 73–5**, on Cruikshank's illustrations.

[. . .] there is no doubt whatever that I did tell this gentleman that I was the originator of the story of *Oliver Twist*, as I have told very many others who may have spoken to me on the subject, and which facts I now beg permission to repeat in the columns of *The Times*, for the information of Mr. Forster[2] and the public generally.

When *Bentley's Miscellany* was first started, it was arranged that Mr. Charles Dickens should write a serial in it, and which was to be illustrated by me; and in a conversation with him as to what the subject should be for the first serial, I suggested to Mr. Dickens that he should write the life of a London boy, and strongly advised him to do this, assuring him that I would furnish him with the subject and supply him with all the characters, which my large experience of London life would enable me to do. My idea was to raise a boy from a most humble position up to a high and respectable one – in fact, to illustrate one of those cases of common occurrence, where men of humble origin by natural ability, industry, honest and honourable conduct, raise themselves to first-class positions in society. And as I wished particularly to bring the habits and manners of the thieves of London before the public (and this for a most important purpose, which I shall explain one of these days), I suggested that the poor boy should fall among thieves, but that his honesty and natural good disposition should enable him to pass through this ordeal without contamination, and after I had fully described the full-grown thieves (the 'Bill Sikes') and their female companions, also the young thieves (the 'Artful Dodgers') and the receivers of stolen goods, Mr. Dickens agreed to act on my suggestion, and the work was commenced, but we differed as to what sort of boy the hero should be. Mr. Dickens wanted rather

---

1 Dickens, Clarendon, *Oliver Twist*, p. 158.
2 Dickens's friend and first biographer.

a queer kind of chap, and although this was contrary to my original idea I complied with his request, feeling that it would not be right to dictate too much to the writer of the story, and then appeared 'Oliver asking for more'; but it so happened, just about this time, that an inquiry was being made in the parish of St. James's, Westminster, as to the cause of the death of some of the workhouse children who had been 'farmed out,' and in which inquiry my late friend Joseph Pettigrew (surgeon to the Dukes of Kent and Sussex) came forward on the part of the poor children, and by his interference was mainly the cause of saving the lives of many of these poor little creatures. I called the attention of Mr. Dickens to this inquiry, and said that if he took up this matter, his doing so might help to save many a poor child from injury and death, and I earnestly begged of him to let me make Oliver a nice pretty little boy, and if we so represented him, the public—and particularly the ladies—would be sure to take a greater interest in him and the work would then be a certain success. Mr. Dickens agreed to that request, and I need not add here that my prophecy was fulfilled; and if any one will take the trouble to look at my representations of 'Oliver' they will see that the appearance of the boy is altered after the two first illustrations, and, by a reference to the records of St. James's parish, and to the date of the publication of the *Miscellany*, they will see that both the dates tally, and therefore support my statement. I had a long time previously to this directed Mr. Dickens's attention to 'Field-lane,' Holborn-hill, wherein resided many thieves and receivers of stolen goods, and it was suggested that one of these receivers, a Jew, should be introduced into the story; and upon one occasion Mr. Dickens and Mr. Harrison Ainsworth[3] called upon me at my house in Myddleton Terrace, Pentonville, and in course of conversation I then and there described and performed the character of one of these Jew receivers, who I had long had my eye upon; and this was the origin of 'Fagan' [*sic*]. Some time after this Mr. Ainsworth said to me one day, 'I was so much struck with your description of that Jew to Mr. Dickens, that I think you and I could do something together,' which notion of Mr. Ainsworth's, as most people are aware, was afterwards carried out in various works. Long before *Oliver Twist* was ever thought of, I had, by permission of the city authorities, made a sketch of one of the condemned cells in Newgate prison; and as I had a great object in letting the public see what sort of places these cells were, and how they were furnished, and also to show a wretched condemned criminal therein, I thought it desirable to introduce such a subject into this work; but I had the greatest difficulty to get Mr. Dickens to allow me to carry out my wishes in this respect, but I said I must have either what is called a Christian or what is called a Jew in a condemned cell, and therefore it must be 'Bill Sikes' or 'Fagan'; at length he allowed me to exhibit the latter.

Without going further into particulars, I think it will be allowed from what I have stated that I am the originator of *Oliver Twist*, and that all the principal characters are mine, but I was much disappointed by Mr. Dickens not fully carrying out my first suggestion.

I must here mention that nearly all the designs were made from conversation

---

3   William Harrison Ainsworth (1805–82), novelist and close acquaintance of Dickens. A so-called 'Newgate' novelist (see **pp. 43–4**).

and mutual suggestion upon each subject, and that I never saw any manuscript of Mr. Dickens until the work was nearly finished, and the letter of Mr. Dickens, which Mr. Forster mentions, only refers to the last etching – done in great haste – no proper time being allowed, and of a subject without any interest in fact, there was not anything in the latter part of the manuscript that would suggest an illustration; but to oblige Mr. Dickens I did my best to produce another etching, working hard day and night, but when done, what was it? Why, merely a lady and a boy standing inside of a church looking at a stone wall!

Mr. Dickens named all the characters in this work himself, but before he had commenced writing the story he told me that he had heard an omnibus conductor mention some one as Oliver Twist, which name, he said, he would give the boy, as he thought it would answer his purpose. I wanted the boy to have a very different name, such as Frank Foundling or Frank Steadfast; but I think the word Twist proves to a certain extent that the boy he was going to employ for his purpose was a very different sort of boy from the one introduced and recommended to him by, Sir, your obedient servant,

GEORGE CRUIKSHANK,
Hampstead-road December 29

From **The Girlhood of Queen Victoria: A Selection from her Diaries Between the Years 1832 and 40,** edited by Viscount Esher, 2 vols (London: John Murray, 1912), Vol. II, pp. 89, 144

Lord Melbourne's initial objections to the low life featured in *Oliver Twist* are an expression of the prejudice Dickens was trying to counter in his 1841 Preface to the novel, that 'low' people had no place in serious art. Though such an assumption is shocking to us now, the novel was written only a few years after the 1832 Reform Bill, so the idea that the lower classes could have political and cultural access was still controversial. It is interesting that the young Victoria enjoyed the novel but saw it as a 'light' book rather than what Lord Melbourne might call 'pure and edifying'.

[. . .]

(1 January 1839) 'Talked to [Lord Melbourne] of my getting on with *Oliver Twist*; of the description of "squalid vice" in it; of the accounts of starvation in the Workhouses and Schools, Mr Dickens gives in his books. Lord M. says, in many schools they give children the worst things to eat, and bad beer, to save expense; told him Mamma admonished me for reading light books.' (ii, 89) [Two days later, she persuaded Lord Melbourne to read *Oliver Twist*.]

(7 April 1839) 'Lord M. was talking of some dish or other, and alluded to something in *Oliver Twist*: [. . .] "It's all among Workhouses, and Coffin Makers, and Pickpockets," he said; "I don't like *The Beggar's Opera*;[1] I shouldn't think it

---

1   John Gay's *The Beggar's Opera* (1728) is a serious artistic treatment of low life and criminality and, like *Oliver Twist*, employed slang. See **pp. 121–2.**

would tend to raise morals; I don't like that low debasing view of mankind."
We defended *Oliver* very much, but in vain. "I don't *like* those things; I wish to
avoid them; I don't like them in *reality*, and therefore I don't wish them represented," he continued; that everything one read should be pure and elevating.
[. . .]'. (ii, 144)

From **Edward Bulwer Lytton, Preface (1840) to *Paul Clifford* (1830),** Copyright edn. (Leipzig: Bernhard Tauchnitz, 1842), Collection of British Authors, Vol. VII, pp. vii–viii

> Edward Bulwer Lytton (1803–73) was a Victorian novelist and politician who,
> like Dickens, was labelled a 'Newgate' novelist and accused of glamorizing crime
> in his novels (see **pp. 43–4**). His novel *Paul Clifford*, referred to in Dickens's
> 1841 Preface to *Oliver Twist* (see **p. 122**), was the first so-called Newgate novel.
> Like Dickens, Bulwer claimed (in the pieces below and in many other writings)
> serious literary and social purposes for his crime fiction.

First, to draw attention to two errors in our penal institutions, viz. a vicious
Prison-discipline and a sanguinary Criminal Code,—the habit of first corrupting
the boy by the very punishment that ought to redeem him, and then hanging the
man, at the first occasion, as the easiest way of getting rid of our own blunders.
[. . .] A second and a lighter object in the novel of 'Paul Clifford' [. . .] was to shew
that there is nothing essentially different between vulgar vice and fashionable
vice,—and that the slang of the one circle is but an easy paraphrase of the cant of
the other.

From **Edward Bulwer Lytton, 'A Word to the Public',** appended to *Lucretia* (1846), reprinted in *Lucretia; or The Children of Night* (London: Chapman & Hall, 1853), pp. 297–334

[. . .]
    [. . .] We come, then, at once, to a question, which common sense and universal
authority ought long since to have decided – viz., 'How far the delineation of
crime is a legitimate object of fictitious composition.'
    [. . .]
    To sum up, I think, then, we must allow—
    1st. That crime, however great and heinous, is an admitted and necessary
agency in tragic fiction, warranted by the employment of the greatest masters, and
the sanction of all ages.
    2ndly. That it is equally admissible in the narrative fiction as the dramatic.
    3rdly. That we may seek for the materials of terror in crime, or *destructive
power*, amidst the present as the past. [. . .]
    I said that we have a right to demand certain stipulations as to treatment and
selection.
    1stly. We have a right to demand that, whatever interest the author bids us to

take in the criminal, we should never by any metaphysical sophistry, be seduced into admiration of the crime. [. . .]

2ndly. The crimes depicted should not be of a nature to lead us through licentious scenes, nor accompanied with descriptions that appeal dangerously to the senses. [. . .]

3rdly. In dealing especially with the coarser and more violent crimes least idealised by remote tradition, least dignified by history above vulgar associations, the author is bound to have some object in view belonging to the purer and more thoughtful principles of art, to which the means he employs are subordinate and conducive.

[. . .]

2

Interpretations

Critical History

'Some of the author's friends cried, "Lookee, gentlemen the man is a villain; but it is Nature for all that;" and the young critics of the age, the clerks, apprentices, &c., called it low, and fell a groaning.' – FIELDING.

In 1841, Dickens reissued *Oliver Twist* with a Preface that defended the novel against charges that it was 'low' and immoral (see **pp. 119–24**). His epigraph, appropriately chosen from Henry Fielding's novel *Tom Jones* (1749), draws attention to what he sees as the snobbery underlying the so-called 'moral' objections of critics to his novel. These kind of objections to *Oliver Twist* reached the upper echelons of the reading public (see Lord Melbourne's comments to Queen Victoria, **pp. 37–8**). *Oliver Twist* was one of a group of crime novels published between 1830 and 1847 which became known as 'Newgate' novels. They were named after the famous Newgate prison that burnt down in 1780 and more specifically after *The Newgate Calendar; or, The Malefactors' Bloody Register*, a popular collection of criminal biographies first published in 1773. All the Newgate novels were, in the words of John Sutherland, 'sensationally popular'.[1] All provoked the criticism that they corrupted readers – and by implication society – by glamorizing crime. As crime novels published previously had not provoked such a controversy, it is tempting to conclude that objections to these novels had as much to do with anxieties about the radical social changes of the 1830s and 1840s (see **pp. 14–18**). Dickens took the attacks personally and artistically, however, and the 1841 Preface was an uncharacteristic defence of his art from a writer who did not generally write much about writing. (See also John, **pp. 89–91** and **pp. 119–24, 137–42, 153–6, 159–60, 164–8**, for an analysis of *Oliver Twist*'s self-reflexive critique of Newgate fiction.)

In a sense, the attacks were personal. *Fraser's Magazine* and one of its main writers, William Makepeace Thackeray, launched a sustained campaign against 'Newgate' fiction and its authors (Dickens, William Harrison Ainsworth and Edward Bulwer Lytton). Radical, Tory, and aggressively middle class, the journal launched a particularly vitriolic campaign against the aristocractic 'Newgate'

1   *The Longman Companion to Victorian Fiction* (Harlow: Longman, 1988), p. 462.

novelist, Sir Edward Bulwer Lytton. Thackeray's advice to 'trust more to the people's description of themselves, than to Bulwer's ingenious inconsistencies, and Dickens's startling, pleasing, unnatural caricatures' (see **p. 57**) sums up his recurrent argument that lack of realism in Dickens's representation of criminal low life was misleading and immoral. Thackeray was a slippery character whose criticism of Dickens may have been informed by rivalry. But the association of Dickens with the 'Newgate' novel was not helped by the fact that the most sensational of them all, Ainsworth's *Jack Sheppard* (1839–40), was published in *Bentley's Miscellany*, the same journal that published *Oliver Twist* (and indeed Ainsworth succeeded Dickens as the editor of that magazine). Both *Oliver Twist* and *Jack Sheppard* were illustrated by George Cruikshank. Dickens does his best to distance himself from the Newgate novelists in the Preface to the Third Edition, whilst carefully avoiding the word 'Newgate' (see **pp. 119–24**). It would be misleading to assume, however, that *Oliver Twist* met a hostile reception from its early critics. As the extracts selected here demonstrate, the opposite was overwhelmingly the case (see **p. 51**).

In 1837, the young G. H. Lewes praised 'One of the peculiar merits of "Boz" ', that 'of bringing before us things which we have all noticed hundreds of times, yet which we never thought of committing to paper' (see **p. 53**). By 1872 however, in his famous essay, 'Dickens in Relation to Criticism', Lewes claimed that there was not 'a single thoughtful remark' in the whole Dickens canon and that his characters were like 'frogs whose brains have been taken out for physiological purposes'.[2] Written just after Dickens's death, 'Dickens in Relation to Criticism' in many ways marks the beginning of a modern criticism of Dickens. Whereas many early commentators were troubled by the content of the novel, Lewes objected to Dickens's style. As the novel was a relatively new genre, both content and style were up for grabs in the nineteenth century. Dickens was at one with Lewes and George Eliot in his view that the novel should be taken seriously as an art form and that it should foreground the plight of ordinary people from the lower and (predominantly) middle classes. Uncontroversial as the latter may seem to us now, Lord Melbourne's comments above (**pp. 37–8**) show the extent to which the conjunction of high art and low-to-middling subject matter seemed an unnatural one in the early nineteenth century. Equally contentious was the question of the ideal style of the novel, and on this Dickens and Eliot differed. Though Dickens saw himself as championing all that was real and 'TRUE', as the 1841 Preface to *Oliver Twist* insists, he was not real and true in the sense that George Eliot, the prime mover in British literary realism, thought advisable. Eliot's criticisms of Dickens essentially echo, and no doubt influenced, her partner G. H. Lewes's influential critique of the recently departed Dickens: for Eliot, Dickens 'scarcely ever passed from the humorous and external to the emotional and tragic, without becoming [. . .] transcendent in his unreality'.[3] For Lewes and Eliot, faithful representation of the inner life was the test of a great realist novelist. To put it crudely, for Eliot and the Lewes of 1872, a great novelist had to be a realist novelist as they defined realism. Most importantly, both Lewes and Eliot

2 *Fortnightly Review*, 11 (February 1872), pp. 141–54.
3 'The Natural History of German Life', *Westminster Review*, 10 (1 July 1856), pp. 51–79.

were influenced by the rise of psychology in the nineteenth century (it was a nineteenth-century science), and their conception of realism involved a psychological conception of character: character in the novel should be represented and analysed by a faithful, organic, evolutionary depiction of the inner mind and emotions. Dickens was a writer in the eighteenth-century tradition, believing that character and the mind could as usefully and 'realistically' be represented externally. Neither was he a realist in the sense the Preface to the Third Edition of *Oliver Twist* might lead us to understand. His subject matter was realistic but his style was typically theatrical, even fantastic. A forerunner of contemporary magic realism, Dickens sought to represent what he called in the Preface to *Bleak House* (1852–3), 'the romantic side of familiar things'.

It would not be feasible here to enter into a labyrinthine discussion of literary realism: Lilian Furst's anthology, *Realism*,[4] is one of the most helpful collections to students in its balanced selection of writings on the topic. What is important to register, however, is that Dickens was never a straightforwardly realist writer in the sense he claims in the *Oliver Twist* Preface, or in the sense implied by Catherine Belsey when she includes him (and *Oliver Twist*) in her influential critique of realism in *Critical Practice*.[5] When you consider the issue of realism, you must think in terms of both content and style: a novel (such as *Oliver Twist*) might include a realistic vision of society – content – but adopt an unrealistic style. But an unrealistic, caricatured or theatrical style can be just as sophisticated, 'deep' or 'profound', to use words commonly favoured by my students, as a work of psychological realism. For many years, however, this was not a commonly accepted vision and Dickens's reputation as a novelist suffered with critics (if not with the public) who consciously or otherwise, used psychological realism as *the* yardstick of great art. Henry James, for example, famously labelled Dickens, 'the greatest of superficial novelists',[6] while F. R. Leavis left Dickens out of the canon of 'great novelists' he formulated in *The Great Tradition*, regarding Dickens as a 'great entertainer' who lacked the seriousness of a great novelist.[7]

Against the backdrop of this critical climate, an important wave of Dickens criticism looked for psychological complexity not primarily in Dickens's characters, but in Dickens himself. This 'biographical' approach to Dickens – incorporating elements of psychology and psychoanalysis – was most influentially adopted by Edmund Wilson in his essay, 'Dickens: The Two Scrooges' (1941), which argued that the tendency of Dickens to veer between absolutely good characters and absolutely bad characters was rooted in his own personality (see **pp. 64–5**). The biographical approach had a significant impact on readings of *Oliver Twist*. In the 1940s, for example, House argued that Dickens's childhood feelings of alienation made him understand outsiders – and criminals – better than he did those who conform (see **pp. 66–7**). Steven Marcus's 1965 essay, 'Who is Fagin?' was another milestone, Marcus speculating that Fagin was named after Dickens's workmate in the blacking factory, Bob Fagin (see **pp. 71–2**). These

4   Lilian Furst, *Realism* (London: Longman, 1992).
5   Catherine Belsey, *Critical Practice* (London: Methuen, 1980).
6   Henry James, '*Our Mutual Friend*', Nation, 1 (21 December 1865), pp. 786–8 (p. 787).
7   F. R. Leavis, *The Great Tradition* (London: Chatto & Windus, 1948); F. R. and Q. D. Leavis, *Dickens the Novelist* (London: Chatto & Windus, 1970), p. 9.

accounts are no doubt interesting but are problematic in a couple of respects. First, they seem to accept that psychological realism is essential to a serious novelist. And second, they do not account for the craft of Dickens's fiction: many people have had difficult childhood experiences, but this does not mean that they can write novels about it. (See also **pp. 7–8.**)

Another approach that has been influential to understandings of *Oliver Twist* is the social realist approach: from his own day onwards, Dickens has had the reputation for being a social reformer. From Humphry House's influential *The Dickens World* onwards,[8] Dickens has been approached via the concerns of his age. There has been a great deal of attention (as in this volume) to his attacks on the New Poor Law, his class attitudes, his attitudes to capital punishment, juvenile delinquency, child prostitution, and many more topical issues in the novel, *Oliver Twist*. A knowledge of the topical concerns of the novel is important to an informed understanding of the text on its own terms. But to concentrate on social realism and social reform as the prime achievements of a Dickens novel is in some ways to miss the point. As Arnold Kettle said of *Oliver Twist* some time ago, 'What is the secret of the power? Is it merely the objective existence of the horror, the fact that such things were, that strikes at our minds? Fairly obviously not or we should be moved in just the same way by a social history.'[9] Dickens was moreover never a great respecter of 'facts', nor was he a consistent social and political analyst. He felt strongly about certain social problems – for example, the New Poor Law – but did not extend the implications of his sympathy with the poor in a theoretically consistent fashion in his work (nearly all the good people in *Oliver Twist*, for example, are middle class and Oliver's goodness seems synonymous with his unlikely gentility).

The dominant influence of classic realism on nineteenth-century literature and its critics eventually provoked some superbly sophisticated analyses of both the kind of realism that actually features in Dickens's novels and of the assumptions of classic realism and its exponents. John Bayley, writing in the 1960s, still has something to tell us about Dickens and the real: like the best work of its time, it is nuanced and multidimensional, exploiting its lack of allegiance to any one particular theoretical school (see **pp. 70–1**). However, the real turning point for Dickens criticism and Dickens's reputation in the twentieth century came with the advent of a theoretical school called 'post-structuralism': to put it simply, this argued that meaning is never fixed or stable because it depends on language, which is itself multiple in its meanings and shaping contexts. Though realists such as George Eliot had never argued, as their opponents like to suggest, that the novel, a linguistic construct, could somehow directly or transparently represent truth or reality, realism did presuppose an imagined causal relationship between the words on the page and a social or psychological reality. Post-structuralism did not, or it did not imagine it in the same way. The reason post-structuralism was good for Dickens was that its exponents – most influentially J. Hillis Miller – managed to make people see the obvious: Dickens was not trying and failing to present a photographically accurate vision of any reality. He was a novelist, a

8   Humphry House, *The Dickens World* (Oxford: Oxford University Press, 1941).
9   'Dickens. Oliver Twist (1837–8)', in *An Introduction to the English Novel* (1951), 2 vols, 2nd edn (London: Hutchinson, 1967; reprinted 1981), Vol. I, p. 116.

word-artist, who was creating his own fictional realities which partly related to the extra-novelistic world and partly related to the world of the novel. Dickens, in other words, was a highly self-conscious craftsman whose work is self-reflexive (reflects on itself) as well as externally focused. He took fiction seriously, but he also played games with it. Hillis Miller's essay 'The Fiction of Realism' (1971) is important to an understanding of *Oliver Twist* and indeed realism (see **pp. 73–5**). For Miller, Dickens's texts (and the illustrations that form part of those texts) foreground the interpretative process that underpins critical and social activity. From this perspective, there is no such thing as 'reality' (let alone realism) in fiction or in life, only something we construct as reality by the selective perception and interpretation of what we observe around us. Post-structuralist criticism has done much to draw attention to the sophistication of Dickens's self-reflexivity, and to counter the crude notion that Dickens was a failed realist or psychologist. However, its characteristic emphasis on the fictionality of both texts and social experience can lead to a neglect of the ideological and ethical values underlying Dickens's fiction, as well as to a divorce of literature from history. In this sense, the resulting criticism can resemble the earlier movement of New Criticism, which divorced texts from contexts and foregrounded questions of literary form.

Post-structuralism (and structuralism) also did much to problematize the notion of character in literature by correctly pointing out that literary characters are not real people but linguistic constructs. For some time, this idea was taken to the extreme in literary studies so that the lesson learnt was not that discussions of character must become more sophisticated but that it was taboo to discuss character at all: to discuss character was to announce one's stupidity and naivety. To think about Dickens without thinking about character is clearly ridiculous, though to imagine that Dickens's characters are best understood only as direct representations of real people is to miss their richness and complexity. Dickens's characters are representations of real people *and* they are fictional and linguistic constructs. They belie the damaging division between 'flat' and 'round' characters formulated by E. M. Forster, as Forster himself recognised.[10] The best critics of character are an eclectic bunch, ranging from some of the early reviewers unfettered by realist criteria, to the wonderful G. K. Chesterton (see **pp. 63–4**), to theorized modern critics such as Brian Rosenberg.[11]

One of the most incisive modern critics of Dickensian character is John Kucich. Influenced by psychoanalysis, Michel Foucault and Marxism, Kucich draws attention to the 'decentering psychological approach' and the 'refractive view of the psyche' presented in Dickens's novels.[12] What he means by this is that characters in Dickens represent individuals, but they also represent aspects of individuals. Dickens's characters are best understood, from this perspective, in groups, clusters or doubles, each individual character distilling a certain emotional or psychological drive. Dickens's vision of identity is thus best understood by observing the interaction between these drives in carefully patterned groups of

---

10 E. M. Forster, *Aspects of the Novel*, Pelican (Harmondsworth: Penguin, 1962).
11 See Rosenberg, *Little Dorrit's Shadows: Character and Contradiction in Dickens* (Columbia, Miss.: University of Missouri Press, 1985).
12 'Dickens', in John Richetti (ed.) *The Columbia History of the British Novel* (New York: Columbia University Press, 1994), pp. 381–406 (p. 400). Not included in this volume.

characters. Kucich is particularly good on the importance of the relationship between violence and repression and between excess and restraint in Dickens: to Kucich, violence is not the stark opposite of repression but exists in a 'metonymic' relationship to it: repression creates violence and vice versa.[13] If we apply this to *Oliver Twist*, for example, the relationship between Fagin and Sikes is not quite as oppositional as it appears. There is a sense of brooding violence beneath Fagin's control, which Sikes embodies.

In some ways, Kucich is updating the pre-realist view of character. For before the advent of the realist novel, it was automatically understood that characters were symbolic of ideas and not simply mirror images of people. Dickens clearly understands Oliver in such a way, announcing in the 1841 Preface to the novel that Oliver represents 'the principle of Good surviving through every adverse circumstance' (see **p. 121**). Thus understood, he is part of the allegorical tradition in literature and is overtly influenced by John Bunyan's religious parable, *The Pilgrim's Progress*.[14] Dickens is also steeped in the moral symbolism of the eighteenth-century novelists, the caricatured satire of the artist Hogarth and the oppositional characterisation of popular stage melodrama. In these genres, characters were not meant to be fully rounded 'grey' people, but entertaining, morally symbolic counters. As the rise of Dickens mirrored the rise of psychology, however, his characterization inevitably reflects interest in the psyche. But for Dickens, the idea that the inner life was reality or the knowable centre of things was a distortion leading to an unhealthily inward-looking understanding of society that was not the reality for many.[15] His novels thus dramatize and symbolize their psychological insights in ways that are both readily accessible and deceptively difficult.

The 'refractive' view of Dickensian identity has been used most controversially by Eve Sedgwick, whose work *Between Men: English Literature and Male Homosocial Desire* was heralded as a ground-breaking text in queer theory as well as in nineteenth-century studies.[16] Though not directly concerned with *Oliver Twist*, her essay on Dickens's *Our Mutual Friend* (1864–5) looks at Dickens's work as reflective of the 'homosocial' relations that existed between men in the nineteenth century: relations between men were much more important, she argues, in this age of separate spheres, than relations between men and women, and they were frequently sexually charged. The most erotically charged relations often involved triangles of desire where a woman was the ostensible but not the real object of desire for two male rivals. The idea that there are sexual (specifically, paedophile) undertones in the relationship between Fagin and his boys has been observed by several critics,[17] but the triangular relationship between Fagin, Sikes and Nancy is perhaps worthy of more attention.

13 'Repression and Representation: Dickens's General Economy', *Nineteenth Century Fiction*, 38 (1983), pp. 62–77 (p. 69).
14 See Janet Larson, *Dickens and the Broken Scripture* (Athens, Ga.: University of Georgia Press, 1985), pp. 47–67.
15 See Juliet John, *Dickens's Villains: Melodrama, Character, Popular Culture* (Oxford: Oxford University Press, 2001).
16 Eve Sedgwick, *Between Men: English Literature and Male Homosocial Desire* (New York: Columbia University Press, 1985).
17 See, for example, Garry Wills, 'The Loves of *Oliver Twist*', *New York Review of Books*, 36 (26 October 1989), pp. 60–7.

Sedgwick's work has grown out of the developing prominence since the 1960s in society as well as in criticism of 'identity politics'. Identity politics is a politics that defines people and their interests through social categories such as class, race, gender, and sexuality, categories that have become increasingly important in the delivery of literature modules. Opponents of such an approach to literature argue that it involves facile populism and political correctness – that it is an easy way to give students a partial understanding of literature. As I hope this brief critical overview has made clear, however, all approaches offer a partial view of a text and real understanding is only arrived at by an understanding of many approaches. Moreover, while an interest in sexuality is relatively recent in criticism, critics of *Oliver Twist* have always been absorbed by its representation of class, race and gender. Indeed, ideas about class are so engrained in criticism of the novel that they speak through various essays in this selection rather than being artificially limited to one. See, for example, Gissing (**p. 62**), Orwell (**pp. 65–6**), D. A. Miller (**pp. 77–9**) and Ingham (**pp. 84–7**). Interestingly, despite the controversy that Dickens's views on Fagin has always provoked, there is relatively little literary critical material available on the topic.[18] I have included here Harry Stone's early controversial attempt to place Dickens's anti-Semitism in context (**pp. 68–70**), and Deborah Heller's rebuttal of his argument (**pp. 82–4**). Adapters, audiences and reviewers of performances of the novel seem to have been far more exercised by the novel's representation of Fagin, however, and the difference between the clamour about the issue surrounding television and film representations and the relative prominence of the issue in literary studies is something you may wish to consider further.

Likewise, gender has not always seemed a natural concern in Dickens. While Dickens's notoriously patriarchal views have traditionally deterred many feminists from critical attention to his work, this has started to change. As Nancy is considered by many to be the most interesting female character in the Dickens canon – a claim I cannot support – *Oliver Twist* has always attracted those interested in gender. For many years, however, the biographical background to *Oliver Twist* has submerged the actual narrative, the story of Dickens's grief over the death of Mary Hogarth preventing the text being read in fresh new ways. Neither Dickens's reaction to the death of Mary Hogarth nor his representation of women was as one-dimensional as has often been implied, however, as John Bowen and Patricia Ingham illustrate (see **pp. 87–9** and **pp. 4–7** respectively).

---

18 See Lauriat Lane, Jr., 'Dickens's Archetypal Jew', *PMLA*, 73 (1958), 94–100 and Edgar Rosenberg's *From Shylock to Svengali: Jewish Stereotypes in English Fiction* (Stanford University Press, 1960). David Paroissien's Annotated Bibliography on *Oliver Twist* in *Dickens Studies Annual*, 35 (2005), 397–514 (pp. 508–11) also notes the following recent essays on Fagin: Murray Baumgarten, 'Seeing Double: Jews in the Fiction of Scott Fitzgerald, Charles Dickens, Anthony Trollope, and George Eliot,' in *Between 'Race' and Culture: Representations of 'the Jew' in English and American Literature*, ed. by Bryan Cheyette (Stanford University Press, 1996), pp. 41–61; Cornelia Cook, ' "The Jew" and the Philosophers', *Dickensian*, 90 (2003), 127–35; Jonathan H. Grossman, 'The Absent Jew in Dickens: Narrators in *Oliver Twist*, *Our Mutual Friend*, and *A Christmas Carol*', *Dickens Studies Annual*, 24 (1996), 37–57; Efraim Sicher, 'Imagining "the Jew": Dickens' Romantic Heritage', in *British Romanticism and the Jews: History, Culture, Literature*, ed. by Sheila A. Spector (New York: Palgrave Macmillan, 2002), pp. 139–55; Juliet Steyn 'Charles Dickens' *Oliver Twist*: Fagin as a Sign', in *The Jew in the Text: Modernity and the Construction of Identity*, ed. and Intro. by Linda Nochlin and Tamar Garb (London: Thames and Hudson, 1995), pp. 42–55.

Much of the best work on Dickens is difficult to identify with a single critical approach, largely because Dickens was an eclectic, self-educated author whose work eludes easy classification. As John Bowen wrote about composing his book *Other Dickens: Pickwick to Chuzzlewit*,[19] trying to use critical theory 'on' Dickens was a bit like 'a pantomime elephant trying to pick up a pea, or indeed at times, like a pea trying to pick up an elephant'.[20] Richard Stein's *Victoria's Year: English Literature and Culture, 1837–38*,[21] excluded here for reasons of copyright, is suggestive of avenues left to explore: genuinely interdisciplinary, it effortlessly analyses the novel and its illustrations in the context of various discourses of the time (for example, science, political economy, materialism, and bestiality).

A huge amount of work on *Oliver Twist* already exists, though, and in an effort to sample as wide a variety of criticism as possible, I have envisaged my selection as an extensive lecture hand-out: each extract is here to give a taste of a larger piece rather than in any way to represent an argument fully. Some pieces were less intelligible as extracts than they were in their original context and several texts in this category are listed under further reading.

---

19 John Bowen, *Other Dickens: Pickwick to Chuzzlewit* (Oxford: Oxford University Press, 1999).
20 Oxford University Press web site ⟨http://www.oup.co.uk/academic/humanities/literature/view-point/john-bowen⟩.
21 Richard Stein, *Victoria's Year: English Literature and Culture, 1837–38* (Oxford: Oxford University Press, 1987).

Early Critical Reception

Oliver Twist was labelled a 'Newgate' novel and accused of glamorizing crime by *Fraser's Magazine* and one of its main reviewers, William Makepeace Thackeray (see **p. 51**). Elsewhere, however, early reviews of the novel were overwhelmingly positive. Some reviews of the early serialized episodes published in pro-government publications unsurprisingly objected to Dickens's treatment of the New Poor Law – see John Forster's *Examiner* review (**p. 52**), for example, or the *Morning Chronicle*'s review of Summer 1837. But reviews of the complete novel were generally silent on this score. Only the 1839 reviewer in the *Quarterly Review* lamented Dickens's anti-Poor Law stance.[1] The early reviews are wide-ranging and eclectic in their interests, though it is notable how many reflect on the reasons for Dickens's popularity, as well as on his ability to depict character and his humour (see editorial headnotes to 'Opening' and 'Oliver Asks for More', **pp. 127–8** and **pp. 129–30**, for an analysis of Dickens's humour).

From **[Charles Buller], 'The Works of Dickens'**, *London and Westminster Review*, 29 (July 1837), pp. 194–215

[. . .]

It is not, indeed, difficult to discover or to enumerate the causes of this popularity. The merits of Mr Dickens, though great, are not very varied; and the range of his subjects has not been large. The qualities for which every body reads and admires him are his humour and wit: and it is well known that he has delighted to employ these powers mostly in describing and commenting on the comic peculiarities of the lower orders of Englishmen. Indeed, the class which has been the peculiar object of his attention is even more limited. It is easy to see that his observations have been mainly confined to London. [. . .] He is the literary Teniers[2] of the metropolis; and he paints the humours of the lower orders of London with all the exactness and all the comic effect with which his prototype has handed to us the comic peculiarities of the Dutch boors of his time. [. . .]

---

1 Tillotson (ed.), Clarendon *Oliver Twist*, p. x.
2 David Teniers (1610–90), a Flemish landscape painter, born in Antwerp and died in Brussels.

[. . .] *Oliver Twist, or the Parish Boy's Progress* [. . .] is indeed remarkable as a specimen of a style rather more serious and pathetic than any other of the author's longer works; and it confirms the impression which we previously had of his powers in this style. His capacity of pathetic description is wonderfully great, and his taste in the selection of his objects seems to be constantly improving. Still the work has, though in a diminished degree, the same fault as we have noticed in the pathetic portions of his writings. They are monotonous. The accumulation of little details of misery and discomfort positively pains, and at last harasses the reader. We must advise the author, in continuing the work, to put in some touches not merely of comedy, which is by no means deficient, but of something descriptive of a little more comfort and happiness. The very accuracy of all these minute details of human wretchedness makes their effect more distressing, and renders such a variation necessary to relieve our feelings.

[. . .]

From [John Forster], review in the *Examiner* (10 September 1837), pp. 581–2

The story of *Oliver Twist*, so far as it has yet proceeded, is its author's masterpiece, and mean as the subject appears to be—the account of the Progress of a Parish Boy—promises to take its place among the higher prose fictions of the language. Appearing in detached portions in a monthly magazine, and written, we presume, as the occasion arises monthly—the variety and vigour of character thrown into each separate part is indeed surprising. The art of copying from nature as it really exists in the common walks of life has not been carried to great perfection, or to finer results in the way of combination, by the most eminent writers. [. . .]

[. . .] The account of his mother's death is a masterly piece of the tragedy of common life—full of deep pathos, and with fine touches of the grotesque. [. . .]

No one can read this without feeling a strong and sudden interest in Oliver, and the interest never after ceases. We think it necessary to observe, at the same time, that in the first two or three chapters of his history, an unwarrantable and unworthy use is made of certain bugbears of popular prejudice and vulgar cant connected with the new poor law, which we are surprised to see such a writer as Mr. Dickens resorting to. The attempt to elevate the pauper in our sympathies at the cost of the struggling labourer—to leave rate-payers lean with their work and hunger, so that the pauper may be stuffed to the proper extent of comfort—which all these allusions in Oliver's case would seem to tend to—is a system of curious philanthropy which we confess we cannot understand. But leaving this, which, as we have said, only colours the first three chapters of Oliver's history, we must admit the force and distinctness with which the various parish authorities are gradually brought upon the scene. [. . .]

[. . .] We feel as deep an interest in little Oliver's own fate, as in that of a friend we have long known and loved. [. . .]

From [G. H. Lewes?], review of *Sketches, Pickwick* and *Oliver Twist,* in the *National Magazine and Monthly Critic* (December 1837), pp. 445–9

[. . .]

'Boz' has perhaps a wiser popularity than any man has enjoyed for many years. Nor alone are his delightful works confined to the young and old, the grave and gay, the witty, the intellectual, the moralist, the thoughtless of both sexes in the reading circles, from the peer and judge to the merchant's clerk; but even the common people, both in town and country, are equally intense in their admiration. [. . .]

If asked by what peculiar talent Boz characterised, we find ourselves at a dead fault—if we feel inclined to say, startling fidelity of observation, his wit and humour rise before us, and compel us to pause; and we are obliged to answer that we cannot fairly say what we think he is greatest in, but that it is a combination of those qualities (before enumerated) that characterises him. [. . .] There is one thing worthy of notice, because it speaks the kindliness of his heart and the sympathy of his nature; and that is the charm which he throws over every nature, making you love it in spite of yourself. [. . .] There is also another thing which is remarkable. Although he takes us into scenes of the lowest description, (more particularly in *Oliver Twist,*) and although he gives us the language of vagabond, thief, footman, ostler,[1] and gentleman, catching their several idioms with the most surprising felicity, yet there is not a single coarse word, or one allusion that could call a blush into the cheek of the most fastidious; [. . .]

'Boz's' satire is the finest that we ever read, because it is generally satire by *implication*, not personality [. . .] and it is done in that style that one might easily suppose an individual under the lash laughing at it himself, and feeling its deep truth at the same time – an effect very different to the satire of the great writers above-mentioned. [. . .]

One of the peculiar merits of 'Boz' is that of bringing before us things which we have all noticed hundreds of times, yet which we never thought of committing to paper. [. . .] Then, too, his language, even on the most trivial points, has, from a peculiar collocation of the words, or some happy expression, a drollery which is spoiled by repeating or reading loud, because this drollery arises from so fine an association of idea that the sound of the voice destroys it. We cannot help remarking, however, in this respect, a continual straining after humorous things, and this straining gives a laboured air to the work, besides which, it gives a want of light and shade, which fatigues the mind, if reading much at a time. While we are finding fault, an ungrateful task, and one which we feel rather reluctant about [. . .] we would notice the incongruity (the more remarkable in one so true to nature) of which he has been guilty in the character of Oliver Twist. To say nothing of the language which this uneducated workhouse-boy ordinarily uses, there are many phrases which amount to positive absurdities in one of his standing.[2] [. . .]

---

1 Stableman at an inn.
2 See **p. 17** and Dickens's 1841 Preface (**pp. 120–21, 123**), for a discussion of Dickens's language and Oliver's received pronunciation.

From **[Thomas Henry Lister], a review of *Sketches* (1st and 2nd Series), *Pickwick, Nickleby* and *Oliver Twist*,** *Edinburgh Review,* 68 (October 1838), pp. 75–97

[. . .] He has put them forth in a form attractive, it is true, to that vast majority the *idle* readers—but one not indicative of high literary pretensions, or calculated to inspire a belief of probable permanence of reputation. [. . .] This is the view which many persons will take of Mr Dickens's writings—but this is not our deliberate view of them. We think him a very original writer—well entitled to his popularity—and not likely to lose it—and the truest and most spirited delineator of English life, amongst the middle and lower classes, since the days of Smollett and Fielding.[1] He has remarkable powers of observation, and great skill in communicating what he has observed—a keen sense of the ludicrous—exuberant humour – and that mastery in the pathetic which, though it seems opposed to the gift of humour, is often found in conjunction with it. Add to these qualities, an unaffected style, fluent, easy, spirited, and terse—a good deal of dramatic power—and great truthfulness and ability in description. We know no other English writer to whom he bears a marked resemblance. [. . .] We would compare him rather with the painter Hogarth. What was in painting, such very nearly is Mr Dickens in prose fiction. The same turn of mind—the same species of power displays itself strongly in each. Like Hogarth he takes a keen and practical view of life—is an able satirist—very successful in depicting the ludicrous side of human nature, and rendering its follies more apparent by humorous exaggeration [. . . .] Mr Dickens is exempt from two of Hogarth's[2] least agreeable qualities—his cynicism and his coarseness. There is no misanthropy in his satire, and no coarseness in his descriptions—a merit enhanced by the nature of his subjects. His works are chiefly pictures of humble life—frequently of the humblest. The reader is led through scenes of poverty and crime, and all the characters are made to discourse in the appropriate language of their respective classes—and yet we recollect no passage which ought to cause pain to the most sensitive delicacy, if read aloud in female society.[3]

[. . .] The tendency of his writings is to make us practically benevolent—to excite our sympathy in behalf of the aggrieved and suffering in all classes; and especially in those who are most removed from observation. He especially directs our attention to the helpless victims of untoward circumstances, or a vicious system [. . .]

Mr Dickens's characters are sketched with a spirit and distinctness which rarely fail to convey immediately a clear impression of the person intended. They are, however, not complete and finished delineations, but rather outlines, very clearly and sharply traced, which the reader may fill up for himself; and they are calculated not so much to represent that actual truth as to suggest it. Analyses of disposition, and explanations of motives will not be found, and, we may add, will

---

1   See the 1841 Preface, **pp. 119–20, 123** and note 18, **p. 123** on Smollett and Fielding and Dickens's sense of his debt to them. See also **pp. 119, 121, 123** for the influence of eighteenth-century satire on Dickens.

2   See **p. 48**, the 1841 Preface, **pp. 121–3** and n. 5, **p. 121** on Hogarth and Dickens's sense of his debt to him.

3   This chimes with Dickens's stated intention (see 1841 Preface, **pp. 121–3**), but the novel does not seem to have had this effect on Lord Melbourne (see **pp. 37–8**).

be little required. His plan is, not to describe his personages, but to make them speak and act,—and it is not easy to misunderstand them. [. . .]

But Mr Dickens's forte perhaps lies less in drawing characters than in describing incidents. He seizes with great skill those circumstances which are capable of being graphically set before us; and makes his passing scenes distinctly present to the reader's mind. [. . .]

[. . .] The author, however, must beware lest he converts a certain Mr Monks who figures in the latter chapters, into a mere melo-dramatic villain of romance. There is such perfect truthfulness in the generality of his characters, that deviations from nature are less tolerable than when found in other works. Unfinished as this tale still is, it is the best example which Mr Dickens has yet afforded of his power to produce a good novel; but it cannot be considered a conclusive one. The difficulties to which he is exposed in his present periodical mode of writing are, in some respects, greater than if he allowed himself a wider field, and gave his whole work to the public at once. But he would be subjected to a severer criticism if his fiction could be read continuedly [. . .].

From **an anonymous review of *Oliver Twist,*** *The Spectator,* 11 (24 November 1838), pp. 1114–16

The numerous readers who have been moved to laughter or to sadness, led to grave reflection, or excited to horror, by some of the passages in *Oliver Twist,* may naturally ask why they and criticism so differ? The answer will be, that they have been moved by *parts*: we are speaking of the work considered as *a whole,* and testing it by a reference to time, and those models of enduring art with which certain over-zealous *clacqueurs*[1] have challenged comparison. Quitting these larger views, we will go a long way with Boz's admiring readers, and endeavour to point out the sources of their admiration, and the reasons of their idol's success. [. . .] That this author exhibits genius in embodying London character, and very remarkable skill in making use of peculiarities of expression, even to the current phrase of the day, is undoubtedly true; but he has higher merits, and other elements of success. His powers of pathos, sadly touching rather than tearful, are great; he has a hearty sympathy with humanity, however degraded by vice or disguised by circumstances, and a quick perception to detect the existence of the good, however overlaid; his truth and nature in dialogue are conspicuous to all; he has the great art of bringing his actors and incidents before the reader by a few effective strokes; though deficient in *narrative*, his *description* is sometimes nicely true, and often powerful; and his command of language considerable, without his style ever appearing forced. In addition to these qualities, he has a manly self-reliance—above all pretence, and all conventional servilities of classes and coteries; nor does he ever, with a sickly vanity, obtrude *himself* upon the reader's attention. Above all, he has genius to vivify his observation. [. . .]

[. . .] When his matter is not sufficiently attractive in itself, he has no objection

---

1   Hired applauder.

to paint up to the flaring tastes of the vulgar great and small; nor does he scruple to avail himself of any current prejudice, whether popular or *fee*losophical,[2] without much regard to critical exactness. Thus, Mr Fang, the Police Magistrate, was a hit at LAING of Hatton Gardens,[3] whilst the functionary's pranks were full in the public mind. The earlier workhouse scenes in *Oliver Twist*, with the hard-hearted indifference of the parochial authorities, the scanty allowance of the paupers, and the brutal insolence of office in the beadle, were intended to chime in with the popular clamour against the New Poor-law:[4] but Boz has combined the severity of the new system with the individual tyranny of the old,—forgetting that responsibility amongst subordinate parish-officers and regularity of management came in with the Commissioners. The scenes of pauper misery, whilst Oliver is on liking with the parish undertaker, appear to have been suggested by some inquests: and there are points thrown out by the Jew to flatter the opponents of capital punishment,—although the tendency of the work is to show that nature and habit cannot be eradicated by a sentimentality which contents itself with substituting a penitentiary[5] for a gallows. These things tell with many readers, but they must detract from the permanence of the writer who freely uses them. [. . .]

From **an unsigned review of *Oliver Twist*,** *Literary Gazette* (24 November 1838), p. 741

[. . .] we would advert to one quality which Mr. Dickens has displayed to an extent altogether unequalled, if we except, perhaps, the mighty names of Shakespere [*sic*] and Scott.[1] We allude to the creation of individual character: to the raising up and embodying of a number of original human beings in so substantial a form, and endowed with such living feelings and passions, and acting in so real and natural a manner, that they immediately become visibly, personally, and intimately known to us; and we no more doubt of their existence than if we had seen them in the flesh, conversed with them, and observed their conduct. [. . .]

What felicity and acuteness of observation does this single feature in his literary course proclaim! And it is, after all, but a single feature. He has dug deep into the human mind; and he has nobly directed his energies to the exposure of evils—the workhouse, the starving school, the factory system, and many other things, at which blessed nature shudders and recoils. As a moralist and reformer of cruel abuses, we have the warmer thanks of the community to offer him. [. . .]

---

2   Philosophical. The implication may be that Dickens's main aim is to gain financially and to ingratiate himself with the public.
3   See **pp. 27–8.**
4   See **pp. 11–13.**
5   Prison.

---

1   The novelist Sir Walter Scott (1771–1832).

From **William Makepeace Thackeray, 'Horæ Catnachianæ'**, [1]
Fraser's Magazine, 19 (April 1839), 407–24 (pp. 407–9)

[. . .]

We (that is, the middling classes) have been favoured of late with a great number of descriptions of our betters, and of the society which they keep; and have had also, from one or two popular authors, many facetious accounts of the ways of life of our inferiors. There is in some of these histories more fun—in all, more fancy and romance—than are ordinarily found in humble life; and we recommend the admirer of such scenes, if he would have an accurate notion of them, to obtain his knowledge at the fountainhead, and trust more to the people's description of themselves, than to Bulwer's ingenious inconsistencies, and Dickens's startling, pleasing, unnatural caricatures.

[. . .]

Our public has grown to be tired of hearing great characters, or even ordinary ones, uttering virtuous sentiments; but put them in the mouth of a street-walker, and straightway they become agreeable to listen to. We are sick of heroic griefs, passions, tragedies; but take them out of the palace, and place them in the thief's boozing ken[2]—be prodigal of irony, or slang, and bad grammar—sprinkle with cant phrases—leave out the h's, double the v's, divide the w's (as may be necessary), and tragedy becomes interesting once more. [. . .].

All these opinions are, to be sure, delivered *ex cathedrá*,[3] from the solemn critical chair; but when out of it, and in private, we humbly acknowledge that we have read every one of Mr. Dickens's tales with the most eager delight [. . .].

[. . .] When we say that neither Mr. Dickens, nor Mr. Ainsworth, nor Sir Lytton Bulwer, can write about what they know not, we presume that not one of those three gentlemen will be insulted at an imputation of ignorance on a subject where knowledge is not, after all, very desirable. [. . .] Dickens's Jew, Fagin, is one of the cleverest actors that ever appeared on the stage; but, like a favourite actor, the Jew is always making points to tickle the ears of the audience. We laugh at his jokes, because we are a party to them, as it were, and receive at every fresh epigram a knowing wink from the old man's eye, which lets us into the whole secret. [. . .] Fagin is only a clever portrait, with some of the artist's mannerism—a mask, from behind which somebody is uttering bitterest epigrams. [. . .]

From **[Richard Ford] 'Oliver Twist; or the Parish Boy's Progress'**,
Quarterly Review, 64 (June 1839), pp. 83–102

His works are a sign of the times; their periodical return excites more interest than that of Halley's comet.[1] They, like good sermons, contribute to our moral health,

---

1   James Catnach junior (1792–1841) was a printer and publisher who was known for publishing sensational ballads and broadsides, many about crime. 'Horae' literally means 'hours'. The title can thus be roughly translated as meaning 'Catnachian pursuits'.
2   House or public house.
3   With the full authority of office.

---

1   A famous comet named after Edmund Halley, who calculated its orbit.

for mirth, cakes, ale, and ginger hot in the mouth do us good, Mr. Froude's negation of negus[2] to the contrary notwithstanding. The works of Boz[3] come out in numbers, suited to this age of division of labour, cheap and not too long—double merits: there is just enough to make us rise from the feast, as all doctors of divinity and medicine do from dinner, with an appetite for more: in fact, Boz is the only *work* which the superficial acres of type called newspapers leave the human race time to peruse. His popularity is unbounded—not that that of itself is a test of either honesty or talent. [. . .] Though dealing with the dregs of society, he is never indelicate, indecent, nor irreligious; he never approves nor countenances the gross, the immoral, or offensive; he but holds these vices up in a pillory, as a warning of the disgrace of criminal excess. Boz, like the bee, buzzes amid honey without clogging his wings; he handles pitch charmingly; the tips of the thumb and fore-finger of the cigaresque señoras of Paraguay are infinitely more dis-coloured. He tells a tale of real crushing misery in plain, and therefore most effective, language; he never *then* indulges in false sentimentality, or mawkish far-fetched verbiage. Fagin, Sikes, and the dog especially, are always in their proper and natural places, always speaking, barking, and acting exactly as they ought to have done, and, as far as we are able to judge, with every appearance of truth. Boz sketches localities, particularly in London, with marvellous effect; he concentrates with the power of a camera lucida.[4] Born with an organic bump[5] for distinct observation of men and things, he sees with the eye, and writes with the pen of an artist—we mean with artistical skill, and not as artists write. He translates nature and life.

Boz fails whenever he attempts to write for effect; his descriptions of rural felicity and country scenery, of which he clearly knows much less than of London, where he is quite at home and wide awake, are, except when comical, over-laboured and out of nature. His 'gentle and genteel folks' are unendurable; they are devoid of the grace, repose, and ease of good society; something between Cheltenham and New York. [. . .] Boz is, nevertheless, never vulgar when treating on subjects which are avowedly vulgar. He deals truly with human nature, which never can degrade; he takes up everything, good, bad, or indifferent, which he works up into a rich alluvial[6] deposit. He is natural, and that never can be ridiculous.

[. . .] This is the great objection which we feel towards Oliver Twist. It deals with the outcasts of humanity, who do their dirty work in work, pot, and watch houses, to finish on the Newgate drop.[7] [. . .] The happy ignorance of innocence is disregarded. Our youth should not even suspect the possibility of such hidden depths of guilt, for their tender memories are wax to receive and marble to retain. These infamies feed the innate evil principle, which luxuriates in the supernatural

2   Richard Hurrell Froude (1803–36) was an Anglican minister who preached against the consump-tion of negus, which is a mixture of wine (usually port or sherry) and hot water, usually sweetened with sugar and nutmeg.
3   Dickens's pseudonym in his early writing career and the name he assumed when he published *Sketches by Boz*.
4   An optical device that projects a precise image of an object onto a plain surface.
5   The pseudoscience of phrenology, which had some credence in Dickens's day, held that bumps on the cranium revealed the character of individuals.
6   Containing sediment deposited by flowing water.
7   The gallows.

and horrid, the dread and delight of our childhood, which is never shaken off, for no man entirely outlives the nursery. We object to the familiarising our ingenious youth with 'slang;' it is based in travestie of better things. [. . .] The jests and jeers of the 'slangers' leave a sting behind them. They corrupt pure taste and pervert morality, for vice loses shame when treated as a fool-born joke, and those who are not ashamed to talk of a thing will not be long ashamed to put it into practice.

Oliver Twist, again, is directed against the poor-law and workhouse system; and in our opinion with much unfairness. The abuses which he ridicules are not only exaggerated, but in nineteen cases out of twenty do not at all exist. Boz so rarely mixes up politics, or panders to vulgar prejudices about serious things, that we regret to see him joining in an outcry which is partly factious, partly sentimental, partly interested.

The whole tale rivals in improbabilities those stories in which the hero at his birth is cursed by a wicked fairy and protected by a good one; but Oliver himself, to whom all these improbabilities happen, is the most improbable of all. He is represented to be a pattern of modern excellence, guileless himself, and measuring others by his own innocence, delicate and high-minded, affectionate, noble, brave, generous, with the manners of a son of a most distinguished gentleman, not only uncorrupted but incorruptible:[8] less absurd would it be to expect to gather grapes on thorns, to find pearls in dunghills, violets in Drury Lane,[9] or make silk purses of sows' ears.

While the romantic approve, and metaphysicians speculate on the abstract possibility of his union of virtue and vice, we all sympathise with Nancy's melancholy fate: her death is drawn with a force which quite appals. This devotedness to her unworthy companion, to whom, notwithstanding her early history, she is clearly constant, forms her redeeming point. [. . .] Nancy is described as aware of her degraded situation: she felt the awe of the undefiledness of virtue, at which vice stands abashed; yet, when Miss Maylie, who, seeing only horror and guilt, calmly reasons, and attempts to save her from Sikes, Nancy, who loves, is faithful and unmoved. We may indeed *speculate* whether such metal, had it been cast in a better mould, would not have run true and clear. We can only *reason* on what of necessity must have been the result of the influences to which she had been exposed form her birth downwards. Notwithstanding that the great tendency in woman towards the gentler affections renders a Nancy somewhat less improbable than an Oliver, we fear that both characters must be considered contrary to the laws of human nature and experience everywhere, and particularly in England. Here, a woman once lost descends instantaneously, as through a trap-door, into unknown depths, to be heard of no more.[10] [. . .] all throw the first stone, all press on the bruised reed,—and her own sex the heaviest: not only those who are themselves unscathed, merely because they have never known want, misery, or temptation; but even the wise, the thoughtful, the experienced, the truly and intrinsically pure,—even they can pardon every crime and cover every shame save that of an erring sister.

It is hardly fair to conclude an article, however brief and desultory upon Oliver

8 See G. H. Lewes's review, p. 53 and n. 2.
9 A street and theatre frequented by prostitutes.
10 See also pp. 31–3.

Twist, without making some allusion to the obligations under which author and reader are laid by the graphic running commentary of Mr. Cruikshank's etchings. This, we suspect, may be as great an artist in his own way as Boz himself—and it is difficult to say, on laying down the book, how much of the powerful impression we are conscious of may be due, not to the pen, but to the pencil.[11] [. . .]

From **William Makepeace Thackeray, *Catherine: A Story*,** *Fraser's Magazine* (May 1839–February 1840); reprinted from *The Oxford Thackeray*, edited by George Saintsbury (Oxford: Oxford University Press, [1908]), pp. 185–6

[. . .] No one has read that remarkable tale of *Oliver Twist* without being interested in poor Nancy and her murderer; and especially amused and tickled by the gambols of the Artful Dodger and his companions. The power of the writer is so amazing, that the reader at once becomes his captive, and must follow him whithersoever he leads; and to what are we led? Breathless to watch all the crimes of Fagin, tenderly to deplore the errors of Nancy, to have for Bill Sikes a kind of pity and admiration, and an absolute love for the society of the Dodger. All these heroes stepped from the novel on to the stage; and the whole London public, from peers to chimney-sweeps, were interested about a set of ruffians whose occupations are thievery, murder, and prostitution. A most agreeable set of rascals, indeed, who have their virtues, too, but not good company for any man. We had better pass them by in decent silence; for, as no writer can or dare tell the *whole* truth concerning them, and faithfully explain their vices, there is no need to give *ex-parte*[1] statements of their virtues.

[. . .] But in the sorrows of Nancy and the exploits of Sheppard,[2] there is no such lurking moral, as far as we have been able to discover; we are asked for downright sympathy in the one case, and are called on in the second to admire the gallantry of a thief. The street-walker may be a very virtuous person, and the robber as brave as Wellington:[3] but it is better to leave them alone, and their qualities, good and bad. [. . .]

From **[Anonymous], 'Charles Dickens and His Works',** *Fraser's Magazine*, 21 (April 1840), pp. 381–400

Few writers have risen so rapidly into extensive popularity as Dickens and that by no mean or unjustifiable panderings to public favour, or the use of low arts of tricking, puffery, or pretence. [. . .]

Now, without asking where Nancy got her fine sentiments, may we not ask where she got her fine English? She talks the common slang of London, in its

---

11 See Cruikshank's 'On the Origin of *Oliver Twist*', **pp. 35–7.**

1 Partisan.
2 Jack Sheppard, a real-life highwayman and jail-breaker (1702–24), who was the hero of Ainsworth's Newgate novel of the same name (1839–40).
3 Arthur Wellesley (1769–1852), Duke of Wellington and leader of the British military in the Napoleonic wars.

ordinary dialect, in the beginning of the novel; at the end no heroine that ever went mad in white satin talked more picked and perfumed sentences of sentimentality. [. . .]

In *Oliver Twist* it is, no doubt, very satisfactory to the lovers of poetical justice that Fagin should be hanged, but the Old Bailey[1] justice that consigned him to the gallows is somewhat peculiar. [. . .] Murder, while advising moderation, is enough to make him an accessory before the fact, and that a clerk of the crown would be found ingenious enough to frame a count in the indictment upon it, and we allow that, if the popular and liberal branch of the legislature proceeds as it has been doing for some time, and the attorney-general continues to display so much dexterity in drawing up warrants there is no saying what we may come to at last,— admit all this, yet still who was to prove it? [. . .]

[. . .] But for this, and many other slips in his stories and style, Boz has offered the adequate excuse, viz. the nature of his publication, in which every thing was to be postponed to the necessity of periodical appearance. We can hardly believe him implicitly when he tells us that the artists designed *after* his hints. In fact, many of his sketches are little more than catalogues of what we find in the pictures, done with the minuteness of an appraiser. The picture, in fact, sold the number, and the writing was a matter of secondary consideration, so far as sale was concerned.[2] [. . .]

But this is the only fault of Boz—if fault it can be called, to make hay while the sun shines. We wish him well; but talking of literature in any other light than that of a hack trade, we do not like this novel-writing by scraps against time. He can never do himself or his readers justice. [. . .] He has one great merit, independent of his undoubted powers of drollery, observation, and caricature—he has not lent his pen to any thing that can give countenance to vice or degradation; and he has always espoused the cause of the humble, the persecuted, and the oppressed. This of itself would cover far more literary sins than Boz has to answer for; and, indeed, we do not remember any of importance enough to require covering at all. [. . .]

From [Anonymous], 'Literary Recipes', *Punch* (7 August 1841), p. 39

A STARTLING ROMANCE

Take a small boy, charity, factory, carpenter's apprentice, or otherwise, as occasion may serve—stew him well down in vice—garnish largely with oaths and flash songs—boil him in a cauldron of crime and improbabilities. Season equally with good and bad qualities—infuse petty larceny, affection, benevolence, and burglary, honour and housebreaking, amiability and arson—boil all gently. Stew down a mad mother—a gang of robbers—several pistols—a bloody knife. Serve up with a couple of murders—and season with a hanging-match.

N.B. Alter the ingredients to a beadle and a workhouse—the scenes may be the

---

1   The central criminal court. There has been some discussion about whether or not Fagin would actually have been hanged for his crimes. See headnote to 'Fagin's Trial, Last Meeting with Oliver, and his Hanging', **pp. 177–8**.
2   See Cruikshank's 'On the Origin of *Oliver Twist*', **pp. 35–7**; see also Richard Ford's review, **p. 60**, n.11.

same, but the whole flavour of vice will be lost, and the boy will turn out a perfect pattern.—Strongly recommended for weak stomachs.

From **George Gissing, 'Oliver Twist'** (c. 1898–1900), in The Immortal Dickens (London: Cecil Palmer, 1925), pp. 76–7

> The novelist Gissing (1857–1903) was one of the foremost early critics of Dickens. The Immortal Dickens is made up of pieces on Dickens written by Gissing between 1898 and 1900. His assertion that Dickens's novels declare 'the democratic tendency of the new age' is contentious but worthy of debate. (See **pp. 14–18**.)

[. . .]

After a long interval during which English fiction was represented by the tawdry unreal or the high imaginative [. . .], a new writer demands attention for stories of obscure lives, and tells his tale so attractively that high and low give ear. It is a step in social and political history; it declares the democratic tendency of the new age. Here is the significance of Dickens's early success, and we do not at all understand his place in English literature if we lose sight of this historic point of view.

[. . .]

Modern Criticism

From **G. K. Chesterton, 'Oliver Twist',** in *Criticisms and Appreciations of the Works of Dickens* (1911) (London: House of Stratus, 2001), pp. 22–7

The writer G. K. Chesterton (1874–1936) is widely regarded as one of the greatest critics of Dickens. His writing is eclectic and wide-ranging, so the sample that follows gives just a taste of many subjects he covered. Here he comments on Dickens's modernity, the mixture of the macabre and the comic in his work and, perhaps most memorably, on Dickens's characterization and 'social revolt'. Chesterton's religious, humanist tendencies are evident in this extract.

[. . .] Dickens mixed up with the old material, materials so subtly modern, so made of the French Revolution, that the whole is transformed. If we want the best example of this, the best example is *Oliver Twist*.

[. . .] With the exception of some gorgeous passages, both of humour and horror, the interest of the book lies not so much in its revelation of Dickens' literary genius as in its revelation of those moral, personal, and political instincts which were the make-up of his character and the permanent support of that literary genius. It is by far the most depressing of all his books; it is in some ways the most irritating; yet its ugliness gives the last touch of honesty to all that spontaneous and splendid output. Without this one discordant note all his merriment might have seemed like levity.

[. . .] There was in Dickens this other kind of energy, horrible, uncanny,[1] barbaric, capable in another age of coarseness [. . .]. This strain existed in Dickens alongside of his happy laughter; both were allied to the same robust romance. Here as elsewhere Dickens is close to all the permanent human things.

---

1   Seemingly supernatural, mysterious or strange. The term was of interest to Freud, who wrote an essay about it, and psychoanalysis. It is often used to convey a sense of ourselves as double, split or at odds with ourselves.

He is close to religion, which has never allowed the thousand devils on its churches to stop the dancing of its bells. He is allied to the people, to the real poor, who love nothing so much as to take a cheerful glass and to talk about funerals. The extremes of his gloom and gaiety are the mark of religion and democracy; they mark him off from the moderate happiness of philosophers, and from that stoicism which is the virtue and the creed of aristocrats. [. . .]

As a nightmare, the work is really admirable. Characters which are not very clearly conceived as regards their own psychology are yet, at certain moments, managed so as to shake to its foundations our own psychology. Bill Sikes is not exactly a real man, but for all that he is a real murderer: Nancy is not really impressive as a living woman; but (as the phrase goes) she makes a lovely corpse. Something quite childish and eternal in us, something which is shocked with the mere simplicity of death, quivers when we read of those footprints. And this strange, sublime, vulgar melodrama, which is melodrama and yet is painfully real, reaches its hideous height in that fine scene of the death of Sikes. [. . .] There is in this and similar scenes something of the quality of Hogarth and many other English moralists of the early eighteenth century. [. . .] It is a sort of alphabetical realism, like the cruel candour of children. But it has about it these two special principles which separate it from all that we call realism in our time. First, that with us a moral story means a story about moral people; with them a moral story meant more often a story about immoral people. Second, that with us realism is always associated with some subtle view of morals; with them realism was always associated with some simple view of morals.

[. . .]

[. . .] Dickens' social revolt is of more value than mere politics and avoids the vulgarity of the novel with a purpose. [. . .] He disliked a certain look on the face of a man when he looks down on another man. [. . .] He saw that under many forms there was one fact, the tyranny of man over man; and he struck at it when he saw it, whether it was old or new. [. . .] This is what makes the opening chapter of *Oliver Twist* so curious and important. The very fact of Dickens' distance from, and independence of, the elaborate financial arguments of his time, makes more definite and dappling his sudden assertion that he sees the old human tyranny in front of him as plain as the sun at noonday. Dickens attacks the modern workhouse with a sort of inspired simplicity as of a boy in a fairy tale who had wandered about sword in hand, looking for ogres and who had found an indisputable ogre. All the other people of his time are attacking things because they are bad economics or because they are bad politics, or because they are bad science; he alone is attacking things because they are bad. All the others are Radicals with a large R; he alone is radical with a small one. He encounters evil with that beautiful surprise which, as it is the beginning of all real pleasure, is also the beginning of all righteous indignation. He enters the workhouse just as Oliver Twist enters it, as a little child.

[. . .]

From **Edmund Wilson, 'Dickens: The Two Scrooges',** in *The Wound and the Bow: Seven Studies in Literature* (1941) (New York: Oxford University Press, 1965), pp. 51–2

Edmund Wilson's seminal biographical reading of Dickens sees the character of Scrooge, the miser who becomes benevolent in *A Christmas Carol*, as symbolic of a lack of balance in Dickens's own personality. His unstable 'emotional constitution', brought on by his traumatic childhood experiences, led to the melodramatic extremes of his novels. (See also Forster, **pp. 34–5**.)

[. . .] Yet Scrooge represents a principle fundamental to the dynamics of Dickens' world and derived from his own emotional constitution. It was not merely that his passion for the theater had given him a taste for melodramatic contrasts; it was rather that the lack of balance between the opposite impulses of his nature had stimulated an appetite for melodrama. For emotionally Dickens *was* unstable. Allowing for the English restraint, which masks what the Russian expressiveness indulges and perhaps over-expresses, and for the pretenses of English biographers, he seems almost as unstable as Dostoevsky.[1] [. . .]

From **George Orwell, 'Charles Dickens',** in *Dickens, Dali and Others* (San Diego, Calif.: Harcourt Brace Jovanovich, 1946), pp. 2–32

In this essay, the socialist novelist George Orwell (1903–50) asks how Dickens has been able to offer a 'radical' critique of British society while remaining so popular. For Orwell, Dickens's social criticism 'is almost exclusively moral'. Dickens's 'moral' standpoint perhaps partly explains the ideological inconsistencies in his attitudes to race, class and national identity.

[. . .] even if Dickens was a bourgeois, he was certainly a subversive writer, a radical, one might truthfully say a rebel. Everyone who has read widely in his work has felt this. [. . .] *Oliver Twist, Hard Times, Bleak House, Little Dorrit*, Dickens attacked English institutions with a ferocity that has never since been approached. Yet he managed to do it without making himself hated, and, more than this, the very people he attacked have swallowed him so completely that he has become a national institution himself. In its attitude towards Dickens the English public has always been a little like the elephant which feels a blow with a walking-stick as a delightful tickling. [. . .] Naturally this makes one wonder whether after all there was something unreal in his attack upon society. Where exactly does he stand, socially, morally and politically? As usual, one can define his position more easily if one starts by deciding what he was *not*.
  [. . .]

1   Fyodor Dostoevsky (1821–81), the Russian novelist. Dostoevsky was an admirer of Dickens's work.

The truth is that Dickens's criticism of society is almost exclusively moral. Hence the utter lack of any constructive suggestion anywhere in his work. [. . .]

[. . .] Dickens is not *in the accepted sense* a revolutionary writer. But it is not at all certain that a merely moral criticism of society may not be just as 'revolutionary' – and revolution, after all, means turning things upside down – as the politico-economic criticism which is fashionable at this moment. [. . .]

[. . .] It is true that he takes it for granted (*Oliver Twist* and *Great Expectations*) that a receiver of stolen goods will be a Jew, which at the time was probably justified. But the 'Jew joke,' endemic in English literature until the rise of Hitler, does not appear in his books, and in *Our Mutual Friend* he makes a pious though not very convincing attempt to stand up for the Jews.[1]

Dickens's lack of vulgar nationalism is in part the mark of a real largeness of mind, and in part results from his negative, rather unhelpful political attitude. He is very much an Englishman, but he is hardly aware of it – certainly the thought of being an Englishman does not thrill him. He has no imperialist feeling, no discernible views on foreign politics, and is untouched by the military tradition. [. . .] It is noticeable that Dickens hardly writes of war, even to denounce it. [. . .]

From **Humphry House, 'The Macabre Dickens'** (1947), in *All in Due Time: The Collected Essays and Broadcast Talks of Humphry House* (1955) (Freeport, NY: Books for Libraries Press, 1972), pp. 183–7

> Both extracts from Humphry House adopt a biographical approach to argue that Dickens's feelings of social alienation as a child worker in the blacking factory explain the imaginative vividness of criminals and outsiders in his novels (and in passages such as 'The Flight of Sikes', **pp. 170–3**). His observation 'It is as if Dickens was afraid of attempting to portray the full complexity of an adult', looks for psychological realism as opposed to allegorical or symbolic meaning in the novels. (See also Forster, **pp. 34–5**.)

The present lively interest in Dickens has in it an element never before prominent in all his hundred years of popularity—an interest in his mastery of the macabre and terrible in scene and character. [. . .] He has worked as much beneath the surface as above it; and he was possibly not himself fully conscious of what he was putting into his books. The floor of consciousness has been lowered. [. . .]

[. . .] Dickens's imagination usually concentrates through all the greater part of a story now on the black, now on the white, exclusively: the two don't interpenetrate. [. . .] It is as if Dickens was afraid of attempting to portray the full complexity of an adult. [. . .] I cannot think of a single instance in which one of the good characters suddenly reveals a streak of evil. [. . .] The startling thing that *does* happen is that the villains suddenly reveal, if not a streak of good, a streak of vivid power, and then an immense depth of intricate confused and pitiable humanity. [. . .]

---

1   See letters to Eliza Davis, **pp. 33–4**, Stone and Heller, **pp. 68–70**, and **pp. 82–4** and 'The Work in Performance,' **pp. 108–13**.

One of the problems that face the critic of Dickens is to explain how this intimate understanding of morbid and near-morbid psychology links on to his apparent optimism, and above all to his humour.

From **Humphry House, 'Introduction' to Charles Dickens, The Adventures of Oliver Twist** (London: Oxford University Press, 1949), pp. x–xi

[. . .] To understand the conjunction of such different moods and qualities in a single man is the beginning of serious criticism of Dickens. The theme of murder, and still more of the murderer being hunted and haunted after his crime, treated not as a detective story, but as a statement of human behaviour, recurs several times in his major work. Both Sikes and Jonas Chuzzlewit[1] are transfigured by the act of murder.

The psychological condition of a rebel-reformer is in many ways similar to that of a criminal, and may have the same origins. A feeling of being outside the ordinary organization of group life; a feeling of being an outcast, or misfit or a victim of circumstance; a feeling of bitter loneliness, isolation, ostracism or irrevocable disgrace—any one or any combination of such feelings may turn a man against organized society, and his opposition may express itself in what is technically crime or what is technically politics: treason, sedition, and armed rebellion manage to be both. Dickens's childhood had been such that all these feelings, at different times in different degrees, had been his: he knew no security and no tenderness: the family home was for a time the Marshalsea prison,[2] and for six months Dickens himself was a wretched drudge in a blacking-factory. These two experiences, and others similar, lie behind the loneliness, disgrace and outlawry which pervade all his novels. These were always his leading psychological themes. [. . .]

The lasting impression left by this novel is one of macabre horror. [. . .]

From **Graham Greene, 'The Young Dickens'**, *Oliver Twist* (London: Hamish Hamilton, 1951), pp. 101–10

The novelist Graham Greene sees 'Manichaeism' in *Oliver Twist* and later novels as a dualism between good and evil in which evil is stronger than good. A Manichee is an adherent of a religious system (third–fifth century) that represented Satan as coeternal with God – a dualist.

[. . .] As for the truth, is it too fantastic to imagine that in this novel, as in many of his later books, creeps in, unrecognized by the author, the eternal and alluring taint of the Manichee, with it simple and terrible explanation of our plight, how the world was made by Satan and not by God, lulling us with the music of despair?

---

1   A murderer in Dickens's *Martin Chuzzlewit* (1843–4).
2   The debtors' prison, which also features in Dickens's *Little Dorrit* (1855–7). See **pp. 7–8**.

From **Harry Stone, 'Dickens and the Jews',** *Victorian Studies,* 2 (1959), pp. 223–53

In this essay, Stone tries to account for the anti-Semitism which many have seen as informing Dickens's characterization of Fagin by relating it to the prevailing anti-Semitism of the times. (See also **pp. 33–4, p. 49, pp. 108–13** and Heller, **pp. 82–4.**)

[. . .] one can understand Dickens' protesting his bewilderment at charges of anti-Semitism, for his attitude toward Jews changed greatly between *Oliver Twist* (1837–39) and *Our Mutual Friend* (1864–65).

[. . .] For Dickens' drift from careless prejudice to at least an intellectual understanding is both a significant personal achievement and a revealing symptom of the evolving patterns of Victorian culture.

Oliver Twist grew out of an era and a literary tradition which was predominantly anti-Semitic. Laws, parliamentary debates, newspapers, magazines, songs, and plays, as well as novels, reflect the latent anti-Semitism which was a part of the early Victorian heritage. In 1830 a Jew could not open a shop within the city of London, be called to the Bar, receive a university degree, or sit in Parliament. Sir Robert Peel,[1] who a few years later championed the Jewish cause, was still in 1830 opposing Jewish emancipation on the strange grounds that the restricted Jew was not like his free compatriots. 'The Jew,' said Sir Robert, speaking against the removal of Jewish disabilities, 'is not a degraded subject of the state; he is rather regarded in the light of an alien—he is excluded because he will not amalgamate with us in any of his usages or habits—he is regarded as a foreigner. In the history of the Jews . . . we find enough to account for the prejudice which exists against them.' That prejudice was accentuated by the occupations Jews were compelled to enter by English law and custom. In 1830 the majority of England's twenty to thirty thousand Jews earned their living through buying and selling old clothes, peddling, and moneylending. Portraits in fiction of Jewish clothesdealers staggering under huge bags of rags, bearded peddlers haggling with country housewives, and miserly usurers gloating over their secret treasures were given reality not only by a long literary tradition but by the intermittent evidence of the London streets. And the exotic evil which the average Londoner of that day felt sure lay hidden in bag or beard or countinghouse was occasionally confirmed by sensational newspaper reports. In the summer of 1830 the respectable citizenry of London were being diverted by the trial of one Isaac (Ikey) Solomons, a Jewish fence who, like Fagin, dealt in stolen jewelry, clothing, and fabrics. Ikey Solomons, although acquitted on all charges of burglary and theft, was finally convicted of possessing stolen goods and sentenced to seven years' transportation. His case was so notorious that a play of the period entitled *Van Diemen's Land* was rechristened *Ikey Solomons*, and one of its minor characters, Barney Fence, a stereotyped stage-Jew, was transformed into Ikey himself.

Such a transformation reflected the ubiquitous anti-Semitism of the period.

---

1   See p. 15.

[. . .]

Oliver Twist, then, was the work of an author who accepted and reflected the anti-Semitism of his milieu. And yet *Oliver Twist* is not as anti-Semitic as one might expect; Fagin is less a premeditated attack upon the Jews than a convenient villain drawn to an ancient pattern. He exhibits, for instance, a number of stereotyped stage-Jew characteristics: red hair and whiskers, hooked nose, shuffling gait, and long gabardine[2] coat and broadbrimmed hat. Furthermore, he is a dealer in secondhand clothes and trinkets, the Jewish occupation par excellence. [. . .] But Fagin is strangely lacking in other traits of the literary Jew. He has no lisp, dialect, or nasal intonation (although Barney, a minor confederate of Fagin, described as 'another Jew: younger than Fagin, but nearly as vile and repulsive in appearance,' talks with a perpetual cold in his head, saying, 'Dot a shoul' for 'Not a soul,' and so forth. And Fagin goes through no act, ritual, or pattern which identifies him as a Jew. Actually, aside from his conventionalized physical traits and old-clothes dealings, his main claim to Jewishness is the fact that Dickens constantly labels him 'the Jew.' It seems fair to assume that Fagin was a Jew because for Dickens and his readers he made a picturesque and believable villain.

But that Dickens could create Fagin is a reflection of his indifference to the implications of his portrait. And this is true even though he attempted here and there to underline the distinction between Fagin the individual and Fagin the Jew. In Fagin's first appearance he is portrayed toasting a sausage—an act which immediately brands him a renegade Jew. And in the condemned cell, in one of the reader's final glimpses of him, Dickens again contrasts him with the Jews as a whole. 'Venerable men of his own persuasion,' he writes, 'had come to pray beside him, but he had driven them away with curses. They renewed their charitable efforts, and he beat them off.' It seems strange that Dickens could believe these touches would offset the implications of the remainder of his portrait, but his attitude toward the Jews was negligent at best, and he probably gave little thought to Fagin's anti-Semitic ramifications.

[. . .] The years 1830 to 1860 witnessed a steady rise in the status of English Jewry. Legal barriers were swept away, commercial restrictions removed, and social antagonisms lessened. Jews held offices in local and national government, became connected through marriage with prominent families, took part increasingly in the social and artistic affairs of the country, and grew in power and numbers. [. . .]

In *Oliver Twist* [Dickens] made hundreds of emendations,[3] but the most important and most numerous by far concern Fagin and the Jews. Beginning with Chapter XXXIX, he went through *Oliver Twist* and eliminated the bulk of the references to Fagin as 'the Jew,' canceling that term entirely, or replacing it with 'he [. . .],' or with 'Fagin.' [. . .]

The effect of these changes is to eliminate, for the most part, the one important link connecting Fagin with the Jews. [. . .]

These final revisions are doubly significant. For Dickens' journey had been the journey of his times. [. . .] And yet by 1864 and *Our Mutual Friend* he was not

---

2   Smooth, durable twill-woven cloth, especially of worsted or cotton.
3   In 1867; see **pp. 33–4**.

merely mirroring; despite his occasional confusions and ambivalences, he was urging forward the Victorian advance toward toleration. For in his relationship with the Jews, as in other areas of his life and art, Dickens was a maker as well as a creature of his times.

From **John Bayley, 'Oliver Twist: Things as they really are'**, in *Dickens and the Twentieth Century*, edited by John Gross and Gabriel Pearson (London: Routledge & Kegan Paul, 1962), pp. 49–52

> John Bayley's nuanced essay explores Dickens's claim to be representing 'things as they really are' in *Oliver Twist*, rightly concluding that the reality of the novel in fact resembles 'the honesty of the dream world'. Bayley's essay is unusual for its time in so far as it undermines the notion that realism and fantasy are opposite kinds of writing. Bayley's undermining of the idea of contrasts and separate worlds in the novel contradicts Lucas (**pp. 72–3**) but picks up on Henry James's observation on Cruikshank's illustrations that 'The nice people and the happy moments [. . .] frightened me almost as much as the low and the awkward'.[1]

Oliver Twist is a modern novel. It has the perennially modern pretension of rejecting the unreality of a previous mode, of setting out to show us 'things as they really are'. But its modernity is more radical and more unsettling than this pretension implies [. . .].

Oliver Twist lacks only one attribute of the modern novel—complete self-consciousness. No novelist has profited more richly than Dickens from not examining what went on in his own mind.[2] [. . .] Dickens recoiled from what he called 'dissective' art, and if he had been able and willing to analyse the relation between our inner and outer selves he could never have created the rhetoric that so marvellously ignores the distinction between them. Unlike us, he had no diagrammatic view of mind, no constricting terminology for the psyche. [. . .]

Their wholeness and harmony have a curious effect on the evil of Dickens's monsters: it sterilizes it in performance but increases it in idea. The energy of Fagin or Quilp[3] seems neutral; there is not enough gap between calculation and action for it to proceed to convincingly evil works. [. . .] We cannot recoil from Dickens's villains: they are the more frightening and haunting because we cannot expel them for what they do; they have the unexpungable nature of our own nightmares and our own consciousness. [. . .]

Oliver Twist is not a satisfying novel—it does not liberate us. In achieving what might be called the honesty of the dream world it has to stay in prison. The sense of complete reality in fiction can perhaps only be achieved by the author's possessing, and persuading his reader to share, a sense of different worlds,

---

1   *A Small Boy and Others* (1913), in Henry James, *Autobiography*, ed. by Frederick W. Dupee (London: W. H. Allen, 1956), pp. 3–236 (p. 69).
2   See letter to G. H. Lewes [?9 June 1838], **pp. 29–30**.
3   The dwarf villain of Dickens's novel, *The Old Curiosity Shop* (1840–1).

different and indeed almost incompatible modes of feeling and being. [. . .] But in *Oliver Twist* there are no such contrasts, no such different worlds. Even the apparent contrast between Fagin's world and that of Rose Maylie and Mr. Brownlow is not a real one, and this is not because the happy Brownlow world is rendered sentimentally and unconvincingly by Dickens, but because the two do in fact co-exist in consciousness: they are twin sides of the same coin of fantasy, not two real places that exist separately in life. [. . .]

That the two worlds are one in the mind appears even in Cruickshank's drawings, where Oliver often has a distinct look of Fagin. [. . .]

From **Steven Marcus, 'Who is Fagin?' in *Dickens: From Pickwick to Dombey*** (New York: Norton, 1985), pp. 358–78

Steven Marcus's essay, 'Who is Fagin?', appended to his book, takes a biographical and psychoanalytic approach to the character of Fagin (as does the work of Wilson and House, **pp. 64–7**). Fagin was named after Bob Fagin, a kindly boy who worked with Dickens at the blacking factory. He was responsible for teaching Dickens factory work when he arrived. The two sometimes worked together at a window in public view and one day Bob offered to walk Dickens home. Dickens was too proud to tell him that his family were in the Marshalsea debtors' prison, so in view of Bob, he knocked on the door of a respectable house as if it were his own and asked whether Robert Fagin lived there. Marcus's theory is that the name Fagin was transferred to the villain of *Oliver Twist* to purge some of the resentment Dickens felt at his life in the blacking factory and the near exposure of his shame. (See also Forster, **pp. 34–5**.)

[. . .] the Bob Fagin whose friendship contained the threat of exposure, and the father whose freedom was a fraud and an outrage while his son slaved in a window, coalesced in Dickens's mind. But they coalesced into an image which has its origin in an earlier phase of Dickens's development, a phase which the London experience re-awakened and which the scene at the window both refers to and conceals. This is the image of the father of infancy and earliest childhood. And it is at this point that Fagin, the terrible, frightening old Jew, becomes relevant. For the traditional popular mythology of the Jew as Devil and Anti-Christ, as the castrator and murderer of good little Christian boys, corresponds itself to this image of the terrible father of infancy and of our primal fantasies, and is indeed one of western culture's chief expressions of it.[1]

[. . .] the boy who suffered passively in the blacking warehouse, who grieved in solitude and felt himself to be Oliver Twist, was also the boy who was not afraid to lie to protect his and his father's poor pride and shame, who acted out that lie with spirit and audacity, and who told stories to amuse and entertain his fellows in the warehouse. He went on lying and telling stories until he became one of the

---

1 [Marcus's note.] See Ernest Jones, *On the Nightmare*, and Norman Cohn, *The Pursuit of the Millenium*, for exhaustive and illuminating illustrations of this subject.

world's great masters of the art, and created those grand imaginative lies which in our perplexed condition somehow approximate the truth. Oliver Twist could never have imagined Fagin, and Dickens could neither have imagined nor created him had Fagin not been part of himself and had he been unable ever to affirm that part of himself with gusto and delight.

From **John Lucas, *The Melancholy Man: A Study of Dickens's Novels*** (London: Methuen, 1970), pp. 32–9

> John Lucas focuses here on the idea of Oliver as a child of nature and on the novel's representation of 'worlds that exist totally distinct from and unknown to each other', in particular the country and the city. Arnold Kettle had previously argued that 'The core of the novel, and what gives it value, is its consideration of the plight of the poor. Its pattern is the contrasted relation of two worlds – the underworld [. . .] and the comfortable world'.[1] Compare Dickens's related comments on the use of contrasts in the novel in Chapter 17, **pp. 151–3** and John Bayley (**pp. 70–1**).

[. . .] Nature is a word that receives a good deal of attention in *Oliver Twist* as it does in most of Dickens's novels, and later in the chapter I shall have something to say about Oliver as the natural child of a natural relationship. Here, however, I want to concentrate on Dickens's hero as a Rousseauistic[2] child of nature.

To begin with, we must note that when Monks and Fagin appear to Oliver he is in the country and happier than he has ever been. And this is not merely a matter of sweet air and climbing plants; Dickens goes out of his way in this section of the book to insist on the educative and healing powers of nature. No doubt much of this passionate identification of Oliver and nature goes back to the novelist's own childhood. Edgar Johnson calls his chapter on the young Dickens at Rochester 'The Happy Time', and he provides quite enough evidence of Dickens's rambles with his father and delighted knowledge of the countryside to persuade us that those years were indeed happy.[3]

They must have looked particularly beautiful seen through a perspective created by the blacking factory, and there is a possible hint of that retrospect when we read that 'Oliver, whose days had been spent among squalid crowds and in the midst of noise and brawling, seemed to enter on a new existence there.'[4] But no matter what autobiographical material may have been fed into the study of Oliver, Dickens's interest in him is proper to the novel. As a child of nature

---

1   Arnold Kettle, *An Introduction to the English Novel* (1951), 2 vols, 2nd edn (London: Hutchinson, 1967; repr. 1981), Vol. I, pp. 115–29 (p. 121).

2   Jean-Jacques Rousseau (1712–78): a Swiss philosopher who believed that people 'in a state of nature' were good and that society corrupted.

3   [Lucas's note.] Edgar Johnson: *Charles Dickens: His Tragedy and Triumph* 2 vols (1952). Vol. I, esp. pp. 14–19.

4   Dickens, *Oliver Twist*, Chapter 33.

Oliver's new existence distinguishes him from those who live 'in the great city, pent 'mid cloisters dim'. [. . .]

[. . .] *Oliver Twist* concerns itself with sets of worlds that threaten each other because, so it seems, they are creations of a society that has lost any sense of shared purpose or identity. [. . .]

It is when we come to register Dickens's rendering of social apartness, its manifestations and consequences, that we inevitably come upon the most frequently noted characteristic of *Oliver Twist*. The novel inaugurates what it is now customary to call Dickens's sense of an atomistic universe, of worlds that exist totally distinct from and unknown to each other. [. . .] In this respect, the novel's topographical precision is important because by means of it Dickens localizes and makes realistic the different worlds and suggests the feel of their self-containment and mutual unknowability. [. . .] But *Oliver Twist* is nevertheless determined to confront its audience with worlds that will not go away no matter how much they may be ignored. Eric Hobsbawm has pointed out that during the period 1820–40, urban development 'was a gigantic process of class segregation' [. . .].[5]

The picaresque element of *Oliver Twist* provides Dickens with the opportunities he needs for confronting his audience with those areas of society from which they have escaped or about which they are plainly ignorant. That is why Oliver is so important to the novel's purpose [. . .].

From **J. Hillis Miller, 'The Fiction of Realism: *Sketches by Boz, Oliver Twist*, and Cruikshank's Illustrations'**, in *Dickens Centennial Essays,* edited by Ada Nisbet and Blake Nevius (Berkeley, Calif.: University of California Press, 1971), pp. 128–53

In this essay, Miller uses post-structuralist theory to explain the relationship between the written text, the illustration and extra-textual 'reality' when we read illustrated texts. Illustrated texts undermine the idea of 'the self-enclosed unity of the literary work. [. . .] Illustrations establish a relation between elements within the work which shortcircuits the apparent reference of the literary text to some real world.' Thus, when we are reading an illustrated text, we should be aware that signs always refer to 'other equally fictional entities'. One of the main aims of Miller's essay is to expose 'the fiction of realism' or the crudity of 'mimetic' understandings of realism which assume a direct relationship between an artistic 'sign' and its referent outside the text. In *A Small Boy and Others* (1913), Henry James seems to separate the illustrations from the text in his description of the effect the illustrations had on him as a boy. See also Cruikshank on the relationship between text and illustration, **pp. 35–7,** and Cruikshank's illustrations, **pp. 142, 146** and **181**. John Jordan's piece, **pp. 79–82**, offers another example of post-structuralist criticism and my own extract, **pp. 89–91,** builds on Miller's work.

---

5 [Lucas's note.] E. J. Hobsbawm, *The Age of Revolution,* 1964, p. 242.

[. . .] To allow a non-verbal element full rights within this structure of meaning is no longer to be able to maintain a now traditional view of the self-enclosed unity of the literary work. Moreover, if the illustrations are as much a part of the text as any of its verbal elements, which has priority over the other in the case of a discrepancy? Which is the 'origin' of the other? Which illustrates which? [. . .]

The relation between text and illustration is clearly reciprocal. Each refers to the other. Each illustrates the other, in a continual back and forth movement which is incarnated in the experience of the reader as his eyes move from words to picture and back again, juxtaposing the two in a mutual establishment of meaning. Illustrations in a work of fiction displace the sign-referent relationship assumed in a mimetic reading and replace it by a complex and problematic reference between two radically different kinds of sign, the linguistic and the graphic. Illustrations establish a relation between elements within the work which shortcircuits the apparent reference of the literary text to some real world outside. [. . .] Here is one way to talk about the self-expressive aspect of Cruikshank's art. It imitates not the real London and not the imaginary world created by Dickens's words, but the special quality of Cruikshank's mind or vision of things. [. . .] Cruikshank is supposed to have told Henry Mayhew[1] that Fagin was copied from a mirrored image of himself crouching in bed, with his hand to his mouth, meditating despairingly on the difficulty of drawing Fagin in the condemned cell. In his later years Cruikshank came increasingly to identify himself with Fagin and to like to play the role of his most famous illustration. In the same way, the preliminary sketches for his illustrations are often marginally decorated with miniature self-portraits. The narcissistic image of Cruikshank drawing his own mirrored face seems an appropriate emblem for the way his art is not copied from the external world or from the literary texts it is supposed to illustrate but is projected outward from his own inner world.

[. . .] Cruikshank's work is in many ways related to an elaborate tradition and may be fully understood only in terms of its references to the conventions of that tradition.[2] The tradition in this case is that of caricature, whether political or comic, drawing, etching, or woodcut. [. . .] E. H. Gombrich has shown how any tradition of graphic representation involves complex conventions whereby three-dimensional objects are signified by marks on a flat surface. These conventions are in no sense realistic but come to be taken for granted as adequate mirrorings of reality by artists and viewers of art who dwell within the conventions. [. . .] Far from being a self-portrait, Cruikshank's Fagin is one of a long line of similar figures by various artists, each one referring back to earlier similar ones, and no one identifiable as the 'archetype.' [. . .] Cruikshank's illustrations are based on complex conventions which include not only modes of graphic representation, but also the stereotyped poses of melodrama and pantomime [. . .]. Rather than imitating some extra-artistic realm, Cruikshank's pictures draw their meaning from their relation to other works of art to which they implicitly refer and on which they depend for the creation of their own significance.

To investigate a given illustration by Cruikshank on the assumption that it is a

---

1   Henry Mayhew (1812–87) journalist and writer, best known for *London Labour and the London Poor* (1851): see 'Fagin in the Condemned Cell', **p. 181**.
2   The tradition of caricature; see **p. 48**.

'sign' pointing to some reality outside itself is to discover that each illustration is the meeting point of a set of incompatible references – the 'real' London, Dickens's text, Cruikshank's 'sensibility,' and the tradition of caricature. [. . .]

[. . .] To raise the question of what it means to have an illustrated book [. . .] is to encounter a contradictory vibration between a mimetic reading sustained by reference to something extra-artistic and a reading which sees both the literary text and its illustrations as fictions. The meaning of such fictions is constituted and maintained only by their reference to other equally fictional entities. This reciprocally sustaining, reciprocally destroying vacillation between literal and figurative interpretations is crucial to the process of explicating both graphic and literary works.

[. . .]

From **Dennis Walder, *Dickens and Religion*** (London: Allen & Unwin, 1981), pp. 42–61

Walder's *Dickens and Religion* argues that, 'In *Oliver Twist* Dickens moves towards the expression of both good and evil as forces having their origin beyond the material world, so that in reading the novel we are often aware of some metaphysical drama hovering about the events of the surface-narrative.' (On the metaphysical Dickens, see Greene, **p. 67**, and Bowen, **p. 109**.) Oliver is saved by genuine Christian charity and goodness, for Walder, by characters who help him because of sympathy and 'Christian love, expressed as a love of God and one's neighbour'. This is not the version of Christianity that allied evangelical ministers with political economists in their support for the Poor Law Amendment Act. Evangelical religion usually entailed intense and public professions of belief which Dickens believed to be extreme and repellent. Evangelicals believed in the inherent sinfulness of human nature and share with Utilitarians a negative view of people that Dickens despises (see Dickens's satire, **pp. 127–34**). Evangelicals, as Walder explains at the end of this extract, held several beliefs that made them more prone to sympathize with the New Poor Law.

The fundamental aim of *Oliver Twist* (1837–9) is to move us [. . .] into sympathy and charity for the poor [. . .].

[. . .] It is one of the abiding strengths of Dickens's vision of life that, unlike most of his great contemporaries in the English novel, such as Thackeray, George Eliot, or Trollope,[1] he has a profound apprehension of evil which extended beyond the domestic or even social.

This is not to ignore (as Greene[2] and later critics ignore) the fact that the hero of *Oliver Twist* is, finally, *saved*. He is saved by the sympathy and charity, the freely given loving aid of those good Christians (explicitly identified as such) into whose hands he is cast 'by a stronger hand than chance' (ch. xlix). If God permits evil to

---

1   The realist novelist Anthony Trollope (1815–82).
2   The novelist Graham Greene (1904–91); see Greene's extract, **p. 67**.

flourish in *Oliver Twist*—and there can be no denying the *initial* power of the parish authorities, of Fagin and his gang—then he also ensures its ultimate failure and destruction. The turning-point is quite clear: not only do we see Bumble, symbol of parish authority, reduced and humbled by his wife (ch. xxxvii), but Sikes and Nancy pale, cadaverous and ill (ch. xxxix), after Oliver's recovery with the Maylies. Thenceforward, evil is set on a downward path. [. . .] He continues to believe not only in the ultimately hopeful ordering of human affairs, despite the suffering of the poor and destitute, but also in the existence of good as a transcendental value, a 'principle' to be embodied in symbolic or 'romantic', rather than realistic form. In *Oliver Twist* Dickens moves towards the expression of both good and evil as forces having their origin beyond the material world, so that in reading the novel we are often aware of some metaphysical drama hovering about the events of the surface-narrative. In so far as *Oliver Twist* insists upon its importance in meeting the needs of the poor, the novel carries a more noticeably Christian hue than most of his fictional works, except perhaps the *Christmas Books* and the last novels. The term means more than the simple human virtue of benevolence, or giving alms to the poor; it implies the more general motive of Christian love, expressed as a love of God and one's neighbour. This distinction has been used to argue that Dickens's charitable characters are not strictly Christian in their performance of benevolent acts towards others, since these seem no more than spontaneous expressions of their good nature, rather than reflections of a will dedicated to God. But Dickens wishes to avoid the premeditativeness of doing good as a duty, as well as any hint of excess – or even merely open—piety, preferring a modest, self-effacing, yet direct goodness which emerges as the natural expression of the personality. He reveals virtue implicitly, in terms of the essential being of a character, rather than in terms of its motivation. If the good people love God—and he often implies that they do—this is revealed only implicitly, through imagery and action, and not by allotting characters overtly Christian motives.

[. . .]

Dickens was critical not only of the New Poor Law as such, but of the whole structure of beliefs concerning the poor which underlay the legal system of his time: 'this ain't the shop for justice', as the Dodger remarks (ch. xliii). The link between the social philosophy of the utilitarian political economists and the religious outlook for the evangelicals, implicit in the new regulations, was forged long before their appearance, and not only among economists or evangelical ministers: it had long been the general conviction that the visible inequality of rewards was a part of the Providential plan; that vice and misery were God-given checks upon population growth; above all, that providing relief for the poor was simply interfering with the severe but necessary conditions for social, economic and moral progress. This is implicit in all that happens before the appearance of the board's new 'system'. [. . .]

From **Helena Michie, *The Flesh Made Word: Female Figures and Women's Bodies*** (Oxford: Oxford University Press, 1987), pp. 76–7

Michie's analysis of Nancy focuses interestingly on the denial of the body and on the emphasis on dress and artificiality in Dickens's representations of her. (The same denial of the body occurs in many female Dickens characters.) See also Ingham, **pp. 84–7**, Bowen, **pp. 87–9** and **pp. 149–50, 163–4**.

[. . .]

The descriptions of Nancy and the other prostitutes in *Oliver Twist* focus far more obsessively on what they put on than on what they take off; Oliver's first observations, that they have 'a good deal of hair' and 'a great deal of colour in their faces', emphasize dress and artificiality over nudity and sensuality. Nancy's costumes proliferate as the novel progresses. With the aid of curlers and an apron from Fagin's 'inexhaustible stock' of disguises, she pretends to be Oliver's sister. Toward the middle of the novel, as she begins to sympathize with Oliver, she spies on Sykes and Fagin, covering herself with a shawl to make herself invisible. Slipping into the novel's dark corners, head and body swathed in her shawl, she becomes a symbol of self-erasure and vicariousness. Her murder is a final dressing, a revelation of her as typological [. . .]. Nancy, neutralized into an 'it', a 'figure', is easy prey. Her last act, the holding up of Rose's handkerchief to Heaven, is a final covering, a gesture that makes metaphorically possible Sykes' denial of her corporeality as he covers his eyes. The reader too sees not Nancy, but the death of a symbol whose function is simultaneously the representation of illicit sexuality and the denial of the body.

The covering of the prostitute's body is reiterated in Victorian paintings of women. [. . .]

From **D. A. Miller, *The Novel and the Police*** (Berkeley, Calif.: University of California Press, 1988), pp. 4–8, 58–60

D. A. Miller's *The Novel and the Police* draws on *Discipline and Punish* by Michel Foucault (see **pp. 16–17**) in which Foucault argues that the shift between the eighteenth and nineteenth centuries away from capital punishment to the use of prisons as the main instrument of the law represents not greater freedom for people but greater 'surveillance' and discipline. The prison, for Foucault, thus becomes the model for the way in which society, its institutions and its discourses monitors, regulates and normalizes behaviour; the label of delinquency becomes a tool of social control. Miller points out that in *Oliver Twist*, delinquency is determined by 'a structured milieu or network' from which delinquents cannot escape. Similarly, the middle classes, who see themselves as above the law and outside the milieu of delinquency, maintain their apparent freedom only by 'absolute submission to the norms, protocols, and regulations of the middle-class family', and 'the burden of an immense internal regulation'.

[. . .]

A large part of the moral shock *Oliver Twist* seeks to induce has to do with the *coherence* of delinquency, as a structured milieu or network. The logic of Oliver's 'career,' for instance, establishes workhouse, apprenticeship, and membership in Fagin's gang as versions of a single experience of incarceration. Other delinquent careers are similarly full of superficial movement in which nothing really changes. [. . .] Nor is it fortuitous that Fagin recruits his gang from institutions such as workhouses and groups such as apprentices, or that Mr. and Mrs. Bumble become paupers 'in that very same workhouse in which they had once lorded it over others'.[1] The world of delinquency encompasses not only the delinquents themselves, but also the persons and institutions supposed to reform them or prevent them from forming. The policemen in the novel—the Bow Street runners Duff and Blathers—belong to this world, too. The story they tell about a man named Chickweed *who robbed himself* nicely illustrates the unity of both sides of the law in the delinquent context, the same unity that has allowed cop Blathers to call robber Chickweed 'one of the family'.[2] Police and offenders are conjoined in a single system for the formation and re-formation of delinquents. [. . .]

In proportion as Dickens stresses the coherence and systematic nature of delinquency, he makes it an *enclosed* world from which it is all but impossible to escape. [. . .] With the exception of Oliver, characters are either appallingly comfortable with their roles or pathetically resigned to them. An elsewhere or an otherwise cannot be conceived, much less desired and sought out. The closed-circuit character of delinquency is, of course, a sign of Dickens's progressive attitude, his willingness to see coercive system where it was traditional only to see bad morals. Yet one should recognize how closing the circuit results in an 'outside' as well as an 'inside,' an 'outside' precisely determined as *outside the circuit*. [. . .] Much of the proof of Nancy's ultimate goodness lies in her awed recognition of the impermeable boundaries that separate her from Rose Maylie. It is this, as much as her love for Bill Sikes (the two things are not ultimately very different), that brings her to say to Rose's offers of help: 'I wish to go back . . . I must go back.'[3] [. . .]

Outside and surrounding the world of delinquency lies the middle-class world of private life [. . .]. What repeatedly and rhapsodically characterizes this world is the contrast that opposes it to the world of delinquency. [. . .] It is systematically unclear which kind of appreciation *Oliver Twist* does most to foster. Much as delinquency is circumscribed by middle-class private life, the indignation to which delinquency gives rise is bounded by gratitude for the class habits and securities that make indignation possible.

The 'alternative' character of the middle-class community depends significantly on the fact that it is kept free, not just from noise and squalor, but also from the police. [. . .] Not to cooperate with the police, therefore, is part of a strategy of surreptitiously assuming and revising their functions. [. . .]

We would call this vigilantism, except that no ultimate conflict of purpose or interest divides it from the legal and police apparatus that it supplants. Such division as does surface between the law and its supplement seems to articulate a

1   Dickens, *Oliver Twist*, Chapter 53.
2   Dickens, *Oliver Twist*, Chapter 31.
3   Dickens, *Oliver Twist*, Chapter 40.

deeper congruency, as though the text were positing something like a doctrine of 'separation of powers,' whereby each in its own sphere rendered assistance to the other, in the coherence of a single policing action. Thus, while the law gets rid of Fagin and his gang, the amateur supplement gets rid of Monks. [. . .] The two systems of regulation beautifully support one another. [. . .]

[. . .]

[. . .] The topic of the carceral in Dickens – better, the carceral as topic – thus worked to secure the effect of difference between, on the one hand, a confined, institutional space in which power is violently exercised on collectivized subjects, and on the other, a space of 'liberal society', generally determined as a free, private, and individual domain and practically specified as the family. Yet clear though the lines of demarcation were, it was alarmingly easy to cross them. [. . .] And in the portrayal of its hero in the workhouse, *Oliver Twist* (1838) dramatized the shameful facility with which such institutions might mistakenly seize upon what were middle-class subjects to begin with. Still, if to witness the horror of the carceral was always to incur a debt of gratitude for the immunities of middle-class life, then to sense the danger from the carceral was already to learn how this debt had to be acquitted. [. . .] The price of Oliver's deliverance from the carceral (either as the workhouse or as Fagin's gang) would be his absolute submission to the norms, protocols, and regulations of the middle-class family, in which he received tuition not just from Brownlow but from the Maylies as well. Liberal society and the family were kept free from the carceral institutions that were set up to remedy their failures only by assuming the burden of an immense internal regulation. [. . .]

From **John O. Jordan, 'The Purloined Handkerchief'**, *Dickens Studies Annual*, 18 (1989), pp. 1–17

In Jordan's own words, 'The title, "The Purloined Handkerchief," aims not only at the scenes of pocket picking and handkerchief thieving in the novel but also [. . .] at Edgar Allan Poe's celebrated detective story of 1845, "The Purloined Letter", and at the important body of critical commentary that Poe's story has received in recent years, notably in essays by Jacques Lacan, Jacques Derrida, and Barbara Johnson'. Influenced by post-structuralist and psychoanalytic theory, Jordan analyses the social and symbolic significance of handkerchiefs in the novel. Using Freudian ideas such as 'castration anxiety' (fears about emasculation or, literally, the loss of the male genitals) and 'Oedipal fantasies' (fantasies about killing the father, or father figure, in order to sleep with, or be closer to, the mother), Jordan offers a figural reading of the text which concludes that 'Oliver himself is a purloined handkerchief circulating through the text of the novel and waiting to be claimed by his rightful owner'. Jordan's emphasis on a network of textual referrals bears some similarity to Hillis Miller's post-structuralist emphasis on the same (see **pp. 73–5**).

The topic of this essay is a small but revealing aspect of Dickens' *Oliver Twist* (1837–39): namely, the motif of pocket-handkerchiefs in the book. [. . .] The term 'purloined' derives largely from this critical tradition.[1] The verb 'to purloin' (from the Anglo-French *pur* + *loigner*) means to set aside or delay and hence, by extension, to steal; but [. . .] the word should properly retain something of its original sense of retardation and displacement in addition to the more straightforward notion of theft, and it is with this broader sense of its meaning that the word is used here. Like the letter in Poe's story, the handkerchiefs in *Oliver Twist* are displaced from their original location and made to circulate through the text and illustrations of the book along a complex network of communication and exchange. [. . .]

Pocket-handkerchiefs abound in *Oliver Twist*. Nearly every major character in the book handles, carries, or wears some form of handkerchief during the course of the narrative. Over fifty separate instances of the word 'handkerchief' or its near-synonyms ('neckerchief,' 'cravat'; also the slang terms 'fogle' and 'wipe') occur in the text, and if we include references to other woven materials such as veils, shrouds, curtains, blankets, coverlets, and so forth, then the number is even greater. In addition, handkerchiefs figure prominently in Cruikshank's illustrations to the novel. At least half of the twenty-four plates[2] in the book contain or suggest the presence of a handkerchief. Moreover, the novel appears at times deliberately to flaunt its preoccupation with handkerchiefs, presenting them not just singly but in astonishing profusion.

The abundance of pocket-handkerchiefs in *Oliver Twist* is of course in large part a function of the plot and of Dickens' decision to place his young protagonist in Fagin's gang of juvenile London pickpockets, for whom the theft of handkerchiefs represents a chief source of livelihood. [. . .]

In addition to documenting a particular class of petty criminals, the handkerchiefs in *Oliver Twist* are themselves part of a specific social and historical formation. During the 1820s and 30s, when the action of *Oliver Twist* presumably takes place, handkerchiefs continued, as they had throughout the eighteenth century, to be an important fashion accessory for well-to-do persons of both sexes. Fine handkerchiefs were considered articles of luxury [. . .].

What begins to emerge from these examples is something like a rudimentary dress code in the book with respect to handkerchiefs. Silk handkerchiefs, carried in the pocket, are the property of the upper classes. Ordinary cotton handkerchiefs, often worn about the neck, belong to the lower classes, especially the thieves. [. . .] Mr. Bumble, a lower-class character whose role as beadle aligns him politically with the upper classes, should have two handkerchiefs: one in his pocket; [. . .] and another that he takes from inside his hat to wipe his brow. There are, of course, exceptions to the handkerchief code. Both Grimwig and Monks, two upper-class characters, wear neckerchiefs, though the case of Monks is complicated by his close association with the thieves and by the special reason he has for covering his throat.

One other aspect of early nineteenth-century handkerchief history deserves mention at this point: a development that I shall call the 'textualization' of the handkerchief. The invention of the roller or cylinder printing machine by Thomas Bell in 1785 was of tremendous importance for the British textile industry at the turn of the century. Printed handkerchiefs, which had previously been relatively difficult

---

1   i.e. writings on Poe by Lacan, Derrida and Johnson, who are mentioned by Jordan (see headnote).
2   Illustrations.

and expensive to manufacture, now became mass-produced articles. In addition to decorative patterns such as the blue and white belcher[3] design, one finds an increasing number of utilitarian, commemorative, literary, and political motifs represented upon nineteenth-century handkerchiefs. Maps, statistical tables, poems, political caricatures, and scenes depicting important social and historical events appear with regularity. Handkerchiefs thus become texts as well as textiles, objects to be read and interpreted as well as used in connection with some bodily function.

[. . .]

The association between handkerchiefs and hanging is confirmed both verbally and visually in *Oliver Twist*. In the passage [. . .] describing Oliver's first arrival at Fagin's den, the silk handkerchiefs are said to be '*hanging*' (emphasis mine) over a clothes-horse, and in the companion scene—describing Field Lane they '*hang dangling* from pegs outside the windows' (emphasis mine). The hanging motif is further reinforced in the illustration that accompanies the first of these scenes. On the wall adjacent to the cascade of handkerchiefs we can recognize a small popular print in which three bodies are shown hanging from a gallows. The hang/handkerchief pun is also apparent in Charley Bates's dumb-show explanation of the word 'scragged.'[4] Here again, Cruikshank's illustration for the scene repeats and thus corroborates the evidence of the verbal text.

The thieves' obsessive fear of hanging may point toward other anxieties as well. Dianne Sadoff, for example, has argued that the thieves' tenderness about the neck represents the displacement upward of a repressed castration anxiety that structures the entire novel.[5] For Sadoff, metaphors of castration at once repress and repeat Oedipal fantasies that underlie Oliver's story. Handkerchiefs and neckerchiefs can thus be understood as signifiers that mark the place of a conspicuous absence in the text—that of the phallus. Likewise, handkerchief stealing can be viewed as a defensive strategy whereby the original conflict is displaced but in which the substitute symptom—pocket picking—repeats in symbolic form the conflict it was intended to resolve.

Castration anxiety is not the only motive for narration in *Oliver Twist*. If handkerchiefs signal a conspicuous absence in the text, then we should consider them as well in relation to Oliver's status as an orphan. [. . .] The search for parents and for parental substitutes is thus an important motivating force behind the story. It is perhaps too much, however, to say that Oliver himself engages actively in this search. Indeed, he remains remarkably passive throughout the book, ready to attach himself to almost any adult figure that the plot tosses his way, but hardly ever an active participant in initiating such attachments. The search for his father, for example, is carried out on Oliver's behalf by a committee of (mostly) older men, all of them aligned in various ways with the paternal order and the rule of law. The place of Oliver's missing father is marked in the text by a series of written documents—the will, the letter, and the ring given by him to Oliver's mother with her name inscribed inside. All of these, along with other unnamed 'proofs,' have

---

3   A spotted handkerchief worn around the neck and named after the boxer Jim Belcher (1781–1811).
4   Hanged.
5   [Jordan's note.] Dianne F. Saldoff, *Monsters of Affection: Dickens, Eliot, and Brontë on Fatherhood* (Baltimore: 1982) pp. 212–14.

been either stolen or destroyed by Monks and his mother in their effort to conceal Oliver's paternal origin. They constitute what we might call the 'purloined letters' of the novel, and they must be recovered before the plot can come to a close.

[. . .]

The hypothesis that Dickens may have been attempting a Newgate *Othello*[6] in *Oliver Twist* is not entirely without foundation. Dickens was of course familiar with all of Shakespeare's work [. . .]. Moreover, Dickens appears to have taken a particular interest in *Othello* during the 1830s. [. . .] The scenes between Sikes and Nancy in *Oliver Twist* thus may well be another effort to revise Shakespeare's tragedy, this time as melodrama rather than burlesque or farce. If this hypothesis is correct, it may also help to explain the shift in narrative perspective that takes place toward the end of the book, when the novel's point of view moves inside the guilty consciousness of Sikes, creating greater sympathy for him and making him, if not a tragic hero, at least briefly the protagonist of a Victorian melodrama.

Finally, and at the risk of giving an overly figural reading to the book, I would submit that Oliver himself is a purloined handkerchief circulating through the text of the novel and waiting to be claimed by his rightful owner. To view Oliver in this way is to consider him not so much a character as a narrative function—a small but valuable piece of portable property shuttled about the story by forces outside of his control, including the narrator [. . .].

From **Deborah Heller, 'The Outcast as Villain and Victim: Jews in Dickens's *Oliver Twist* and *Our Mutual Friend*',** in *Jewish Presences in English Literature*, edited by Derek Cohen and Deborah Heller (Montreal: McGill-Queen's University Press, 1990), pp. 40–9

> Deborah Heller's essay is a direct rebuttal to what she sees as a tendency to imply that 'Fagin's Jewishness is somehow incidental to his conception'. See also Stone, **pp. 68–9**, Dickens's letters to Eliza Davis, **pp. 33–4**, **p. 49** and **pp. 108–13**.

[. . .] Whether as the incarnation of Vice or of Virtue, however, the two most important Jews in Dickens's work are defined in the context of the conflict between innocence and worldly evil. [. . .]

[. . .]

The claim that Fagin's Jewishness is somehow incidental to his conception, that it is a kind of historical accident, would be almost too preposterous to take seriously had it not been advanced by Dickens himself and treated seriously by many critics since his time. However, the fact remains that Dickens chose to stress unremittingly Fagin's Jewishness. One cannot but be struck by the persistence with which Fagin is referred to through the novel as 'the Jew'. If Dickens – or any other writer – were consistently to refer to a villain as 'the Frenchman' or 'the

---

6   First performed in 1604, Shakespeare's tragedy features the Moor soldier who murders his wife because he has been tricked into believing her guilty of adultery using a handkerchief as 'proof'.

Chinaman', no reader could be faulted for supposing the writer was making a considered point about the generic nature of the French or the Chinese.

Moreover, the claim that the rest of the wicked characters are Christians, besides overlooking a minor Jewish character, the repulsive Barney (Fagin's associate), simply ignores the extent to which Dickens was willing to draw on the long history of anti-Semitic associations and stereotypes to provide added resonance to Fagin's particular villainies. In addition, Fagin has certain prominent physical characteristics of the stereotyped stage Jew, notably his red hair, which is repeatedly referred to; in Cruikshank's illustrations, Fagin is also shown with hooked nose, broad-brimmed hat, and long gown. Frequently described by Dickens as skulking or creeping stealthily through the back alleys of London, Fagin is frightening and repulsive as well. Furthermore, he is a dealer in second-hand clothes and trinkets, one of the few occupations open to Jews at the time of *Oliver Twist*. However, Dickens does withhold from Fagin other characteristics of the stage-Jew stereotype, for example, the supposedly characteristic gestures and 'Jewish' speech patterns such as local dialect, or nasal intonation displayed by other Jews in Dickens's fiction (including Barney in *Oliver Twist*). Fagin's English is as improbably pure as Oliver's.

More fundamental to Fagin's conformity to the popular Jewish stereotype, however, are his clear identification with the devil (shared with Shylock[1]) and his ominous role as an abductor of children and violator of childhood innocence. Both associations have been credited with providing much of the impetus to anti-Semitism from medieval times through our own. Fagin resembles the devil first of all in appearance. The red beard worn by Fagin was worn by the devil in medieval drama, before being transferred to the Jew. [. . .]

[T]he insistence on Fagin's unremitting evil, however, is pervasive. The evil that Fagin represents is, indeed, so inclusive – one might even say, so generic – that although we are treated to a highly dramatic trial scene in the penultimate chapter, no specific *charge* against Fagin is ever mentioned. The omission is significant. It suggests that something as finite as an explicit charge could only mitigate or trivialize the enormity of the villain's all encompassing evil. [. . .]

Fagin, in fact, as Dickens makes plain, has cut himself off from any specifically Jewish community as well. When we first met him, it is *sausages* he is roasting over that fire, and later we watch him breakfasting on ham.[2] The night before his execution we are shown a glimpse – for the first and only time – of a different kind of Jew: 'Venerable men of his own persuasion had come to pray beside him, but he had driven them away with curses. They renewed their charitable efforts, and he beat them off.'[3] The fact that Fagin is a bad Jew, a voluntary outsider to the Jewish community, does not detract from the fact that his badness through the novel is presented as inextricable from his identity as 'the Jew'. Fagin's villainy, as we have seen, gains resonance and added horror from Dickens's insistence on Fagin's Jewishness and Dickens's readiness to exploit the whole compendium of terrifying associations that have clustered around the stereotype of the Jew in the popular imagination from the Middle Ages onward.

1   The Jewish protagonist of Shakespeare's *The Merchant of Venice* (1600).
2   Dickens, *Oliver Twist*, Chapters 8 and 9.
3   Dickens, *Oliver Twist*, Chapter 52.

[. . .] This is not to suggest – nor has it ever seriously been suggested – that Dickens was attempting to incite anti-Semitic feeling or to fan the fires of anti-Semitism. Rather, Dickens seems to have been appealing to an anti-Semitism already present in his readers, which he was simply willing to exploit in creating his first major representation of evil in its confrontation with childhood innocence. Of course taken as a whole, Dickens's novels present a wide array of evil characters, only one of whom is a Jew. But it must be acknowledged that in his portrayal of Fagin's villainy, Dickens, as a young writer, chose to rely on ready-made, deeply rooted associations to a supposedly specifically Jewish brand of villainy.

From **Patricia Ingham, *Dickens, Women and Language*** (Hemel Hempstead: Harvester Wheatsheaf, 1992), pp. 45–59

Ingham's book acts as a much-needed corrective to simplified biographical interpretations of Dickens's attitudes to women. Ingham analyses the way in which Dickens invokes and undermines recognizable 'signs' of femininity in both his novels and his biographical writings. In this section, Ingham analyses the way in which Nancy is associated with more than one such 'sign': the 'womanly woman' the 'nubile girl' and the 'fallen girl'. Ingham also analyses the class implications of the shifts in Nancy's speech throughout the novel and the way in which her death 'sweeps away the traditional significance of the death of a prostitute as cleansing'. (See also **pp. 31–3**, Michie, **p. 77** and Bowen, **pp. 87–9**.)

[. . .]

Fallen girls in the novels are not, of course, mere penitents but are charged with other unexpected meanings. Nancy [. . .] is not obviously distinguished from a stereotypical group encountered by Fagin in a public house, who attract attention by their repulsiveness. [. . .] Moreover, Nancy willingly undertakes the recapture of Oliver after he has escaped from Fagin's gang. And yet eventually she reveals characteristics proper to the womanly woman, from whom she is patently dissociated by dress, manners, speech. She preserves a commitment to Sikes paralleling the loyalty expected of even a wronged wife till death. [. . .]

More striking than this shadowing of a wife's role is Nancy's conversion to womanly compassion when she comes to feel Oliver's innocence and vulnerability. This is still described in terms of an unwomanly 'passion of rage' potentiated by 'recklessness and despair',[1] traditional enough words to apply to a prostitute but here relating to the passionate rages of an unexpected and long-sustained womanly virtue. The rewriting of her as not totally evil, while still using these familiar terms, eases the transition obviously felt by the narrator to be a difficult one. He attempts to theorise it in a confused passage before Nancy's interview with Rose Maylie about the plan to save Oliver. He starts with a bold

---

1   Dickens, *Oliver Twist*, Chapter 16. See **pp. 149–51**.

assertion that her life 'had been squandered in the streets, and among the most noisome of the stews and dens of London, but here was something of the woman's original nature left in her still'. But he soon modifies this by a reference to her evil and contradictory pride, since 'even this degraded being felt too proud to betray a feeble gleam of the womanly feeling which she thought a weakness'.[2]

But this conflict of meaning attaching to Nancy and Martha[3] undermines the dichotomy between the two signs of Virgin and Whore/nubile girl and fallen girl, which is central to a whole system of signification that is frequently used to contain anxieties relating to class as well as gender.[4] Prostitutes are typically presented as lower class, and fallen women become declassed. As Walkowitz shows, prostitutes *were* predominantly from the lower classes of society; but there is an interesting divergence between the facts as she presents them and the significance attached to them in the 'literary' language. The reasons for prostitution, as Walkowitz shows in some detail, are largely economic: it was the 'best of a series of unattractive alternatives'.[5] The correlation with working-class females, however, was traditionally interpreted as a manifestation of depravity of the masses. As late as 1862 Hemyng was arguing that 'To be unchaste amongst the lower classes is not always to be the subject of reproach . . . the depravity of manners . . . begins so very early, that they think it rather a distinction than otherwise to be unprincipled'.[6]

[. . .]

[. . .] There was by the 1830s a clear convention, in relation to the speech of characters in novels, requiring that those 'of dignity and moral worth' speak 'a language fit for heroes to speak', free of lower-class markers.[7] This accounts for the middle-class speech of Oliver Twist, brought up in a brutalising workhouse but representing the principle of Good, and happily accommodated finally among the Maylies. The convention is not to be taken as implying that all users of middle-class forms of speech are morally worthy; but the more limited implication it carries (that those of moral worth must use them) maintains the connection between a specific class and specific moral values.

The flaws inherent in such a novelistic convention are revealed whenever Dickens is making the point that virtue is independent of social status – in female characters like Lizzie Hexam.[8] They also surface in the figure of Nancy precisely because she represents the two conflicting versions of the prostitute. Initially, since she is the female representative of the 'dregs of life', a 'pupil' of Fagin, a streetwalker and a thief, she shares the languages of Sikes and Fagin. When these

2   Dickens, *Oliver Twist*, Chapter 40, **pp. 163–4.**
3   Martha Endell, the prostitute who saves Emily from a brothel in Dickens's *David Copperfield* (1849–50).
4   Lynda Nead, *Myths of Sexuality: Representations of Women in Victorian Britain* (Blackwell: Oxford, 1988), p. 94.
5   Judith R. Walkowitz, *Prostitution and Victorian Society: Women, Class and the State* (Cambridge: Cambridge University Press, 1980), p. 31.
6   Henry Mayhew, *London Labour and the London Poor: A cyclopedia of those that will not work, those that cannot work, and those that will not work* (London: Griffin, Bohn; repr. New York: Mayhew, 1968), p. 221.
7   Norman Page, *Speech in the English Novel* (London: Longman, 1973), p. 97.
8   The good, lower-class woman who marries an aristocrat in Dickens's *Our Mutual Friend* (1864–5).
9   Dickens, *Oliver Twist*, Chapter 13.

two press her early on to recapture Oliver she is reluctant on prudential grounds. Her refusal is uttered in their own language: 'It won't do; so it's no use a-trying it on, Fagin.'[9] When Sikes urges her, saying that she is not known locally and would not be recognised by anyone, her reply is equally colloquial: 'And as I don't want 'em to neither, it's rather more no than yes with me, Bill.'[10] Her rare early utterances are sprinkled with thieves' cant, the mark of the criminal insider: 'The young brat's been ill and confined to the crib.'[11] With her adoption of womanly middle-class compassion Dickens comes up against the problem of how to make her speak a language fit for heroines, or at least for a (partly) virtuous woman. Like the related problem with Lizzie Hexam described in chapter 1, this one is dealt with by modifications of her speech away from its originally tainted type. Her first defence of Oliver is still slightly coloured by forms like *'em* and *aye*. Gradually, as she grows more voluble about her views on the cruelty of Sikes and Fagin towards the boy, the lower-class markers become fewer. And by the time of her encounters with Rose Maylie she is as articulate and as middle-class in her speech as her auditor [. . .]. This would be the middle-class moral assessment of Nancy and must therefore be dissociated from the group she belongs to, which is lower class and immoral. Paradoxically, she must now speak of herself in a speech free of 'vulgar' markers and characterised by a middle-class control of syntax. The gradual changes made in the form of her language serve to reveal the illogicalities in the convention relating to speech in the novel and in doing so draw attention to the ideological subterfuge on which it is based.

[. . .]

But it is above all Nancy, the first prostitute in the novels, who sustains a central place in the main plot and effectively determines its course in a way which suggests the appropriateness of the title 'Sikes and Nancy' that Dickens chose for the famous reading version of the novel with which he became so obsessed. In the struggle between the forces of good and evil for Oliver himself it is she who, unknown at first to the other thieves, liaises with the middle-class forces of good and virtually brings about the identification of the boy and his preservation from the evil intended by his wicked brother, Monks. Her actions, though depending on knowledge that she has acquired because of her criminal connections, alter the direction of a sequence of events unconnected with her fallen state. She is more autonomous, more active and more continuously an agent than any other fallen or nubile girl. Power, or at least a degree of power, is thus returned, ironically not to the womanly woman but to the outcast who is normally inscribed only in the underplots and margins of the text. Such a change also diminishes the emphasis usually reserved in the traditional story for the event which stands for both peripety and closure: the harlot's death. The death remains important but not uniquely so.

[. . .]

Nancy, through her actual death, however, becomes Dickens' Tess.[12] She dies, but not in any of the traditional ways. Despite her prediction that she will end like most of her sort in the river, she also realises that a return to Sikes may mean her

10 *ibid.*, Chapter 13.
11 *ibid.*, Chapter 15.
12 The tragic and fallen heroine of Thomas Hardy's *Tess of the D'Urbervilles* (1891).

death: 'I am drawn back to him through every suffering and ill-usage and should be . . . if I knew that I was to die by his hand at last.'[13] The escape route that Martha takes,[14] or perhaps a more comfortable one, is offered to Nancy by Rose Maylie and Mr Brownlow. As this declaration shows, she rejects it, and in doing so exerts the same autonomy that she has shown in the defence of Oliver. Like Tess, she is exercising an option when she chooses death. Perhaps all that their choice amounts to is a choice of *how* they will die. But by choosing the path that ends in her murder by Sikes, Nancy invokes a death that sweeps away the traditional significance of the death of a prostitute as cleansing, restitution, divine justice, merciful oblivion. She remains unambiguously a victim. The brutal death she undergoes fundamentally alters the apparently ineluctable force of the harlot's progress, putting traditional meanings in question. All this is at the beginning of Dickens' career as a novelist and was never repeated, but it serves to indicate the subtext that always develops when a woman falls and so becomes sexualised: a kind of agency accompanies the changes.

From **John Bowen, *Other Dickens: Pickwick to Chuzzlewit*** (Oxford: Oxford University Press, 2000), pp. 86, 98–9

John Bowen's analysis of Nancy argues that Dickens identifies Nancy 'with truth itself', whereas in many nineteenth-century texts, the hysterical woman stands for a corruption of rational and scientific (masculine) truth. His argument about Nancy (influenced by post-structuralism and psychoanalysis) is tied to his more general assertion that *Oliver Twist* most distrusts 'not philosophy, but the claim of discursive reason to be able to stand outside human society'. Bowen's claims are interesting given Dickens's reservations about Utilitarianism (see **pp. 13–14**). On Nancy, see Michie, **p. 77** and Ingham, **pp. 84–7**.

[. . .] What the book most seems to distrust is not philosophy, but the claim of discursive reason to be able to stand outside human society. [. . .]

The figure of the hysterical woman and its relation to the male pursuit of knowledge is important in the writing of the nineteenth century, both in fiction and in scientific and medical discourses, most notably the work of Freud. Indeed, for Freud, it has been argued, the problem of knowledge is itself hysterical. In many of these texts, as Jacqueline Rose has argued in relation to George Eliot's *Middlemarch*, 'the woman stands . . . for a corruption of the visible and a degradation of the scientific pursuit of truth'.[1] In the preface to *Oliver Twist*, by contrast, Nancy is identified with truth itself: true to Oliver and her love for Sikes, a contradictory and impossible love, but nevertheless 'TRUE', and part of her wider

---

13 Dickens, *Oliver Twist*, Chapter 40.
14 Emigration.

---

1 [Bowen's note.] Jacqueline Rose, 'George Eliot and the Spectacle of the Woman', in *Sexuality in the Field of Vision* (London: Verso, 1986), 110.

Figure 2 Alma Taylor as Nancy, in Thomas Bentley (dir.), *Oliver Twist* (Hepworth, 1912).

truth, which is not scientific, but literary, paradoxical, and contradictory. Dickens, like George Eliot, sees 'the link between male truth and a woman's failing' in Agnes's love for Oliver's father, and Nancy's love for Sikes, but it is a very different truth, which does not displace but focuses 'questions about social inequality and misery'.[2] This pursuit of truth, of Nancy, and of Nancy's truth is also a complex and potentially fatal business—fatal to her, to Sikes, to Fagin, and perhaps to Dickens too. One of Cruikshank's illustrations will be called 'Recovering Nancy', a scene that has more than a passing resemblance to Charcot's

2   [Bowen's note.] Jacqueline Rose, *Sexuality in the Field of Vision*, pp. 111, 113.

hysterical demonstrations at Salpêtrière;[3] but it is not clear that Nancy can be recovered in this, or in any other, way.

Readers have disagreed sharply about the portrayal of Nancy in the novel. [. . .] These disagreements between men about Nancy, disagreements about real wenches and 'female nature', about shadows, existence, and all sides of a woman's character, begin not in criticism but in the novel itself, whose characters, narrator, and readers often ask what she means and what she is doing, whether she is speaking truthfully or not, whether she is acting.

From **Juliet John, _Dickens's Villains: Melodrama, Character, Popular Culture_** (Oxford: Oxford University Press, 2001), pp. 129–40

This extract examines Dickens's self-reflexive examination in _Oliver Twist_ of so-called 'Newgate' fiction and the debate that arose from it. (See also Bulwer-Lytton on the Newgate novel, **pp. 38–9** and **pp. 43–4**.) My argument is that Dickens is not just interrogating the power of written narratives and fictions in _Oliver Twist_; he is as concerned with the power of a variety of specifically _popular_ cultural forms that appeal to the literate and illiterate alike. The extract also contains an analysis of the function of emotion and pleasure in Dickens's novels. Several of the Key Passages discussed in the following pages concern Dickens's self-reflexive treatment of the Newgate debate: the 1841 Preface, **pp. 119–24**, 'Oliver's First Experience of the Artful Dodger, London, Fagin and his Gang', **pp. 137–42**, 'Oliver is Given a Lesson in Pickpocketing', **pp. 143–5**, 'Oliver's Education in the Thieves' Den', **pp. 153–5**, 'Oliver Reads a Book Resembling the Newgate Calendar', **pp. 155–6**, 'Blathers and Duff; Conkey Chickweed', **pp. 159–60** and 'Fagin Consoles Charley Bates over the Capture of the Artful Dodger; The Trial of the Artful Dodger', **pp. 164–8**.

[. . .]

Oliver Twist is alone among the Newgate novels in analysing the role of the storyteller, entertainer, or purveyor of fictions in the power dynamics of 1830s Britain. For _Oliver Twist_ offers a sustained self-reflexive exploration of both Newgate fiction and the function of the entertainer in social structures of oppression. Crucial in this investigation is the relationship between 'reality' and fiction, and the role of each in the construction of the other. Contrary to the propagandist 1841 preface,[1] the 'realism' of the novel (in the sense of its photographic truth-to-life) is largely irrelevant to Dickens's ideological and moral scheme in _Oliver Twist_. The most sophisticated layer of commentary depends, not on its exact representation of life, but on its self-referential, textual investigation of the ideological and moral complexity of the relationship between life and fiction.

---

3   Jean-Martin Charcot (1825–93), the first professor of neurology, operated the Salpêtrière School of Hypnosis, which influenced Freud. He believed that hypnosis was due to a form of hysteria.

1   See p. 119.

Fagin is central to this critique in so far as he possesses an acute understanding of this complexity and of the way fictions can be manipulated to achieve one's purposes—i.e. to achieve power. Fagin's cynical deconstruction of life/fiction boundaries is compelling precisely because his construction as a character arrives from a similarly sophisticated play with the same boundaries. Though based on real-life prototype Ikey Solomons,[2] the character of Fagin obviously borrows heavily from the stereotype of the stage Jew and the reader's response to Fagin relies on his or her recognition of, and openness to, well-worn theatrical, literary (and racist) conventions. Thus, to reapply Roland Barthes's[3] term, the 'reality effect' created by the character/caricature of Fagin is highly dependent on the reader's knowledge of the medium of fiction from the beginning.

It is through Fagin's relationship with the Artful Dodger and Charley Bates, above all, that Dickens answers the accusations that were to be leveled at him in the Newgate debate. The Artful Dodger and Charley Bates can be seen as fictional representations of the kind of boys investigated in the 1852 House of Commons inquiry into 'the situation of Criminal and Destitute Juveniles' who blamed their corruption on stage adaptations of Newgate novels. Bates and the Dodger are also the only characters in *Oliver Twist* who appear to be *overtly* attractive criminals in the same way as Robin Hood or the protagonists of the contemporary Newgate novels. They are thus crucial to Dickens in his textualized critique of Newgate fiction on two basic levels.

But to return to Fagin. Fagin is conscious from the outset that fiction, drama, and comic entertainment have the power to corrupt. There are six instances that I wish to examine of Fagin playing a key role in Dickens's self-reflexive analysis of the Newgate controversy [. . . contained in *OT*, Chapters 9, 18, 20, 43].[4]

[. . .] Historicizing the text from this perspective brings an important textual detail into focus. Dickens is not just interrogating the nature of narratives and fictions in *Oliver Twist* (as some of this analysis of self-reflexivity, inspired by post-structuralism, is inclined to suggest); he is as concerned with the power of a variety of specifically *popular* cultural forms. When the novel self-reflexively alludes to the Newgate debate, Newgate myths are nearly always disseminated via cultural vehicles that are accessible to the lowbrow and highbrow alike. In the first example [. . .], Fagin directs an inverted morality play in which the Artful Dodger and Charley Bates attempt to teach Oliver how to pick pockets. In the second, the two boys act out a 'pantomimic representation' of the joys of money on the one hand and the horrors of the gibbet on the other; next, Fagin resorts to oral narrative, telling comic tales; then the Dodger sketches Newgate on a table-cloth; and when Master Bates is on the point of realizing that the romance of crime is a myth, Fagin draws on a variety of popular cultural modes, acting, narrating, conjuring up the Dodger's performances in the law courts (a favourite source of entertainment for the Victorians) and the newspaper reports of the same, to convince Master Bates of the Dodger's inevitable honour and fame.

It is conspicuous that the least visibly effective of all these attempts to corrupt

---

2   See **pp. 15, 68** and Stone, **pp. 223–53**.
3   Roland Barthes (1915–80): a French theorist influential in both structuralism and post-structuralism.
4   See **p. 165** for a discussion of some of these instances.

using Newgate myths is the famous instance when Oliver is given the volume resembling *The Newgate Calendar*.[5] When faced with the written word in the physically substantial form of a book, Oliver takes the book almost as a warning of its own power and falls down on his knees to pray. When indoctrination is disguised as pleasure or entertainment, by contrast, Oliver is far more susceptible [. . .].

[. . .]

If the text is read closely, what seems to be consistently at stake is the function of emotion and pleasure as tools of power: amusement, laughter, and play are the ultimate ideological vehicles. In the context of Newgate debate, this has several repercussions. First, the genres central to the Newgate controversy were romance and melodrama, both of which (and often the two combined) relied on emotion and pleasure for their popular appeal. Second, the potentiality and dangers of the mass market for culture which was emerging in the 1830s are under scrutiny. Dickens seems to be exploring theories that had been put forward by W. J. Fox[6] in the radical *Monthly Repository* in the 1830s, about the possibilities for emotion, pleasure, and also drama as democratic vehicles of communication which would prevent the divorce of intellectual from mass culture. Fox was the editor of the radical Benthamite paper the *True Sun*, for which Dickens worked in his early days as a journalist. The question of the function of emotion and pleasure in the dynamics of mass culture also has acute relevance, of course, to Dickens's own art, whose enduring popularity and cultural centrality have remained in many ways inscrutable to academic enquiry. The main problem critics seem to have had from the 1830s to the present is in reconciling Dickens's accessibility with his 'greatness' as a novelist.

Dickens obviously felt strongly that art should be inclusive, and that art which was pleasurable, entertaining, and emotionally engaging would achieve this— essays like 'The Amusements of the People'[7] and a novel like *Hard Times* prove this beyond doubt. However, his dislike of the exclusivity of the literary elite and his desire to be popular do not necessarily suggest a belief in a fully democratic art of the kind W. J. Fox seeks to define. The implicit relevance of Fagin's role as 'a generalized Newgate novelist'[8] to Dickens's own art is no accident. To Dickens, the storyteller is in a position of power; the comic entertainer who can manipulate the reader's emotions and evoke pleasure is all-powerful. This power is not necessarily a bad thing *per se* as long as (a perennial problem) power does not fall into the wrong hands; in the early Victorian period, when truths and realities seemed to be up for grabs, to sell your own reality convincingly was arguably a radical and proactive act from middle-class writers who had never before had such power. If you do not put your ideological spin on the world then, to quote the Artful Dodger, 'some other cove will'.[9] From the perspective of author–reader dynamics then, for Dickens, inclusive art is not necessarily democratic.

[. . .]

5   See **pp. 43–4**; see also, 'Oliver Reads a Book Resembling the Newgate Calendar', **pp. 155–6**.
6   The Editor of the *Monthly Repository*.
7   In *Household Words*, Vol. I (30 March 1850), pp. 13–15 and (13 April 1850), pp. 57–60.
8   This quotation is taken from Robert Tracy's article ' "The Old Story" and Inside Stories: Modish Fiction and Fictional Modes in Oliver Twist', *Dickens Studies Annual*, 17 (1988), pp. 1–33 (p. 20).
9   Chapter 18, see **p. 154**.

3

The Work in Performance

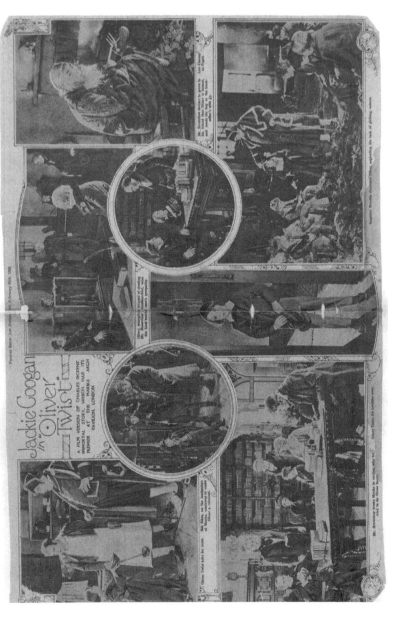

Figure 3 Photo-strip from Frank Lloyd (dir.), *Oliver Twist* (Jackie Coogan Productions, 1922).

Introduction

It is arguable that adaptations of *Oliver Twist* have had more impact on the public than Dickens's original novel. It is indisputable that, without the many adaptations of *Oliver Twist*, the story and its characters would not have become part of the British cultural consciousness. If the mythical person in the street has an image of Fagin or of Oliver asking for more, that person, in the twenty-first century at least, need not have read the novel. My own first experience of *Oliver Twist* was of a school production in the 1970s of Lionel Bart's musical *Oliver!*, and in this I seem typical of my generation and my students' generation. Bart's musical, and Carol Reed's 1968 film of the musical, have had phenomenal mass appeal: the stage musical once ran for 774 performances in one production in New York, and the film made 210 million pounds worldwide, winning six Oscars.[1] If this particular musical version has been the most commercially successful in the history of the novel's adaptation, however, it has not been the most controversial. For the surprising thing about the work's history in performance – surprising at least to those weaned on the carnivalesque cheer of *Oliver!* – is that it has been fraught with controversy. Dickens himself sounded a note of protest when he lay on the floor of the theatre during one of the first stage adaptations unable to bear the desecration of his writing. More seriously, there was such concern about the negative impact that *Oliver Twist* – and other 'Newgate' dramas – may have on vulnerable youths, that the play was effectively censored from the stage for the best part of twenty years in the mid-nineteenth century. The release of David Lean's *Oliver Twist* in 1948 occasioned violent riots in Berlin until the film was withdrawn (it had been banned in New York): the objection was to the film's alleged anti-Semitism, a particularly sensitive charge in the aftermath of the Second World War. Even the BBC managed to cause offence with its first television adaptation of *Oliver Twist* in 1962: questions were raised in parliament about the appropriateness of violence in a Sunday teatime serial with particular reference to the scene with the murder of Nancy.[2] The issue of violence and its possible impact on

---

1 H. Philip Bolton, *Dickens Dramatized* (London: Mansell, 1987), p. 6; Emily Sheffield, *Evening Standard*, 16 November 1999, pp. 28–9.
2 Michael Pointer, *Charles Dickens on the Screen: The Film, Television, and Video Adaptations* (Lanham, Md.: Scarecrow Press, 1996), p. 80.

children, an issue that also arose in Dickens's day, resulted in the BBC cutting a shot showing the shadow of Sikes's body hanging on a rope.[3] Dickens had, himself, worried about the impact of the violence of the scene when he chose to make it the centrepiece of his public readings of his novels. According to Philip Collins: 'Probably no episode in Victorian fiction has had such a stormy theatrical history.'[4]

It is highly unusual for adaptations of a novel to arouse such frequent controversy at such different moments in history. It is also unusual for a text whose adaptations have proved so persistently controversial to be so often adapted. For it is not just the occasioning of riots that has made the performance history of *Oliver Twist* unusual. Dickens is the most frequently adapted novelist in history and *Oliver Twist*, along with *A Christmas Carol*, is his most adapted work. There are more adaptations of *A Christmas Carol*, but *Oliver Twist* was the most adapted of Dickens's texts during the nineteenth century (despite the years of censorship). While there is truth in Alistair Cooke's comment that 'a silent Dickens [. . .] is as much of a contradiction as a talkative statue',[5] Dickens was crucial to the silent-film industry and to the rise of the moving image that this industry occasioned. *Oliver Twist* was the first of Dickens's novels to be adapted (*The Death of Nancy Sykes* in 1897) and the most popular with the silent film industry; six adaptations had been released by 1910.[6] The facts of the performance history beg questions we can only begin to answer here: why has Dickens proved so attractive to film-makers and why has *Oliver Twist* proved especially so? Why has a Victorian allegory, a realist fairy tale about an orphaned boy, proved so controversial in generic translation?

One factor is that Dickens adaptation is a multi-media industry, which scholars and students must ponder seriously if they are to understand Dickens's continued appeal in a mass cultural age. Dickens of course understood that his own age was witnessing the birth of mass culture and embraced an optimistic vision of good quality popular culture that could help to effect education and social cohesion (see Gissing **p. 62** and John, **pp. 89–91**). Drama was central to his vision of popular culture as a force for good, helping to diminish the forces of fragmentation at work in industrialized Britain. This belief in the power of drama indeed contributed to Dickens's decision to embark on high-profile public-reading tours in which he gave solo 'performances' or readings from his novels. Dickens's two-part essay 'The Amusements of the People' is one of his clearest statements of his belief in, and vision of, popular culture (see John, **pp. 89–91**); more importantly, at a time of high rates of illiteracy, it is a lucid articulation of his vision of 'dramatic entertainments' as the most effective instrument of cultural cohesion and somehow the natural imaginative outlet for the 'common people'. 'It is probable,' he begins, 'that nothing will ever root out from among the common people an innate love they have for dramatic entertainment in some form or other. It

---

3 *ibid.*, p. 81.
4 Philip Collins (ed.), *Charles Dickens: The Public Readings* (Oxford: Clarendon Press, 1975), p. 466.
5 Quoted by Pointer, *Charles Dickens on the Screen*, p. 23.
6 *ibid.*, pp. 7, 21. *The Death of Nancy Sykes*, made by the American Mutoscope Company, was a depiction of the murder scene rather than what we would now regard as a complete film.

would be a very doubtful benefit to society, we think, if it could be rooted out.'[7]
'The lower we go,' he continues, 'the more natural it is that the best-relished provision for this [imagination] should be found in dramatic entertainments; as at once the most obvious, the least troublesome, and the most real, of all the escapes out of the literal world.'[8] It is of course in Chapter 17 of *Oliver Twist* that Dickens's narrator introduces an uncharacteristic, self-reflexive comment on his own narrative technique, comparing it to that of 'the custom on the stage, in all good murderous melodramas' (see **pp. 151–3**). Dickens believed that the future of literature depended on its popular appeal and that drama had a key role in this appeal, just as culture was crucial to the well-being of the populace. In a letter to his biographer, John Forster, he voiced his reservations about realist fiction, concluding that: 'I have an idea [...] that the very holding of popular literature through a kind of popular dark age, may depend on such fanciful treatment,'[9] 'Fanciful' or imaginative treatment in Dickens is generally synonymous with a 'dramatic' or externalized 'manner of stating the exact truth'.[10]

This does not mean that Dickens was happy about all adaptations of his work, however. Dickens volunteered to adapt the novel for the stage, but his offer was, interestingly, not taken up by his friend, the actor and theatre manager William Macready. Several adaptations of *Oliver Twist* appeared on stage before the original serial had even run its course, and Dickens objected to both the quality of the entertainment and to the lack of protection given him by copyright law. There is a significant difference between adaptations before and after the de-facto ban on the novel, an 1855 version announcing its cleanliness: it was 'An Entire New Version of Mr Charles Dickens's Tale of Oliver Twist, in Two Acts, Carefully Avoiding All the Repulsive Matter of the Tale' (see **p. 98**). Dickens was as worried about his bank balance and artistic reputation as he was about 'repulsive matter'. His vision of 'popular' culture did not extend to the free distribution of the fruits of his labour, even if the audiences of the popular melodramas of the day were composed in large part of the artisans and workers about whom he was so concerned. Dickens was a strange hybrid of capitalist entrepreneur, socialist reformer, populist and self-created celebrity. His controversial decision, in late career, to tour Britain and America giving readings of his own novels thus arose from a complex range of motives: a genuinely populist vision of art and a sense of the importance of drama to that populism; a modern sense of his own celebrity and of the marketing mechanisms needed to maintain it; and a growing sense of anxiety about his own ability to write at a time of ill health and a troubled personal life.

The murder of Nancy was Dickens's favourite reading piece, and biographical commentators have made great play of the fact that Dickens insisted on re-enacting the murder again and again, despite the dangerously high pulse rate it provoked and against his doctor's advice. At least as interesting in this context,

---

7 Dickens, 'The Amusements of the People', *Household Words*, I (30 March 1850), 13–15, I (13 April 1850), 57–60 (p. 13).
8 *ibid.*
9 John Forster, *The Life of Charles Dickens*, edited by J. W. T. Ley (London: Cecil Palmer, [1928]), p. 728.
10 See, for example, the 'Streaky Bacon' passage, **pp. 151–3**, 'Oliver's First Experience of the Artful Dodger, London and Fagin and his Gang', **pp. 137–42**, and 'Bill Sikes', **pp. 145–7**.

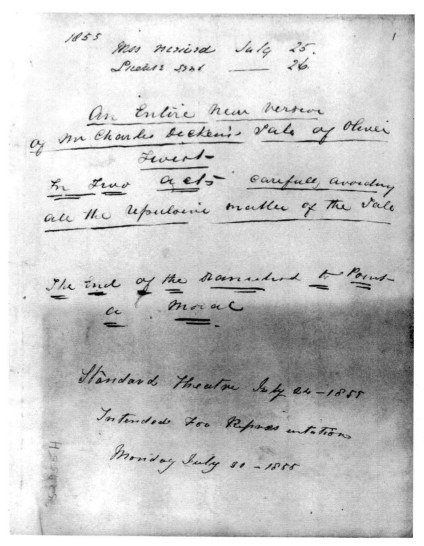

Figure 4 Manuscript of a version of *Oliver Twist* submitted to the Lord Chancellor in 1855. It announces 'An Entire New Version of Mr Charles Dicken's Tale of Oliver Twist, in Two Acts, Carefully Avoiding All the Repulsive Matter of the Tale'!

however, is Dickens's decision to undertake the reading tours in the first place, against the advice of many, including Forster. At the heart of Dickens's disagreement with Forster (and of modern debates about adaptations of classic novels), is the concept of artistic quality. While Forster believed that Dickens would vulgarize his art and cheapen his reputation by reading his novels for money and in public, Dickens's main anxiety was that he might 'petrify an audience' by his reading of 'Sikes and Nancy' (see **pp. 105–6**). Macready's response that the murder reading was as powerful as 'two Macbeths' was exquisite praise to Dickens and seemed to justify his decision 'to leave behind [him. . .] something very passionate and dramatic, done with simple means, if the art would justify the theme' (see **p. 105**).

Dickens never saw populist art as a paradoxical category, and this is perhaps one of the reasons why his works have proved so adaptable to modern popular media such as television and film. His populist vision of drama did not, of course, encompass the idea of filmed drama that could be mass produced. It is ironic, given Dickens's populism, that even his adapters have been troubled, perhaps even baffled, by the possibility of 'art' that is mass produced, copied and disseminated. As a new medium in the 1890s, film had to grapple with its own sense of self as the novel had done earlier in the century and, in the case of film, the populist possibilities were infinite. The sense that mechanized copies of drama could be art was very new in the context of a century steeped in Romantic theories of art that positioned the mechanical as 'common' and antithetical to art. Thus, Sol Lesser, the producer of Frank Lloyd's pioneering silent movie of *Oliver Twist* (1922), recalled why he allowed the destruction of the film's negatives: 'I never realized the value of old negatives. [. . .] I had no sense then that it [film] was an art form. The revivals of the old pictures make me just about the most surprised man in the world.'[11]

Pioneering film-makers have been proud to announce the influence of Dickens on their work. Perhaps ironically, given Dickens's ambiguous status in the eyes of some literary critics, Dickens's reputation as a novelist has been used to strengthen the association between film and art, the film-maker and the artist. Thus, D. W. Griffith, the 'world-dominating pioneer of film "grammar" and the multi-reel film' named Dickens publicly as his 'formal inspiration (and justification) in every one of his films'.[12] Sergei Eisenstein, the great Soviet director and author of the seminal essay, 'Dickens, Griffith, and Ourselves', names Dickens as the father of film and inventor of the film technique of montage. Eisenstein uses a reading of *Oliver Twist* to demonstrate 'That Dickens should be so close to the features of cinema—in his method, his manner, in his particular way of seeing, and in his exposition—is truly amazing'.[13] Chapter 17 of the novel is regarded as Dickens's own 'treatise' on the principles of 'montage' in the construction of story (see **pp. 151–3**). Eisenstein is most interested in two kinds of montage: 'montage exposition' to convey the atmosphere of a particular scene of the inner psychological traits of a character and a 'montage progression' of parallel scenes, in which separate episodes of plot intercut with each other.[14] Tracing Dickens's influence on film through Griffith, he argues: 'our cinema is not entirely without

11 Quoted by Pointer, *Charles Dickens on the Screen*, p. 46.
12 Joss Marsh, 'Dickens and Film', in *The Cambridge Companion to Charles Dickens* (Cambridge: Cambridge University Press, 2001), pp. 204–23 (p. 221).
13 Sergei Eisenstein, 'Dickens, Griffith, and Ourselves' [1942], in *Selected Works*, edited by Richard Taylor and William Powell, 4 vols (London, British Film Institute, 1996), III, 193–238 (p. 199). The essay title is sometimes translated as 'Dickens, Griffith, and the Film Today'.
14 *ibid.*, p. 209.

an ancestry and a pedigree, a past and traditions, or a rich cultural heritage from earlier epochs.'[15]

Eisenstein's use of Dickens to claim 'pedigree', 'a past', and 'rich cultural heritage' has been echoed by the BBC. Despite the controversy aroused by its first production of *Oliver Twist* in 1962, Dickens has become a stalwart of that great British institution, the Sunday teatime serial, largely because of the 'pedigree' that literary success and the passage of time has given him (and other pre-twentieth-century authors). The association between Dickens and the BBC has largely been a happy one, though there are downsides to the relationship. My experience as a teacher has convinced me that BBC serializations have done much to associate Dickens in the minds of students with the ideas of respectability, seriousness and conservatism, but that they have done less to highlight his radicalism, humour and surrealism. Thus, while critics of Dickens and film can be disdainful of the success of the musical *Oliver!*, the musical has kept fresh the idea of Dickens the entertainer and its appeal has reached beyond the nuclear middle-class family. In 1999, Alan Bleasdale's ITV adaptation of *Oliver Twist* was an interesting project. Famous for the gritty realist drama *Boys from the Black Stuff* (1982), Bleasdale brought a socialist sensibility to Dickens, radically rewriting the original: the serial opened with the story of Oliver's mother, and Fagin is more Eastern European conjuror than Jewish pariah. Somewhat disappointingly, reviews focused predominantly on the 'politically correct' portrayal of Fagin (see **pp. 111–13** below).

Years earlier, of course, Jewish protestors had shed blood to prevent the screening of David Lean's classic film of *Oliver Twist* (see **pp. 109–11**). Alec Guinness's portrayal of Fagin in the film seems heavily based on Cruikshank's original illustrations of the novel, and in many ways is faithful to the unthinking anti-Semitism of the novel. The fact that Lean's adaptation, like his brilliant *Great Expectations* (1946), is rated by some as one of the best films ever made, suggests somewhat problematically that Lean did more for the reputation of film in 1948 than for harmonious race relations. What Lean understood about Dickens, of course, is that he speaks through the visual. The visual vocabulary of Dickens's novels has roots in the nineteenth century: as Martin Meisel showed extensively in *Realizations: Narrative, Pictorial and Theatrical Arts in Nineteenth Century England*,[16] there was a mutually constitutive relationship between the novel, the theatre and art in the nineteenth century. Thus 'tableaux' and 'tableaux vivants' were common on the nineteenth-century stage, whereby the stage imitated a picture for a moment, actors freezing to symbolize an important moral or moment of crisis. The melodramatic, externalized poetics of Dickens's novels, though often criticized as somehow lacking by certain literary critics, translate beautifully and meaningfully onto film. And it is indeed through film that we can discover the point of Dickens's externalized stylistic technique. Ideas in Dickens speak through images, surfaces and symbols. Thus, Lean's stylized frames, his stark dramatic use of black and white, reinscribe the emotional and moral vocabulary of Dickens's original novel and Cruikshank's illustrations. Lean wanted to recapture what he

15 *ibid.*, p. 222.
16 Martin Meisel, *Realizations: Narrative, Pictorial and Theatrical Arts in Nineteenth Century England* (Princeton, NJ: Princeton University Press, 1983).

called 'that larger-than-life picture which is really most characteristic of Dickens' kind of writing' and his 'impressions on first reading the two stories'.[17] Of all adaptations, Lean's films do indeed bring us closest to the experience of reading a Dickens novel. They convey 'the expressionism of the moral imagination'.[18]

Figure 5 **Alec Guinness as Fagin in David Lean (dir.),** *Oliver Twist* **(Cineguild, 1948).**

17 Quoted by Pointer, *Charles Dickens on the Screen*, pp. 66–7.
18 Peter Brooks, *The Melodramatic Imagination: Balzac, Henry James, Melodrama and the Mode of Excess* (New Haven, Conn.: Yale University Press, 1976), p. 55. Brooks's phrase originally describes the workings of melodrama at its most ambitious.

The iconography and visual vocabulary of Dickens's novels must be one of the main reasons for their appeal to film-makers. However, the fact that *Oliver Twist* has been reworked by both David Lean and Walt Disney – *Oliver and Company* (1988) – suggests that Dickens's commercial potential is also not insignificant in his continued visibility. Dickens was a shrewd businessman with a modern sense of himself as a 'brand' as well as a sincere populist whose dramatic, visual aesthetics translated well into other media. Even in the nineteenth century, Dickens was a Dickens industry. He was (and is) also a great novelist. But the continued prominence of Dickens owes as much to the 'snowball' economics of the modern culture (and heritage) industry, whereby if you are Dickens, Disney or Barbie, your past success is a kind of guarantee of future commercial success. Fascinatingly, early pressbooks for silent movies are full of ideas on how the film can be used to 'exploit' consumers (see **pp. 106–7**). Many make great play of the line that audiences of *Oliver Twist* will 'ask for more' of merchandise associated with the film. 'Oliver asking for more' can be framed as an iconic capitalist moment.

Where literary critics have felt uneasy about Dickens's larger-than-life characters, these same characters must be immensely attractive to theatrical adapters. In Dickens, we decode characters by examining how they look, speak and act, and such characters can emigrate from stage to page with comparatively little fuss. The lasting appeal of such characters to modern, secular audiences weaned on psychoanalysis is intriguing. Indeed, it is perhaps the very uncertainty and complexity of modern, western models of identity that make Dickens's characters so appealing. Is their seeming solidity and simplicity reassuring in an age of virtual reality? Or are Dickens's characters the products of a 'photographic' sensibility? In their seeming autonomy, are they superficial, easy to categorize and portable? Are they very real, sur-real, or like some postmodern versions of reality, lacking in 'content'? My own feeling is that they negotiate the relationship between surfaces and depths in a way that is perhaps unique, suggesting a reality that is tangible and physical at the same time as problematizing it. That Dickens's characters raise such questions is proof of their modernity, their integral relationship to the world of the moving image and the moving text.

From **letter to Frederick Yates [?29 November 1838],** Pilgrim edn, Vol. I, p. 463

> This letter to the actor and producer Frederick Yates concerns Yates's production of *Nicholas Nickleby,* which had opened on 19 November 1838 at the Adelphi Theatre. Although Dickens approves of this production, the letter explains some of the reasons why Dickens objects to adaptations of his novels that appear before the novel's serialization has ended. Several productions of *Oliver Twist* appeared before serialization was complete.

[. . .]

My general objection to the adaptation of any unfinished work of mine simply is, that being badly done and worse acted it tends to vulgarize the characters, to destroy or weaken in the minds of those who see them the impressions I have

endeavoured to create, and consequently to lessen the after-interest in their progress. No such objection can exist for a moment where the thing is so admirably
done in every respect as you have done it in this instance. I felt it an act of common
justice after seeing the piece, to withdraw all objection to its publication, and to
say this much to the parties interested in it, without reserve.

[. . .]

From **George Almar, Oliver Twist: A Serio-Comic Burletta,** Dicks' Standard Plays, 293 (London: John Dicks, [n.d.]), pp. 5, 8, 24, 26

George Almar's version of *Oliver Twist* (19 November 1838) was one of several
that appeared before the serialized novel had run its course. It was the most
successful of the contemporary stage adaptations but Dickens disliked it so
much that when he saw it at the Surrey Theatre, 'he laid himself down upon the
floor in a corner of the box and never rose from it until the drop-scene fell'.[1]
Reviewers agreed with Dickens. Almar's version omitted the trial of Fagin.

From Act 1, Scene 1

[. . .]

Mrs. C. The dear, good man – why, he is quite overtaken with grief at the story!

Bum. As who would not be? The way in which you told it would have melted
the heart of our overseer. Mrs. Corney, you are not only a Wenus[2] but a Genus![3]
Oh! when shall we become one flesh, Mrs. Corney? Say but the word, and I'll put
up the banns immediately, for there's nothing like wedlock and cannibal happiness. Oh! pictur to yourself ourselves standing at the porochial[4] altar, before
the porochial priest, the charity-boys a-singing, and all the bells ringing. Oh,
Mrs. Corney!

[. . .]

From Act 1, Scene 7

[. . .]

*Outside of the house of Mrs. Mann, a plain white dwelling, with a little garden
before it.*

Enter OLIVER, *with a small bundle.*

Oli. The coal-cellar would not hold me long, and I have escaped them. I listened

---

1   Forster, *The Life of Charles Dickens*, p. 125.
2   Venus.
3   Genius.
4   Parochial; of the parish.

to their taunts without an angry look. I bore the lash without a cry; but when they spoke wild thoughts about my mother, I—I—well, well! I mustn't think. Where am I? As I live, before the very house where, with orphans like myself, I was brought up upon the parish bounty. Hard was it and scanty, like my lodging. Yet it *was* my home, and in my heart I hallow it. How lonesome it is to be unloved in this great world. Ah! when from here I went, there was one who wept to see it, and he made me cry, too. The doctor said the orphan had consumption in his look—like—like enough—poor little Dick, my only friend, is dead.

Enter CHILD.

[. . .]

Oli. I feel cold, stiff, and hungry, and my last penny is gone. If I ask charity, in most of the villages through which I pass large painted boards are put up, warning all persons who do so that they shall be sent to gaol; and if I go into a shop, they talk of the beadle, and put my heart into my mouth. Ah me, I am so tired, I think I could lie down and die.

[. . .]

From Act 3, Scene 9

[. . .]

The garret of Sikes.

[. . .]

Nan. The good lady and gentleman told me of a home where I could end my days in solitude and peace. Let me see them again, and beg them on my knees to show the same mercy and goodness unto you, and—let us never see each other more—let us lead better lives, and forget how we have lived, except in prayer! It is never too late to repent—never!

Sik. You will not loose your hold.

Nan. No—I will hold you till you kiss me and forgive.

Sik. Perdition!

> [*Music. He drags her off,* D. F.
> —*A scream is heard, then a fall.*—*Sikes*
> *re-enters, pale and trembling.*

There is blood upon these hands and she is dead!

> [*Rushes out.*

[. . .]

From Act 3, Scene 12

[. . .]

Sik. But the eyes!—the eyes! Wherever I go they follow and look upon me! I can trace her shadow in the gloom—and how stiff and solemn it seems to stalk along! I could hear its garments rustling in the leaves, and every breath of wind came laden with its last low cry? Well, what are you all staring at? Toby, your hand. (*He turns away.*) Ah, Bates, give me yours!

From **John Forster, *The Life of Charles Dickens*,** edited by J. W. T. Ley (London: Cecil Palmer, 1928), pp. 799–800, 801

These extracts from Forster's biography document first the anxieties that Dickens had about performing public readings of his work before the reading tours and, second, the effect of the 'Sikes and Nancy' reading on ladies in the audience (who fainted) and his friend, the famous actor William Macready. (See also pp. **97–9**.)

[. . .] 'I have made a short reading of the murder in *Oliver Twist*. I cannot make up my mind, however, whether to do it or not. I have no doubt that I could perfectly petrify an audience by carrying out the notion I have of the way of rendering it. But whether the impression would not be so horrible as to keep them away another time, is what I cannot satisfy myself upon. What do you think? It is in three short parts: 1, Where Fagin sets Noah Claypole on to watch Nancy. 2, The scene on London Bridge. 3, Where Fagin rouses Claypole from his sleep to tell his perverted story to Sikes: and the Murder, and the Murderer's sense of being haunted. I have adapted and cut about the text with great care, and it is very powerful. [. . .] I wanted to leave behind me the recollection of something very passionate and dramatic, done with simple means, if the art would justify the theme.' [. . .]

[. . .] The *Sikes and Nancy* scenes, everywhere his prominent subject, exacted the most terrible physical exertion from him. In January he was at Clifton, where he had given, he told his sister-in-law, 'by far the best Murder yet done;' while at the same date he wrote to his daughter: 'At Clifton on Monday night we had a contagion of fainting; and yet the place was not hot. I should think we had from a dozen to twenty ladies taken out stiff and rigid, at various times! It became quite ridiculous.' He was afterwards at Cheltenham. 'Macready is of opinion that the Murder is two Macbeths.'

From **the reading text of Dickens's 'Sikes and Nancy',** in Philip Collins (ed.), *Charles Dickens: The Public Readings* (Oxford: Clarendon Press, 1975), pp. 482–3

This is an extract from the text used by Dickens for his public reading of the 'Sikes and Nancy' scene from *Oliver Twist*. An examination of the passage in its entirety raises interesting questions about the relative requirements of drama and the novel. Dickens includes, for example, the meeting between Nancy, Rose and Mr Brownlow but omits description of Jacob's Island. The effect of the image of Nancy's eyes is minimized after the murder. Throughout, novelistic connectives like 's/he says' are omitted.

[. . .]

The girl was lying, half-dressed, upon the bed. He had roused her from her sleep, for she raised herself with a hurried and startled look.

'Get up!'

'It *is* you, Bill!'

'*Get up*!!!'

There was a candle burning, but he drew it from the candlestick, and hurled it under the grate. Seeing the faint light of early day without, the girl rose to undraw the curtain.

'*Let it be.* There's light enough for wot I've got to do.'———

'*Bill, why do you look like that at me?*'

The robber regarded her, for a few seconds, with dilated nostrils and heaving breast; then, grasping her by the head and throat, dragged her into the middle of the room, and placed his heavy hand upon her mouth.

'You were watched to-night, *you she-devil; every word you said was heard.*'

'Then if every word I said was heard, it was heard that I spared you. Bill, *dear Bill*, you cannot have the heart to kill me. Oh! Think of all I have given up, only this one night, for *you*. Bill, *Bill*! For dear God's sake, for your own, for mine, stop before you *spill my blood*!!! I have been *true* to you, *upon my guilty soul I have*!!! The gentleman and that dear lady told me to-night of a home in some foreign country where I could end my days in solitude and peace. Let me see them again, and beg them, on my knees, to show the same mercy to you; and let us both leave this dreadful place, and far apart lead better lives, and forget how we have lived, except in prayers, and never see each other more. It is never too late to repent. They told me so—I feel it now. But we must have *time*—we must have a *little, little time*!'

The housebreaker freed one arm, and grasped his pistol. The certainty of immediate detection if he fired, flashed across his mind; and he beat it twice upon the upturned face that almost touched his own.

She staggered and fell, but raising herself on her knees, *she drew from her bosom a white handkerchief—Rose Maylie's,—and holding it up towards heaven, breathed one prayer, for mercy to her Maker.*

It was a ghastly figure to look upon. The murderer staggering backward to the wall, and shutting out the sight with his hand, seized a heavy club, and struck her down!!

[. . .]

From **pressbook, William Cowen (dir.), Oliver Twist** (USA, 1933, Pathé Pictures)

This fascinating extract from the pressbook for an early film version of *Oliver Twist* gives distributors instructions about how to use the film for 'exploitation' (advertising). It is a marvellously crude example of the ease with which Oliver's asking for more was framed as capitalist ideology.

TIE-UPS WITH DEALERS.

The very name "Oliver Twist" suggests endless tie-ups with local dealers. Confectioners, for example, will gladly link up with the picture. For example, a little window display of BROWN'S CHOCOLATES:

Like "OLIVER TWIST."

you'll ask for more of

BROWN'S CHOCOLATES.

Take a box with you, and doubly enjoy

"OLIVER TWIST"

at

. . . .

Grocers in particular are likely to welcome the opportunity. Dairymen, too, A gummed disc on the glass milk-bottles will bring 'Oliver Twist' right into the home. Work in the 'baby' idea.

'Baby—like "Oliver Twist"—asks for more of So-and-So's Milk. Baby, alas! can't see "Oliver Twist" at the   . . . .   Theatre; but you can—and enjoy this marvellous film of the Dickens story."

There are endless possibilities for local tie-ups, all the more likely to be welcomed since they are certain to prove mutually helpful.
[. . .]

—AND THE SCHOOLS.

Get into touch with the headmasters and headmistresses of the local elementary schools, intimate when you are showing the film, and advise them of your charge for parties of children, large and small. A slight expenditure of time and trouble is certain to yield a rich reward.

[. . .]

From **pressbook, David Lean (dir.), Oliver Twist** (UK, 1948, Cineguild)

This outline of the plot of David Lean's film adaptation of *Oliver Twist* starts to raise interesting questions about adaptation and the relationship between the novel and film. The film (like other adaptations) should obviously be viewed in order to attempt a serious understanding of the issues raised by adaptations.

Lean's version does not include the Maylies but it does include Monks. The opening scene, featuring Oliver's mother in a thunderstorm arriving at the workhouse, in many ways surpasses the opening of the novel, and the ending, in which Sikes, Fagin and the gang are together when they are caught, is arguably more imaginatively coherent than the ending of the novel. (Good clearly triumphs over evil.) Lean does not dramatize Fagin's trial, however, and it is hard to imagine that he could convey the many layers of meaning conveyed by Dickens's prose in the novelistic scene in which not much actually happens. (See also 'Fagin's Trial', pp. 177–8.)

The story begins in a squalid, drab parish workhouse on a wild winter's night in England in the early part of the last century. An unknown girl (JOSEPHINE STUART) lies dying after giving birth to a son. As the doctor places her baby in her arms she tries to speak, but she has no strength left and dies without saying who she is or where she has come from.

[. . .]

Meanwhile, Bill Sikes has joined the others in their hiding place. His reception by the gang is mixed, but he is armed with a pistol and they all do as he says.

As the angry crowd below batter the doors of the house, the boys work feverishly to strengthen the barricades. Petrified with fear, Fagin gets shut out on the staircase. His cries for help go unheeded because the Dodger – the memory of Nancy's battered body still imprinted on his mind – has shouted from the window denouncing Sikes to the crowd. Sikes, completely enraged, flies at him. Knocking him down, Sikes curses the crowd and, turning back to the room, orders Oliver to get some rope and accompany him to the roof.

As Sikes and Oliver reach the roof, the police break into the house and overpower Fagin and the boys. At pistol point, Sikes forces Oliver to fasten the rope to the chimney stack. Pulling at the rope, Oliver dislodges part of the chimney stack. The splash, as it falls into the canal below, attracts the crowd's attention. Spellbound they watch the two on the roof.

Sikes is just about to slide down the rope when he is hit by a rifle, fired by a police officer below. For a moment the crowd is hushed as he falls from the roof to his death.

Rescued from his precarious perch, Oliver is reunited with Mr. Brownlow, who, explaining his true identity is allowed to take him home. Shortly afterwards Oliver is safe once more with Mrs. Bedwin and a new life of comfort and security opens up before him.

Reviews of Screen Adaptations

The reviews of screen adaptations of the novel included here focus heavily on the representation of Fagin and the issue of anti-Semitism. From the reports of the riots in Berlin when David Lean's 1948 adaptation was first shown to the reviews of Alan Bleasdale's 'politically correct' 1999 television series, reviewers show the political bias of the papers they write for. Thus, the *Telegraph* calls the Jewish protestors in Berlin 'black market operators' and the *Evening Standard* in 1999 associates Bleasdale's downplaying of Fagin's Jewishness to a populist dumbing-down of quality literature. Like Robert Lindsay in Bleasdale's 1999 adaptation, George C. Scott had also been criticized for his 'sanitized' performance as Fagin in a 1982 TV adaptation.[1] John Bowen's *Times Literary Supplement* review is unusual in downplaying the race issue to argue that in Dickens 'what really matters is [. . .] particular scenes of dreamlike hallucinatory clarity [. . .]. What may be missing in Bleasdale's ample and generous adaptation is a sense of the metaphysical stage on which Dickens's characters play out their roles, the novel's belief in pure good and unmitigated evil.'[2] One reason for the high profile of the issue of anti-Semitism in newspapers (as opposed to literary criticism) must be that controversy about race is likely to sell papers and increase viewer numbers. But the impact of the visual and the different ideological traditions of literary and screen studies are also important factors. (See **pp. 95–102** for a discussion of screen adaptations.)

From **[Anonymous], 'Berlin Cinema Fight'**, *Guardian* (21 February 1949)

'Oliver Twist'

JEWS STOP FIRST
PERFORMANCE
BERLIN, FEBRUARY 20.

A crowd of Polish Jews, estimated to number fifty to eighty, forced its way into a cinema in the British sector here to-day and prevented the first showing of the British film 'Oliver Twist.' Mr. Henry Durban, Berlin representative of Eagle-Lion Distributors, said later that the showing had been put off on his instructions 'in the interests of public safety,' but he said that to-morrow he would ask Major General G. K. Bourne, British Commandant here, for 'adequate protection' so that the première might take place in the evening.

Shouting, 'This film is anti-Semitic' and 'We will not allow this film to be shown,' the Polish Jews burst open all the exit doors of the Kurbel Cinema and fought with members of the audience who protested against their action. Cinema seats were broken and several people were injured before order was restored by British military police and Western sector German police.

Mr. Walter Jonigkeit, manager of the cinema, stated that shortly before the performance was due to begin the Polish Jews sent a six-man delegation to his office to demand that it be cancelled.

[. . .]

---

1   John J. O'Connor, "TV: George C. Scott in *Oliver Twist*", *New York Times* (23 May 1982).
2   John Bowen, *Times Literary Supplement*, 24 December 1999, p. 16.

From **[Anonymous], 'Baton Charge on Berlin *Oliver Twist* Objectors'**, *Daily Telegraph* (22 February 1949)

FROM OUR OWN CORRESPONDENT

BERLIN, Monday.

Fewer than 100 Polish Jews, many of whom are known to the Berlin police as black market operators, again stopped the showing at a British sector cinema here to-day of the British film 'Oliver Twist.'

They staged a demonstration outside the cinema, in the course of which German police made baton charges, used a fire hose, and fired warning shots from revolvers. Jews yesterday forced the withdrawal of the film in protest at the portrayal of Fagin in what they regard as a rôle discreditable to Jews.

A British statement issued tonight said: 'If the German public does not wish the film to continue either the cinema proprietor or the distributor can arrange to withdraw it. This has now been done.'

Shortly before to-day's performance began 50 or 60 Jews, many of them clad in tight-waisted coats, carefully creased trousers and snap-brim felt hats, approached the building shouting in broken German: 'Down with Fascism,' and 'Hitler has come to Berlin.' They began tearing down a 10ft-high placard advertising the film.

SERIES OF SCUFFLES

About 120 German police, who had been detailed to protect the cinema, intervened and a general mêlée developed. The police used their truncheons freely in a series of scuffles.

Several of the demonstrators received head wounds from truncheon blows. A number of policemen were also injured.

Meanwhile, on the instructions of Mr. Henry Durban, Berlin manager of J. Arthur Rank Ltd., the performance in the cinemas, which was two-thirds full, began.

More Jews arrived and the crowd in the square was increased by sight-seers to between 2,000 and 3,000. British Public Safety officers, none of whom spoke German, tried to give instructions to German police.

[. . .]

As the police fought their way down one side-street the demonstrators reappeared through another. One spat on a British major of the Public Safety branch. A police cordon across one road drew revolvers and advanced on the Jews, many of whom ran forward baring their chests with theatrical gestures and shouting: 'Shoot. Shoot.'

[. . .]

Scenes were recorded by many American photographers and film operators, who posed injured demonstrators with blood running down their faces.

GERMAN INDIGNATION

The entire episode has made an extremely painful impression here. Although the wisdom of showing 'Oliver Twist' in Berlin is open to question, in view of the opposition which it received in the United States[1], British prestige has suffered severely by allowing the film to be twice forced off the screen by an organised demonstration of a handful of foreigners.

German bystanders openly expressed their indignation at the inability of the police to deal with 'foreign spivs[2] and black market operators.'

[. . .]

From **Rhoda Koenig on political correctness and Bleasdale's *Oliver Twist*,** *Evening Standard* (7 July 1999), 13

Vulgarity and greed—masquerading as sweetness and light—have struck a great classic yet again, with the ITV announcement that its new version of Oliver Twist will have a Fagin who is not all that Jewish. [. . .] David Liddiment, the ITV director of programmes, explains: 'We don't want a Fagin that is a Shylock caricature.'

Is this concern for Jewish viewers, and indeed for all victims of prejudice? Actually, no. The alteration, by the people who brought us Who Wants to Be a Millionaire? (new series on the way),[1] exemplifies not only a lack of understanding of our literary heritage but a contempt for the past itself. It is also an example of sentimentality, arrogance and cowardice that are now passed off as 'sensitivity' and 'responsibility'.

[. . .]

Why have we become so illiterate, so phony and so craven? As an American it grieves me to say that one must simply turn west. Presumably, ITV does not want any trouble when it sells its programme to a much bigger market than Britain, so it is ensuring that its film will appeal to the United States. [. . .] taste in that nation has been debased by sentimentality. [. . .]

From **James Rampton, 'Keep your nose out of it'**, *Independent Review* (1 December 1999), 10

ALAN BLEASDALE ADVISED ROBERT LINDSAY TO ABANDON THE STEREOTYPES FOR HIS TELEVISION FAGIN. THIS TIME, IT'S STRICTLY BY THE BOOK.

[. . .]

By his own admission, Robert Lindsay has become a world expert at what he calls 'nose acting'.

[. . .]

---

1 See **p. 95**.
2 Person living on their wits without regular work or one who engages in black-market dealing.

1 A quiz programme offering up to a million pounds in prize money.

'As I've got older, I've tended to bury myself in prosthetics.[1] I enjoy changing myself,' Lindsay admits. 'But Alan wrote on his script, "Fagin will certainly not have a long nose, Robert".'

Bleasdale's chief concern was to steer clear of what he calls 'the perhaps accidental anti-Semitism' of the original novel. 'The character is obviously territory I'm very familiar with,' says the actor, 'but the Fagin in the Lionel Bart musical is very different from the Fagin in Alan's script. My problem was that I had to get rid of that whole musical performance, get it right out of my head.

'Alan told me right from the start that he wanted to avoid the stereotypical Yiddish[2] Fagin that is so prevalent in the Bart version. The whole rhythm of the language of the musical makes it like that. You can't say phrases like "Oliver, my dear" in any other way. When Alan says that he doesn't want Fagin to be Jewish, I understand completely. This Fagin is a magician from Bohemia[3] who just happens to be Jewish. Alan doesn't want me to overplay it.'

And he doesn't. Lindsay delivers a finely nuanced performance; his Fagin here – who is never directly referred to as Jewish – is magnetic without slipping into 'gotta pick a pocket or two'[4] clichés. On being introduced to Oliver, he conjures flames, multi-coloured silks and doves out of thin air before declaring with a flourish and a twinkle: 'Pleased to meet you. Oliver Twist.' According to Lindsay, 'the fact that Fagin is foreign is beguiling and romantic to the children. He lures them to him with some kind of exotic charisma.'

Some critics have suggested this spills over into child abuse.[5] When Oliver (Sam Smith) first wakes up in the den. Lindsay's Fagin certainly has an insinuating air about him: 'You see, Oliver, you're in my dreams already,' he leers.

But paedophilia remains at a subtextual level – Lindsay denies playing this Fagin as an overt child molester. 'There's always been this big question, hasn't there? Is he a paedophile? Well, he's not in Charles Dickens's novel.' (Bleasdale may get brownie points for playing it by the book here, but purists may be less forgiving about his invention of a two-hour prologue.)

'This man has a coven of boys at his beck and call,' Lindsay continues. 'As kids, we've all been under the influence of some strange men. But I've made up my mind that Fagin is sexless. The big thing for Oliver is that Fagin's den is his first real home, offering food, warmth and sociability. For that boy, it must have been so welcoming after being alone for so long. To tamper with that and play up the sexual angle would be to kill Dickens.'

Bleasdale, who has enjoyed a fruitful partnership with Lindsay over the last decade, echoes the actor: 'Fagin is a Pied Piper,[6] and the young children are drawn to him because of his charm and his magic tricks. I wanted to create a character who was charming and seductive without it being in any way sexual.'

---

1   Originally a surgical term to denote the making up of deficiencies (e.g. false teeth or artificial limbs), it can also refer to the parts thus supplied.
2   Language used by the Jews in or from central and eastern Europe; originally a Middle Rhine dialect with words from Hebrew and several modern languages.
3   Now an area of the Czech Republic.
4   A song from Lionel Bart's musical *Oliver!* and Read's film version.
5   For example, Garry Wills; see 'The Loves of *Oliver Twist*', *New York, Review of Books*, 36 (26 October 1989), 60–7.
6   The central character of the folk story, 'The Pied Piper of Hamelin', about a man who played the flute in such a way that it put a spell on children who followed him and were not seen again.

'There should be no ugliness about Fagin, even though he does things which we know are morally wrong. The fact is that he is an immigrant, and the laws of this country at that time refused to allow Jews to hold property. So often the only way they could make a living was either through loans or through criminal actions. This part is just perfect for Robert.'

It certainly is. It plays to Lindsay's greatest strength – being attractive and repulsive in the same breath. [. . .]

4

Key passages

Introduction

Even those who have not read *Oliver Twist* may feel that they know the novel's 'story'. Oliver is an illegitimate child who is born in a workhouse and, after the speedy death of his mother, he becomes an orphan. After asking for more food in the corrupt and abusive workhouse, he is apprenticed to an undertaker but flees to London after his mother's memory is insulted and he fights to defend her good name. Once he reaches London, he falls in with a gang of child thieves controlled by Fagin who is helped by the violent Bill Sikes and his prostitute partner Nancy. After being wrongly accused of stealing, Oliver is cared for by the kindly, middle-class Mr Brownlow, before he is kidnapped by the gang and returned to Fagin. When he is forced to participate in a robbery, he is shot and captured, then subsequently cared for by the benevolent Maylies in the country. Nancy takes pity on Oliver and reveals some of what she knows about his background to Rose Maylie and Mr Brownlow, a betrayal for which she is murdered by her partner Sikes. Sikes is pursued by the law and ultimately takes his own life, albeit by accident. Fagin is tried and sentenced to death by hanging. Oliver discovers that he is Rose's nephew and the son of the woman Brownlow had loved; Oliver is adopted by Brownlow and hence achieves a respectable position among the middle classes. The second half of the novel features Oliver's evil but legitimate half-brother, Monks, and his attempts to cheat Oliver out of his inheritance, a cumbersome plot which clogs up the ending of the novel. In artistic terms, Monks has not been viewed as a successful character, though some of the ideas that Dickens was trying to express through his characterization are worthy of attention. (Monks is animalistic and subject to fits, yet he is 'legitimate'. Oliver's illegitimacy seems less important than his innate goodness and sturdy spirit.)

In many ways, the details of the plot of *Oliver Twist* are less important than its outline. Its outline, inherited from fairy tale, melodrama and allegory, is that of good triumphing over evil. This particular variation on a theme has achieved mythic status for many reasons, one of which is its consonance with the capitalist myth that has dominated western democracies for the last two centuries, that individuals who want more can get more, and that even the dispossessed can achieve their dreams. The novel's ideological drift is no different from that of many other Victorian novels in this respect, however, and not all of these have achieved the popular acclaim of *Oliver Twist*. To understand *Oliver Twist*'s accessibility, therefore, it is important to study the detail of the text itself, and to understand the means by which that text has been adapted and disseminated in a mass cultural age. The selection of passages included in this section is no substitute for a reading of the novel as a whole. Every passage in *Oliver Twist*, or indeed any novel, is 'key', and therefore the act of selecting 'key passages' is necessarily and largely random. The key passages and commentaries included below are intended to open up the text for readers and to enable them to work towards individual yet grounded new readings.

Key Passages

The Author's Preface to the Third Edition of
Oliver Twist, 1841

The Preface to *Oliver Twist* is commonly acknowledged to be an attempt by Dickens to divorce himself from the Newgate novelists with whom he had been grouped by the hostile *Fraser's Magazine* (see **pp. 43–4**), and to clarify the moral, artistic and class issues surrounding the representation of crime in fiction. Two of the principal charges that Dickens was defending himself against were, first, that his subject matter was *essentially* immoral and, second, that it was 'low' (see Queen Victoria's diaries, **pp. 37–8**). His choice of epigraph from Fielding mocks the stupidity of critics who automatically assume that because the subject matter of a novel is 'low', it is also immoral. The implication of Fielding and Dickens is that no subject – however immoral or 'low – is innately good or evil, beneficial or harmful. Writers' treatment of their subject matter, artistic method or style, should be the true object of critical scrutiny, for the moral bias of a work depends on this.

This reading of the Preface is largely self-evident. But what is not often noticed is that nowhere in the Preface does Dickens mention the term 'Newgate' apart from one particularly dishonest and slippery reference to Edward Bulwer Lytton's 'Newgate' novel *Paul Clifford* (1830). Bulwer Lytton's novels obviously do have a bearing on the subject in every respect, but Dickens, by a rhetorical sleight of hand, chooses to divorce himself from such literary midgets by listing precedents for his own moral art set by giants like 'Fielding, De Foe, Goldsmith, Smollett, Richardson, Mackenzie' and Hogarth (see notes 18 and 5). No doubt the fact that Dickens deliberately avoids the word 'Newgate' can be explained if we acknowledge that the Preface is on one level a piece of literary propaganda designed literally to erase any associations between *Oliver Twist* and the Newgate novels and to carve a niche for Dickens the novelist among the literary greats. But there is also a second, and far more important, reason why Dickens avoids mentioning Newgate and that is because he substitutes for it another key term: 'romance'. The term 'romance' lies at the heart of the Newgate controversy, underlying what was a debate about the relationship in fiction between the romantic and the real. That is, Newgate novelists and critics were grappling semi-consciously with forms and concepts of 'realism' before the word emerged as a literary critical term later in the century (see **pp. 44–5**).

In the Preface, the term 'romance' is closely associated with fiction that glamorizes crime and distorts reality; the term is in fact almost a convenient shorthand for 'Newgate novels'. Dickens declares himself to be an opponent of romance and an exponent of a comparatively realistic style of writing. Dickens's emphatic response to critics of Nancy – 'It is useless to discuss whether the conduct and character of the girl seems natural or unnatural, probable or improbable, right or wrong. IT IS TRUE' (see **p. 124**) – is remarkably similar to the pronouncement by the forefather of French realism, Balzac, on his character, Le Père Goriot: 'This drama is not fiction or romance. *All is true,*—so true that every one can discern the elements of the tragedy in his own house, perhaps in his own heart.'[1] However, although on a superficial level the Preface to *Oliver Twist* can be read as dramatizing a straightforward debate between romance and a burgeoning 'realism', things are not quite that simple. After all his fierce talking, for example, Dickens significantly qualifies his presentation of *Oliver Twist* as realistic by repeatedly claiming that its characters' speech should not 'offend the ear'. Perhaps more problematic for his argument is the fact that he describes Oliver in allegorical terms as representing 'the principle of Good'. Dickens's description of himself as a realistic writer is not strictly accurate; it is the defensive response of a writer under attack in a local critical debate. While there is much that is realistic about his subject matter, his theatrical style is in the eighteenth-century tradition he invokes. His technique is perhaps more thoughtfully described in the Preface to *Bleak House* as representing 'the romantic side of familiar things'.

The Preface also touches on, but does not fully resolve, the thorny issue of the relationship between nature and nurture in the development of criminals. Discussing Sikes, he neatly avoids the issue he is nominally addressing of why there are people like Sikes. He is surer of his ground when it comes to Nancy, though when he discusses her, he confines himself to the question of whether she might exist and not the more challenging question of why such women are as they are. (See **pp. 31–3**, and Michie, **p. 77**, Ingham, **pp. 4–7** and Bowen, **pp. 87–9**.)

'Some of the author's friends cried, "Lookee, gentlemen the man is a villain; but it is Nature for all that;" and the young critics of the age, the clerks, apprentices, &c., called it low, and fell a groaning.'—FIELDING.[2]

---

1   Honoré de Balzac, *Le Père Goriot (1834–5)*, translated by Ellen Marriage (London: Dent, 1896), p. 2.
2   This epigraph is taken from Henry Fielding's novel, *Tom Jones* (1749), 7.1.

THE greater part of this Tale was originally published in a magazine. When I completed it, and put it forth in its present form three years ago, I fully expected it would be objected to on some very high moral grounds in some very high moral quarters. The result did not fail to prove the justice of my anticipations.

I embrace the present opportunity of saying a few words in explanation of my aim and object in its production. It is in some sort a duty with me to do so, in gratitude to those who sympathised with me and divined my purpose at the time, and who, perhaps, will not be sorry to have their impression confirmed under my own hand.

It is, it seems, a very coarse and shocking circumstance, that some of the characters in these pages are chosen from the most criminal and degraded of London's population; that Sikes is a thief, and Fagin a receiver of stolen goods; that the boys are pickpockets, and the girl is a prostitute.

I confess I have yet to learn that a lesson of the purest good may not be drawn from the vilest evil. I have always believed this to be a recognised and established truth, laid down by the greatest men the world has ever seen, constantly acted upon by the best and wisest natures, and confirmed by the reason and experience of every thinking mind. I saw no reason, when I wrote this book, why the very dregs of life, so long as their speech did not offend the ear, should not serve the purpose of moral, at least as well as its froth and cream. Nor did I doubt that there lay festering in Saint Giles's[3] as good materials towards the truth as any flaunting in Saint James's.[4]

In this spirit, when I wished to shew, in little Oliver, the principle of Good surviving through every adverse circumstance, and triumphing at last; and when I considered among what companions I could try him best, having regard to that kind of men into whose hands he would most naturally fall; I bethought myself of those two figures in these volumes. When I came to discuss the subject more maturely with myself, I saw many strong reasons for pursuing the course to which I was inclined. I had read of thieves by scores—seductive fellows (amiable for the most part), faultless in dress, plump in pocket, choice in horseflesh, bold in bearing, fortunate in gallantry, great at a song, a bottle, pack of cards or dice-box, and fit companions for the bravest. But I had never met (except in HOGARTH[5]) with the miserable reality. It appeared to me that to draw a knot of such associates in crime as really do exist; to paint them in all their deformity, in all their wretchedness, in all the squalid poverty of their lives; to shew them as they really are, for ever skulking uneasily through the dirtiest paths of life, with the great, black, ghastly gallows closing up their prospect, turn them where they may; it appeared to me that to do this, would be to attempt a something which was greatly needed, and which would be a service to society. And therefore I did it as I best could.

In every book I know, where such characters are treated of at all, certain allurements and fascinations are thrown around them. Even in the Beggar's Opera,[6] the

---

3 A poor area of London known for its criminal fraternity, which was originally a village north-west of London until the expansion of London eroded the fields that had separated it from the city.
4 A fashionable area of London; one of seven parishes belonging to the City of Westminster.
5 Painter of the *The Rake's Progress* and *The Harlot's Progress*. See **p. 48** and **p. 54**.
6 See **pp. 37–8**, n. 1.

thieves are represented as leading a life which is rather to be envied than otherwise; while MACHEATH,[7] with all the captivations of command, and the devotion of the most beautiful girl and only pure character in the piece,[8] is as much to be admired and emulated by weak beholders, as any fine gentleman in a red coat who has purchased, as VOLTAIRE says, the right to command a couple of thousand men, or so, and to affront death at their head.[9] Johnson's question, whether any man will turn thief because Macheath is reprieved,[10] seems to me beside the matter. I ask myself, whether any man will be deterred from turning thief because of his being sentenced to death, and because of the existence of Peachum and Lockit;[11] and remembering the captain's roaring life, great appearance, vast success, and strong advantages, I feel assured that nobody having a bent that way will take any warning from him, or will see anything in the play but a very flowery and pleasant road, conducting an honourable ambition in course of time, to Tyburn Tree.[12]

In fact, Gay's witty satire on society[13] had a general object, which made him careless of example in this respect, and gave him other, wider, and higher aims. The same may be said of Sir Edward Bulwer's admirable and most powerful novel of Paul Clifford,[14] which cannot be fairly considered as having, or being intended to have, any bearing on this part of the subject, one way or other.

What manner of life is that which is described in these pages, as the every-day existence of a Thief? What charms had it for the young and ill-disposed, what allurements for the most jolter-headed of juveniles? Here are no canterings upon moonlit heaths, no merry-makings in the snuggest of all possible caverns, none of the attractions of dress, no embroidery, no lace, no jack-boots, no crimson coats and ruffles, none of the dash and freedom with which 'the road' has been, time out of mind, invested. The cold, wet, shelterless midnight streets of London; the foul and frowsy dens, where vice is closely packed and lacks the room to turn; the haunts of hunger and disease, the shabby rags that scarcely hold together: where are the attractions of these things? Have they no lesson, and do they not whisper something beyond the little-regarded warning of a moral precept?

But there are people of so refined and elevated a nature, that they cannot bear the contemplation of these horrors. Not that they turn instinctively from crime; but that criminal characters, to suit them, must be, like their meat, in delicate disguise. A Massaroni[15] in green velvet is quite an enchanting creature; but a Sikes in fustian is insupportable. A Mrs. Massaroni, being a lady in short petticoats and

---

7 The highway-man hero of *The Beggar's Opera*.
8 Peachum's daughter (see note 11), Polly.
9 A reference to the attack on the purchasing of commissions in the army and high appointments in the law in Voltaire's (1694–1778) philosophical tale *The World as it Goes* (1748).
10 Dr Samuel Johnson (1709–84) did not in fact comment on the effect of Macheath's pardon but disputed the idea that the play had a moral purpose.
11 In *The Beggar's Opera*, Peachum is a thief-taker who is also a criminal and Lockit is a Newgate warder.
12 The wooden gallows named after Tyburn, until 1783 the place of public execution for Middlesex and London, and situated at the junction of the roads now called Oxford Street, Bayswater Road and Edgware Road.
13 John Gay's *The Beggar's Opera*. See pp. 37–8, n. 1.
14 See 'Contemporary Documents', p. 121, n. 6.
15 Alessandro Massaroni is the hero of James Robinson Planché's *The Brigand: A Romantic Drama* (1829).

a fancy dress, is a thing to imitate in tableaux[16] and have in lithograph[17] on pretty songs; but a Nancy, being a creature in a cotton gown and cheap shawl, is not to be thought of. It is wonderful how Virtue turns from dirty stockings; and how Vice, married to ribbons and a little gay attire, changes her name, as wedded ladies do, and becomes Romance.

Now, as the stern and plain truth, even in the dress of this (in novels) much exalted race, was a part of the purpose of this book, I will not, for these readers, abate one hole in the Dodger's coat, or one scrap of curl-paper in the girl's dishevelled hair. I have no faith in the delivery which cannot bear to look upon them. I have no desire to make proselytes among such people. I have no respect for their opinion, good or bad; do not covet their approval; and do not write for their amusement. I venture to say this without reserve; for I am not aware of any writer in our language having respect for himself, or held in any respect by his posterity, who ever has descended to the taste of this fastidious class.

On the other hand, if I look for examples, and for precedents, I find them in the noblest range of English literature. Fielding, De Foe, Goldsmith, Smollett, Richardson, Mackenzie[18]—all these for wise purposes, and especially the two first, brought upon the scene the very scum and refuse of the land. Hogarth, the moralist, and censor of his age—in whose great works the times in which he lived, and the characters of every time, will never cease to be reflected—did the like, without the compromise of a hair's breadth; with a power and depth of thought which belonged to few men before him, and will probably appertain to fewer still in time to come. Where does this giant stand now in the estimation of his countrymen? And yet, if I turned back to the days in which he or any of these men flourished, I find the same reproach levelled against them every one, each in his turn, by the insects of the hour, who raised their little hum, and died, and were forgotten.

Cervantes laughed Spain's chivalry away,[19] by showing Spain its impossible and wild absurdity. It was my attempt, in my humble and far-distant sphere, to dim the false glitter surrounding something which really did exist, by shewing it in its unattractive and repulsive truth. No less consulting my own taste, than the manners of the age, I endeavoured, while I painted it in all its fallen and degraded aspect, to banish from the lips of the lowest character I introduced, any expression that could by possibility offend; and rather to lead to the unavoidable inference that its existence was of the most debased and vicious kind, than to prove it elaborately by words and deeds. In the case of the girl, in particular, I kept this intention constantly in view. Whether it is apparent in the narrative, and how it is executed, I leave my readers to determine.

It has been observed of this girl, that her devotion to the brutal house-breaker

16 See **p. 100**.
17 A print by lithography, which obtains prints from a stone or metal surface so treated that what is to be treated can be inked but the remaining area rejects ink.
18 Henry Fielding, Daniel Defoe, Oliver Goldsmith, Tobias Smollett, Samuel Richardson and Henry Mackenzie are all respected eighteenth-century writers who featured rogues and low life for moral purposes.
19 Miguel de Cervantes is best known for his picaresque novel *Don Quixote* (1603). William Harrison Ainsworth's Newgate novel *Rookwood* (1834), includes this phrase which is a misquote of Byron's 'Cervantes smiled Spain's chivalry away' (13.11) in *Don Juan* (1818–24).

does not seem natural, and it has been objected to Sikes in the same breath—with some inconsistency, as I venture to think—that he is surely overdrawn, because in him there would appear to be none of those redeeming traits which are objected to as unnatural in his mistress. Of the latter objection I will merely say, that I fear there are in the world some insensible and callous natures that do become, at last, utterly and irredeemably bad. But whether this be so or not, of one thing I am certain: that there are such men as Sikes, who, being closely followed through the same space of time, and through the same current of circumstances, would not give, by one look or action of a moment, the faintest indication of a better nature. Whether every gentler human feeling is dead within such bosoms, or the proper chord to strike has rusted and is hard to find, I do not know; but that the fact is so, I am sure.

It is useless to discuss whether the conduct and character of the girl seems natural or unnatural, probable or improbable, right or wrong. IT IS TRUE. Every man who has watched these melancholy shades of life knows it to be so. Suggested to my mind long ago—long before I dealt in fiction—by what I often saw and read of, in actual life around me, I have for years, tracked it through many profligate and noisome ways, and found it still the same. From the first introduction of that poor wretch, to her laying her bloody head upon the robber's breast, there is not one word exaggerated or over-wrought. It is emphatically God's truth, for it is the truth He leaves in such depraved and miserable breasts; the hope yet lingering behind; the last fair drop of water at the bottom of the dried-up weed-choked well. It involves the best and worst shades of our common nature; much of its ugliest hues, and something of its most beautiful; it is a contradiction, an anomaly, an apparent impossibility, but it is a truth. I am glad to have had it doubted, for in that circumstance I find a sufficient assurance that it needed to be told.

DEVONSHIRE TERRACE,
April, 1841.

Preface to the Cheap Edition of *Oliver Twist* (1850)

After a second epidemic of cholera hit London in 1848–9, Dickens added this Preface to the cheap edition of the novel, urging the need for better sanitary conditions for the poor as the essential basis for further social improvement. The low-life area Jacob's Island, which Dickens describes so vividly in the novel, was a low-lying, waterside district on the south bank of the Thames. It was one of the main sites of the cholera outbreaks of 1832 and 1848–9 (see **pp. 173–7**) The particular butt of Dickens's satirical wrath in this Preface is Sir Peter Laurie, a businessman who became Lord Mayor of London in 1832. Laurie is reported to have mocked the Bishop of London's claims that it would be relatively inexpensive to remedy the sanitary problems of Jacob's Island, as well as his belief that the location Dickens calls Jacob's Island in the novel actually exists. Dickens mocks Laurie's disbelief in the actuality of Jacob's Island by essentially arguing that if Jacob's Island does not exist, then neither does Laurie. Laurie's ignorance of the place and its problems is disturbing evidence of the deep divide between rich and poor in Victorian society.

At page 267 of this present edition of OLIVER TWIST, there is a description of 'the filthiest, the strangest, the most extraordinary, of the many localities that are hidden in London.' And the name of this place is JACOB'S ISLAND.

Eleven or twelve years have elapsed, since the description was first published. I was as well convinced then, as I am now, that nothing effectual can be done for the elevation of the poor in England, until their dwelling-places are made decent and wholesome. I have always been convinced that this Reform must precede all other Social Reforms; that it must prepare the way for Education, even for Religion; and that, without it, those classes of the people which increase the fastest, must become so desperate and be made so miserable, as to bear within themselves the certain seeds of ruin to the whole community.

The Metropolis (of all places under Heaven) being excluded from the provisions of the Public Health Act,[1] passed last year, a society has been formed called the Metropolitan Sanitary Association,[2] with the view of remedying this grievous mistake. The association held its first public meeting at Freemason's Hall,[3] on Wednesday the sixth of February last: the Bishop of London[4] presiding. It happened that this very place, JACOB'S ISLAND, had lately attracted the attention of the Board of Health, in consequence of its having been ravaged by cholera; and that the Bishop of London had in his hands the result of an inquiry[5] under the Metropolitan Sewers Commission,[6] shewing, by way of proof of the cheapness of sanitary improvements, an estimate of the probable cost at which the houses in JACOB'S ISLAND could be rendered fit for human habitation – which cost was stated at about a penny three farthings per week per house. The Bishop referred to this paper, with the moderation and forbearance which pervaded all his observations, and did me the honour to mention that I had described JACOB'S ISLAND. When I subsequently made a few observations myself,[7] I confessed that soft impeachment.

Now, the vestry of Marylebone[8] parish, meeting on the following Saturday, had

---

1   The Public Health Act of 1848 was the Government's first attempt to confront cholera nationally. The Act established a General Board of Health and allowed local authorities to set up local boards to ensure supplies of clean water by proper disposal of sewage.
2   See p. 81, n. 3.
3   The headquarters of Freemasonry in London and the site of many famous public meetings. These were held from the adjoining Freemasons' Tavern from 1786.
4   Charles James Blomfeld was Bishop of London from 1828 to 1856. He was active and respected, but Dickens disliked some of his views (see Paroissen, *Companion to OT*, **pp. 27–8**).
5   The 'Report from the General Board of Health on the Supply of Water to the Metropolis 1850'.
6   Before the Public Health Act of 1848, twelve unpaid committee members decided on all matters relating to the Sewers Commission, though their power was localized.
7   See *The Speeches of Charles Dickens*, edited by K. J. Fielding (Oxford: Clarendon Press, 1960), pp. 104–10 (6 February 1850). They are repeated, almost verbatim, in the second paragraph of the extract.
8   Now a central London address, Marylebone had been a Middlesex village noted for its park before the city engulfed it; the population more than doubled between 1801 and 1871.

the honour to be addressed by SIR PETER LAURIE; a gentleman of infallible authority, of great innate modesty, and of a most sweet humanity. This remarkable alderman, as I am informed by *The Observer* newspaper, then and there delivered himself (I quote the passage without any correction) as follows:

'Having touched upon the point of saving to the poor, he begged to illustrate it by reading for them the particulars of a survey that had been made in a locality called "Jacob's Island"—[a laugh]—where, according to the surveyor, 1,300 houses were erected on forty acres of ground. The surveyor asserted and laid down that each house could be supplied with a constant supply of pure water—secondly, that each house could be supplied with a sink—thirdly, a water-closet—fourthly, a drain—fifthly, a foundation drain—and, sixthly, the accommodation of a dust bin [laughter], and all at the average of 13*s*. 4*d*. per week [oh, oh, and laughter].

'Mr. G. Bird: Can Sir Peter Laurie tell the vestry where "Jacob's Island" is [laughter].

'Sir P. Laurie: That was just what he was about to tell them. The Bishop of London, poor soul, in his simplicity, thought there really was such a place, which he had been describing so minutely, *whereas it turned out that it* ONLY *existed in a work of fiction, written by Mr. Charles Dickens ten years ago* [roars of laughter]. *The fact was admitted by Mr. Charles Dickens himself at the meeting*, and he (Sir P. Laurie) had extracted his words from the same paper, the *Morning Herald*. Mr Dickens said "Now the first of these classes proceeded generally on the supposition that the compulsory improvement of these dwellings, when exceedingly defective, would be very expensive. But that was a great mistake, for nothing was cheaper than good sanitary improvements, as they knew in this case of 'Jacob's Island' [laughter], which he had described in a work of fiction some ten or eleven years ago." '

[. . .] Reflecting upon this logic, and its universal application; remembering that when FIELDING described Newgate, the prison immediately ceased to exist; that when SMOLLETT took Roderick Random[9] to Bath, that city instantly sank into the earth; that when SCOTT exercised his genius on Whitefriars,[10] it incontinently glided into the Thames; that an ancient place called Windsor was entirely destroyed in the reign of Queen Elizabeth by two Merry Wives of that town, acting under the direction of a person of the name of SHAKESPEARE;[11] and that Mr. POPE, after having at a great expense completed his grotto at Twickenham,[12] incautiously reduced it to ashes by writing a poem upon it;—I say, when I came to consider these things, I was inclined to make this preface the vehicle of my humble tribute of admiration to SIR PETER LAURIE. But, I am restrained by a very painful consideration—by no less a consideration than the impossibility of *his* existence. For SIR PETER LAURIE having been himself described in a book (as I understand

---

9 The eponymous protagonist of Smollett's novel (1748) of that name.
10 In Sir Walter Scott's novel *The Fortunes of Nigel*, Nigel Olifaunt flees to Whitefriars to avoid arrest. The area between Fleet Street and the Thames was a notorious criminal haven.
11 In Shakespeare's comedy, *The Merry Wives of Windsor*, Mrs Ford and Mrs Page both live in Windsor.
12 The poet Alexander Pope moved to Twickenham in 1719, where he renovated a riverside villa to include a grotto. He was helped by one of the leading garden designers of the day.

he was, one Christmas time, for his conduct on the seat of Justice), it is but too clear that there CAN be no such man!
[. . .]

DEVONSHIRE TERRACE.
March, 1850.

The Opening

The parodic tone and convoluted syntax of the opening of *Oliver Twist* is best explained with reference to its origins as a serial publication. As discussed in the 'Contextual Overview', *Oliver Twist* was not contracted as a novel but as a series of articles to be published in the journal, *Bentley's Miscellany*. When this passage was first published as an article in *Bentley's Miscellany*, the town mentioned in the opening sentence to which the narrator will 'assign no fictitious name', is named as 'Mudfog'. The reference to Mudfog relates this passage, therefore, to a piece that preceded *Oliver Twist* called 'The Public Life of Mr. Tulrumble, Once Mayor of Mudfog'. 'The Public Life of Mr. Tulrumble' was a humorous satire on a public official who, once in office, 'contracted a relish for statistics, and got philosophical'. Thus, Dickens's rather tortured syntax in the opening of *Oliver Twist* and his first-person narrative are perhaps best understood as a parodic imitation of the voice of a pompous, local politician. On first appearance, readers of *Bentley's Miscellany* would have understood *Oliver Twist*'s opening as a continuation of the 'Mudfog' essays rather than as a completely new narrative. When the text was edited for publication as a novel, Dickens edited out the 'Mudfog' references to create a sense of novelistic autonomy for a novel whose origins were as confused as those of Oliver himself. As Dickens's 'The Public Life of Mr. Tulrumble' essay had strongly identified Mudfog with his home town of Chatham, this led to some topographical inconsistency in *Oliver Twist* the novel. (When Oliver leaves the undertakers, he walks south to London, whereas he would have had to walk north from Chatham.) The uncertain beginnings of the novel as well as its protagonist are further in evidence in the opening passage when the narrator calls Oliver's story 'memoirs' and (less directly) 'biography'. In affecting factual status for his narrative, Dickens is imitating the kind of eighteenth-century prose fiction he admits to admiring in the 1841 Preface; as prose fiction was not held in great esteem before the nineteenth century, writers like Henry Fielding frequently pretended that their fictional narratives were grounded in fact, even if this was patently not the case.

This opening passage introduces the workhouse system to which Dickens objects throughout the novel and, in the voice of the narrator, it conveys the more subtle effects of a poor-relief scheme founded on the principles of utilitarianism (see **pp. 13–14**). The fact that the opening of the novel is probably set around 1827–8, shifting to a direct attack on the 1834 Poor Law in Chapter 2 (when Oliver is eight or nine years old) does not stop Dickens's hostility to the spirit of the 1834 Act pervading the opening passage. The rambling, bureaucratic, political (with a small 'p') voice of the narrator clearly shows the mistaken priorities of those in control of Oliver's story and the official narratives of others like him, and the distance between those in authority and those in their care. The unnamed child is referred to as 'it' and 'an item of mortality'; the details of his history the narrator 'need not trouble to repeat' as they 'can be of no possible consequence to the reader, in this stage of *the business* at all events' (italics mine). The first-person narrator conveys no sense of intimacy, feeling or compassion; the logic of the political economy of the New Poor Law thus informs not just the arguments of its architects or victims, but also the subjectivities of those in between. The ideas of 'Nature' and the nature/nurture debate, which surface throughout the novel, are introduced in this passage too, raising philosophical ideas influenced by the philosopher Rousseau (see Lucas, **pp. 72–3**, n. 2) about whether people are born 'in a state of nature' and corrupted by society, or whether people (and Nature) are governed by the principle of self-interest, as Bentham and utilitarianism maintained (see **pp. 13–14** and Lucas, **pp. 72–3**). Interestingly, the narrator's persona becomes more human and less distant as the first person disappears, though there is a continued indirectness. See also G. K. Chesterton, **pp. 63–4**, who argues that the power of the opening passage comes from Dickens's 'distance from, and independence of, the elaborate financial arguments of his time', and Dennis Walder, **pp. 75–6**.

CHAPTER I
TREATS OF THE PLACE WHERE OLIVER TWIST WAS BORN; AND OF THE CIRCUMSTANCES ATTENDING HIS BIRTH

AMONG other public buildings in a certain town, which for many reasons it will be prudent to refrain from mentioning, and to which I will assign no fictitious name, there is one anciently common to most towns, great or small: to wit, a workhouse; and in this workhouse was born: on a day and date which I need not trouble myself to repeat, inasmuch as it can be of no possible consequence to the reader, in this stage of the business at all events: the item of mortality whose name is prefixed to the head of this chapter.

For a long time after it was ushered into this world of sorrow and trouble,[1] by the parish surgeon,[2] it remained a matter of considerable doubt whether the child could survive to bear any name at all; in which case it is somewhat more than probable that these memoirs would never have appeared; or, if they had, that being comprised within a couple of pages, they would have possessed the inestimable merit of being the most concise and faithful specimen of biography, extant in the literature of any age or country.

Although I am not disposed to maintain that the being born in a workhouse, is in itself the most fortunate and enviable circumstance that can possibly befall a

---

1 From the Book of Common Prayer, service of Holy Communion, Prayer for the Church Militant.
2 A local surgeon contracted by parish authorities for an agreed fee. Originally, they were of lower status than physicians, and the surgeons who attended workhouses were often the cheapest available.

human being, I do mean to say that in this particular instance, it was the best thing for Oliver Twist that could by possibility have occurred. The fact is, that there was considerable difficulty in inducing Oliver to take upon himself the office of respiration, – a troublesome practice, but one which custom has rendered necessary to our easy existence; and for some time he lay gasping on a little flock mattress,[3] rather unequally poised between this world and the next: the balance being decidedly in favour of the latter. Now, if, during this brief period, Oliver had been surrounded by careful grandmothers, anxious aunts, experienced nurses, and doctors of profound wisdom, he would most inevitably and indubitably have been killed in no time. There being nobody by, however, but a pauper old woman, who was rendered rather misty by an unwonted allowance of beer;[4] and a parish surgeon who did such matters by contract; Oliver and Nature fought out the point between them. The result was, that, after a few struggles, Oliver breathed, sneezed, and proceeded to advertise to the inmates of the workhouse the fact of a new burden having been imposed upon the parish, by setting up as loud a cry as could reasonably have been expected from a male infant who had not been possessed of that very useful appendage, a voice, for a much longer space of time than three minutes and a quarter.

[. . .]

Oliver Asks for More

Chapter 2 contains the most concentrated attack on the myriad of abuses Dickens perceived to have arisen or intensified because of the Poor Law Amendment Act of 1834 (see **pp. 11–13**). Though the novel's action starts before the Act was in place, Oliver's ninth birthday, mentioned in the fourth paragraph of this chapter, is timed to coincide with this major legislative change, and thereafter in the novel, the satire on the New Poor Law is unrelenting. In this chapter, the deteriorating system of baby-farming is highlighted through the selfish, grasping character of the significantly named Mrs Mann who, unbeknown to herself, epitomizes what Dickens sees as the evils of Benthamite philosophy (whereby people are motivated by self-interest). The most vulnerable in society, poor women and children, are allowed no voice. This is the main reason, of course, why Oliver's request for more, the dramatic highpoint of this chapter, is so powerful. This symbolic moment (as represented in text and illustration) is no doubt intended as a radical questioning of the status quo and its institutional structures.[1] The fact that Oliver is forced by a group of his peers to become the voice of protest perhaps undermines the subsequent appropriation of this moment as symbolic of individualism and capitalism, though the

---

3   Mattress containing rags or wool refuse.
4   Nurses and midwives were drawn from the lower classes and did not require knowledge or official training.

1   See also Stein, *Victoria's Year*, pp. 135–40 on the illustration.

rags-to-riches movement of the plot reinforces the virtues of asking for more. The prediction that 'that boy will be hung' from 'the gentleman in the white waistcoat' is the more likely outcome of Oliver's life. Like several of the protagonists of the Newgate novels of the 1830s and 40s, however, (see **pp. 43–4** and John, **pp. 89–91**), Oliver is rewarded for his virtue and courage rather than punished for his transgressions.

The satire of this passage is effected by the use of the narrative voice, which metamorphoses throughout the novel (see Lewes's 1837 *National Magazine* review on satire, **p. 53**). Dickens employs metamorphic, free indirect discourse, by which he adopts and parodies the language and attitudes of those he criticizes. Like Jane Austen's novels, Dickens's are peppered with what can be imagined as invisible (or 'intonational') quotation marks, phrases that are, to varying degrees, tongue-in-cheek. Thus, when we are told that the parish authorities enquired 'with dignity', that the workhouse authorities replied 'with humility', and that Mrs Mann is 'a very great experimental philosopher', we know that the opposite is in fact the case and that Dickens is mocking and thereby exposing the attitudes of the those implementing the Poor Law Amendment Act. The examples in this chapter are too numerous to cite, but it would be a useful exercise to highlight the parodic and ironic narrative discourse through which Dickens's social critique operates. The use of free indirect style allows him to pinpoint the abuses of the system he is attacking at the same time that his own ideologies are unfixed by the chameleonic narrative persona: in other words, we are clearer about what Dickens dislikes than about what he would put in its place.

CHAPTER II
TREATS OF OLIVER TWIST'S GROWTH,
EDUCATION, AND BOARD

FOR the next eight or ten months, Oliver was the victim of a systematic course of treachery and deception. He was brought up by hand.[1] The hungry and destitute situation of the infant orphan was duly reported by the workhouse authorities to the parish authorities. The parish authorities inquired with dignity of the workhouse authorities,[2] whether there was no female then domiciled in 'the house' who was in a situation to impart to Oliver Twist, the consolation and nourishment of which he stood in need. The workhouse authorities replied with humility, that there was not. Upon this, the parish authorities magnanimously and

---

1   He was dry-nursed, or fed by artificial food as opposed to breast milk. There may also be the implication here that Oliver was physically abused. (See Dickens's *Great Expectations*, where the phrase is used in this way.)
2   The idea of a partnership between two sets of authorities, by which civil as opposed to ecclesiastical authorities were made responsible for the well-being of the poor, pre-dates the 1834 New Poor Law, which centralized poor relief.

humanely resolved, that Oliver should be 'farmed,'[3] or, in other words, that he should be despatched to a branch-workhouse some three miles off, where twenty or thirty other juvenile offenders against the poor-laws, rolled about the floor all day, without the inconvenience of too much food or too much clothing, under the parental superintendence of an elderly female, who received the culprits at and for the consideration of sevenpence-halfpenny per small head per week. Sevenpence-halfpenny's worth per week is a good round diet for a child; a great deal may be got for sevenpence-halfpenny: quite enough to overload its stomach, and make it uncomfortable. The elderly female was a woman of wisdom and experience; she knew what was good for children; and she had a very accurate perception of what was good for herself. So, she appropriated the greater part of the weekly stipend to her own use, and consigned the rising parochial generation to even a shorter allowance than was originally provided for them. Thereby finding in the lowest depth a deeper still;[4] and proving herself a very great experimental philosopher.[5]

Everybody knows the story of another experimental philosopher who had a great theory about a horse being able to live without eating, and who demonstrated it so well, that he got his own horse down to a straw a day,[6] and would unquestionably have rendered him a very spirited and rampacious animal on nothing at all, if he had not died, four-and-twenty hours before he was to have had his first comfortable bait of air. Unfortunately for the experimental philosophy of the female to whose protecting care Oliver Twist was delivered over, a similar result usually attended the operation of *her* system; for at the very moment when a child had contrived to exist upon the smallest possible portion of the weakest possible food, it did perversely happen in eight and a half cases out of ten, either that it sickened from want and cold, or fell into the fire from neglect, or got half-smothered by accident; in any one of which cases, the miserable little being was usually summoned into another world, and there gathered to the fathers it had never known in this.[7]

Occasionally, when there was some more than usually interesting inquest upon a parish child who had been overlooked in turning up a bedstead, or inadvertently

---

3 Originally, the practice of farming or contracting out pauper infants to the care of paid local matrons was meant to compensate for inadequate hospital facilities and to combat high metropolitan child mortality rates. As supervision of the foster carers deteriorated, however, the practice became counter-productive. The elimination of outdoor poor relief in 1834 meant a further deterioration in infant care, and many unmarried mothers placed their children in baby farms in return for money. There was a scandalously high mortality rate for such children during the Victorian period.

4 Milton, *Paradise Lost*, 4.75–7:
    Which way I flie is Hell; myself am Hell;
    And in the lowest deep a lower deep
    Still threatening to devour me opens wide [. . .]

5 The idea of the 'experimental philosopher' had acquired generally negative connotations by the nineteenth century because of its association with reason and lack of feeling. Dickens certainly compounds this impression, as throughout *Oliver Twist* he repeatedly associates the label with Bentham and Utilitarianism. Mrs Mann here confirms Bentham's view that human beings are essentially selfish.

6 This seems to be a fictitious story, though scientific experiments on live animals in the nineteenth century were not uncommon.

7 Judges 2:10: 'And also all that generation were gathered unto their fathers: and there arose another generation after them, which knew not the Lord [. . .].'

scalded to death when there happened to be a washing; though the latter accident was very scarce,—anything approaching to a washing being of rare occurrence in the farm—the jury would take it into their heads to ask troublesome questions, or the parishioners would rebelliously affix their signatures to a remonstrance. But these impertinences were speedily checked by the evidence of the surgeon, and the testimony of the beadle;[8] the former of whom had always opened the body and found nothing inside (which was very probable indeed), and the latter of whom invariably swore whatever the parish wanted; which was very self-devotional. Besides, the board[9] made periodical pilgrimages to the farm, and always sent the beadle the day before, to say they were going. The children were neat and clean to behold, when *they* went; and what more would the people have!

It cannot be expected that this system of farming would produce any very extraordinary or luxuriant crop. Oliver Twist's ninth birth-day[10] found him a pale thin child, somewhat diminutive in stature, and decidedly small in circumference. But nature or inheritance had implanted a good sturdy spirit in Oliver's breast. It had had plenty of room to expand, thanks to the spare diet of the establishment; and perhaps to this circumstance may be attributed his having any ninth birth-day at all. Be this as it may, however, it *was* his ninth birth-day; and he was keeping it in the coal-cellar with a select party of two other young gentlemen, who, after participating with him in a sound threshing, had been locked up therein for atrociously presuming to be hungry, when Mrs. Mann, the good lady of the house, was unexpectedly startled by the apparition of Mr. Bumble, the beadle, striving to undo the wicket of the garden-gate.

[. . .]

Poor Oliver! He little thought, as he lay sleeping in happy unconsciousness of all around him, that the board had that very day arrived at a decision which would exercise the most material influence over all his future fortunes. But they had. And this was it:—

The members of this board were very sage, deep, philosophical men;[11] and when they came to turn their attention to the workhouse, they found out at once, what ordinary folks would never have discovered – the poor people liked it! It was a regular place of public entertainment for the poorer classes; a tavern where there was nothing to pay; a public breakfast, dinner, tea, and supper all the year round; a brick-and-mortar elysium, where it was all play and no work. 'Oho!' said the board, looking very knowing; 'we are the fellows to set this to rights; we'll stop it all, in no time.' So, they established the rule, that all poor people should have the alternative (for they would compel nobody, not they,) of being starved by a

---

8 A minor parish official with a range of duties. However, by the nineteenth century, he was mainly responsible for supervising paupers and maintaining public order.
9 A group of locally elected parish officials who, according to the 1834 Poor Law Amendment Act, were responsible for administering relief to the poor.
10 In *Bentley's Miscellany*, this read 'eighth'. It was revised in 1838 to read ninth because this was the age when paupers were required to work. According to Kathleen Tillotson (Clarendon edition), the main action of the novel covers about four years.
11 According to David Paroissien (*Companion*), 'Dickens's focus appears to shift in this passage from the local guardians, before whom Oliver appears, to the three Poor Law Commissioners, who, from 1834 onwards, also sat as a board in London, where they initiated some of the sweeping changes to which Dickens objects. As the attack develops, national policies become his target' (pp. 50–1).

gradual process in the house, or by a quick one out of it. With this view, they contracted with the water-works to lay on an unlimited supply of water; and with a corn-factor to supply periodically small quantities of oatmeal; and issued three meals of thin gruel a day, with an onion twice a week, and half a roll on Sundays. They made a great many other wise and humane regulations, having reference to the ladies, which it is not necessary to repeat; kindly undertook to divorce poor married people,[12] in consequence of the great expense of a suit in Doctors' Commons;[13] and, instead of compelling a man to support his family, as they had theretofore done, took his family away from him, and made him a bachelor![14] There is no saying how many applicants for relief under these two last heads, might have started up in all classes of society, if it had not been coupled with the workhouse; but the board were long-headed men, and had provided for this difficulty. The relief was inseparable from the workhouse and the gruel; and that frightened people.

For the first six months after Oliver Twist was removed,[15] the system was in full operation. It was rather expensive at first, in consequence of the increase in the undertaker's bill, and the necessity of taking in the clothes of all the paupers, which fluttered loosely on their wasted, shrunken forms, after a week or two's gruel. But the number of workhouse inmates got thin as well as the paupers; and the board were in ecstasies.

The room in which the boys were fed, was a large stone hall, with a copper[16] at one end: out of which the master, dressed in an apron for the purpose, and assisted by one or two women, ladled the gruel at meal-times. Of this festive composition each boy had one porringer,[17] and no more—except on occasions of great public rejoicing, when he had two ounces and a quarter of bread besides. The bowls never wanted washing. The boys polished them with their spoons till they shone again; and when they had performed this operation (which never took very long, the spoons being nearly as large as the bowls,) they would sit staring at the copper, with such eager eyes, as if they could have devoured the very bricks of which it was composed; employing themselves, meanwhile, in sucking their fingers most assiduously, with the view of catching up any stray splashes of gruel that might have been cast thereon. Boys have generally excellent appetites. Oliver Twist and his companions suffered the tortures of slow starvation for three months; at last they got so voracious and wild with hunger, that one boy: who was tall for his age, and hadn't been used to that sort of thing, (for his father had kept a small cook's shop): hinted darkly to his companions, that unless he had another basin of gruel *per diem*,[18] he was afraid he might some night happen to eat the boy who slept next him, who happened to be a weakly youth of tender age. He had a

---

12 The separation of married couples to prevent promiscuous relations between the sexes in the workhouses was another unpopular measure of the Poor Law Amendment Act.
13 This was the only legal court through which divorces could be obtained.
14 The new Poor Law absolved men of the care of their children in an effort to discourage women (who were presumably viewed as the prime movers in sexual misconduct) from promiscuity. As women with children to care for would be hard pushed to work, this aspect of the law seems unfair at best, misogynistic at worst.
15 The Bentley's edition reads three months.
16 The copper, shown in the left-hand side of the novel's accompanying illustration, was a large copper vessel in a brick or stone structure, which could be heated by a fire underneath.
17 A small bowl.
18 Latin for 'each day'.

wild, hungry, eye; and they implicitly believed him. A council was held; lots were cast who should walk up to the master after supper that evening, and ask for more; and it fell to Oliver Twist.

The evening arrived; the boys took their places. The master, in his cook's uniform, stationed himself at the copper; his pauper assistants ranged themselves behind him; the gruel was served out; and a long grace was said over the short commons. The gruel disappeared; the boys whispered each other, and winked at Oliver; while his next neighbours nudged him. Child as he was, he was desperate with hunger, and reckless with misery. He rose from the table; and advancing to the master, basin and spoon in hand, said: somewhat alarmed at his own temerity:

'Please, sir, I want some more.'

The master was a fat, healthy man; but he turned very pale. He gazed in stupefied astonishment on the small rebel for some seconds; and then clung for support to the copper. The assistants were paralysed with wonder; the boys with fear.

'What!' said the master at length, in a faint voice.

'Please, sir,' replied Oliver, 'I want some more.'

The master aimed a blow at Oliver's head with the ladle; pinioned him in his arms; and shrieked aloud for the beadle.

The board were sitting in solemn conclave, when Mr. Bumble rushed into the room in great excitement, and addressing the gentleman in the high chair, said,

'Mr. Limbkins, I beg your pardon, sir! Oliver Twist has asked for more!'

There was a general start. Horror was depicted on every countenance.

'For *more*!' said Mr. Limbkins. 'Compose yourself, Bumble, and answer me distinctly. Do I understand that he asked for more, after he had eaten the supper allotted by the dietary?'

'He did, sir,' replied Bumble.

'That boy will be hung,' said the gentleman in the white waistcoat. 'I know that boy will be hung.'

[. . .]

Oliver at Mr Sowerberry the Undertaker's; Noah Claypole

After Oliver dares to ask for more, he is packed off to work for the undertaker Mr Sowerberry. Oliver's spell at the undertaker's gives Dickens ample opportunity to indulge his liking for the Gothic mode (characterized by heightened emotions, the macabre, the marginal, and the uncanny). Where Gothic novels and melodramas were set in exotic dungeons and castles, however, Dickens frequently domesticates the Gothic, bringing it into surreal collision with domestic and realistic settings. From as early in his career as his first 'novel', *The Pickwick Papers*, he experimented with inserting Gothic scenarios into his texts via the imaginings of his characters, a technique that enables him to ground the far-fetched in the believable. The fears of death that inevitably shadow an orphan and social outcast like Oliver are here both grounded in the

Figure 6 **George Cruikshank, 'Oliver Asking for More', Dickens House Museum.**

real and attended by the unreal as Oliver imagines that the corpses might come alive and that the coffin boards look like 'high-shouldered ghosts with their hands in their breeches-pockets'. Dickens commonly used this technique of animating the inanimate world and vice versa.[1]

1   See Stefanie Meier, *Animation and Mechanization in the Novels of Charles Dickens* (Zurich: Francke Verlag Bern, 1982).

Noah Claypole is the charity boy working at Mr Sowerberry's who bullies Oliver. Though Dickens is renowned for the visual element in his characterization, Dickens's introduction of Noah, like that of Mr Bumble in Chapter 2, relies more on the character's words and actions than it does on visual detail. The most prominent feature of this description of Noah is his obsession with his social status, or perhaps the lack of it, his need to make himself feel important, where society has made him feel unimportant. Noah has been branded by his 'leathers' (see **p. 137** n. 7), the visible symbol of his poverty and dependence on charity; the reader sees the term rather than the physical reality of the leathers, a term that becomes his uniform even without the uniform itself. This lack of status obviously motivates Noah's bullying of Oliver, a 'nameless orphan' to whom Noah can feel superior. Dickens again uses free indirect discourse to great effect in this passage, imitating and thereby undermining Noah's voice and attitudes ('No chance-child was he, for he could trace his genealogy all the way back to his parents'). The heavily ironic last two sentences, where the narrator claims to uphold Noah's treatment of Oliver as an example of 'what a beautiful thing human nature sometimes is' revives the novel's interest in the question of whether human beings are 'naturally' good or, as Bentham maintained, selfish. Claypole's bullying can in fact be attributed as much to nurture as to nature, while Oliver's goodness seems to be the result of an improbable immunity to social conditioning.

CHAPTER V

OLIVER MINGLES WITH NEW ASSOCIATES. GOING TO A FUNERAL FOR THE FIRST TIME, HE FORMS AN UNFAVOURABLE NOTION OF HIS MASTER'S BUSINESS

OLIVER, being left to himself in the undertaker's shop, set the lamp down on a workman's bench, and gazed timidly about him with a feeling of awe and dread, which many people a good deal older than he will be at no loss to understand. An unfinished coffin on black tressels, which stood in the middle of the shop, looked so gloomy and deathlike that a cold tremble came over him, every time his eyes wandered in the direction of the dismal object: from which he almost expected to see some frightful form slowly rear its head, to drive him mad with terror. Against the wall, were ranged, in regular array, a long row of elm boards cut into the same shape: looking, in the dim light, like high-shouldered ghosts with their hands in their breeches-pockets. Coffin-plates,[2] elm-chips, bright-headed nails, and shreds of black cloth, lay scattered on the floor; and the wall behind the counter was ornamented with a lively representation of two mutes in very stiff neckcloths, on duty at a large private door:[3] with a hearse drawn by four black steeds, approaching in the distance. The shop was close and hot; and the atmosphere seemed

---

2   Metal name plates in coffin lids, usually bearing the dates of birth and death.
3   Attendants who (for middle- and upper-class funerals) were hired to stand each side of the door of the house where the corpse lay waiting for burial and who accompanied the coffin for burial. Funerals were extravagant affairs in the Victorian period.

tainted with the smell of coffins. The recess beneath the counter in which his flock mattress was thrust, looked like a grave.

[. . .]

Noah was a charity-boy,[4] but not a workhouse orphan. No chance-child was he, for he could trace his genealogy all the way back to his parents,[5] who lived hard by; his mother being a washerwoman, and his father a drunken soldier: discharged with a wooden leg, and a diurnal pension of twopence-halfpenny and an unstateable fraction.[6] The shop-boys in the neighbourhood had long been in the habit of branding Noah, in the public streets, with the ignominious epithets of 'leathers,'[7] 'charity,' and the like; and Noah had borne them without reply. But, now that fortune had cast in his way a nameless orphan, at whom even the meanest could point the finger of scorn, he retorted on him with interest. This affords charming food for contemplation. It shows us what a beautiful thing human nature sometimes is; and how impartially the same amiable qualities are developed in the finest lord and the dirtiest charity-boy.

[. . .]

Oliver's First Experience of the Artful Dodger, London and Fagin and his Gang

After a fight with Noah Claypole over the abuse Noah directs at Oliver's dead mother, Oliver flees Mr Sowerberry's for London. This chapter narrates Oliver's meeting with the young pickpocket, the Artful Dodger, who offers Oliver somewhere to stay and guides him through the streets of London to Fagin's den. Unbeknown to Oliver, Fagin 'the elderly gentleman' is a fence who trains children to steal for his profit. Typical Dickensian techniques of character-ization are demonstrated when Oliver first meets the Artful Dodger and Fagin: both first strike us as caricatures whose characters are immediately intelligible through symbolic visual detail. I do not use the word 'caricature' negatively, as Dickens, like the artist Hogarth, uses caricature to achieve effects as complex and profound as more analytical techniques such as those employed by a philo-sophical novelist like George Eliot. Debate has always surrounded Dickens's use of caricature, some commentators arguing that Dickens's externalized char-acters are superficial and 'flat' and others arguing that Dickens's characters evade the psychological realist tradition and in many ways transcend it (see pp. 44–8). To understand the way that Dickens's characterization works, it is essential to grasp that Dickens thinks through images and that his descriptions

---

4   A pupil at a school funded by charitable bequests of voluntary contributions, for the free or cheap education of the poor. Dickens viewed these schools critically.

5   The mention of Noah's genealogy parodies that of his biblical namesake whose ancestors went back to Adam.

6   Wounded veterans from the Napoleonic Wars were commonly seen in the naval town of Chatham. Amputations were more frequent then than now, employed to prevent gangrene. The Claypoles would have lived on his mother's meager salary and his father's pension.

7   Leather breeches, a distinctive part of the charity-school uniform which made pupils stand out.

are vehicles for ideas. The vividness of the descriptions of the Artful Dodger and Fagin is partly achieved because Oliver is an innocent child, seeing the world for the first time; but the secret to Dickens's characterization is that we always feel as if we are seeing people and the world they inhabit for the first time when we read a Dickens novel. The dirty, snub-nosed boy in adult clothes called the Artful Dodger is thus both surreal and somehow familiar: we know the type but had not truly seen the type before Dickens saw him for us. In fact, the Artful Dodger is in the tradition of the likeable rogues who inhabited the Newgate novels of the 1830s and 1840s (see **pp. 43–4**); he also has much in common with the kind of juvenile delinquents it was feared that books like *Oliver Twist* would corrupt during the Newgate debate (see **pp. 43–4** and John, **p. 90**). Despite Thackeray's criticisms that Dickens could not possibly know how low-life thieves looked and spoke (see **p. 57**), Dickens's background and his penchant for walking the streets of London suggest that Thackeray was very much mistaken. His use of street slang or 'flash' here is not original – it was evident in other fashionable crime fiction – but given Dickens's ear for dialect, we cannot assume that it was inaccurate.

There is a sense in which the Artful Dodger is sanitized, however. Though a cog in an abhorrent system of exploitation, viewed in isolation, he possesses what Chesterton may call an 'innocence'. The attractiveness of Dickens's deviants and villains has long been a matter for critical debate, of course, ever since Edmund Wilson and Humphry House argued that Dickens's childhood gave him an emotional and imaginative affinity with deviants and outcasts (see **pp. 64–7**). According to this line of argument, even (especially?) Fagin engages Dickens more than his good characters, his imaginative energy outweighing his moral repulsiveness (see Marcus, **pp. 71–2**). Dickens indeed repeatedly deployed the phrase 'the attraction of repulsion', which he believed to be 'a metaphysical truth'.[1] If one accepts the Wilson/House line on Dickens and deviance, then the moral thrust of the novel would be undermined by the sheer imaginative power of the villains and deviants. Before we accept this line unquestioningly, however, it is worth imagining what the novel would be like without the dull but worthy good characters and remembering the kind of outcome we desire for Oliver at the end. Despite his unbelievable goodness and miraculous ability to speak in received pronunciation, it is surely true that most of us, trained in myth and fairy tale, want the villains to be defeated and Oliver to live happily and comfortably ever after.

Though some critics have argued for sophisticated, self-reflexive readings of Fagin as 'a generalized Newgate novelist' (for example, Robert Tracy, see **p. 91**, n. 8), the most immediate literary associations of Fagin are stereotypical. With his matted red beard and his toasting fork, Fagin draws on recognizable stereotypes: the stage Jew dating back to medieval drama, Shakespeare's Shylock and the Devil. The fact that the characterization of Fagin draws on an anti-Semitic tradition has caused heated debate from Dickens's own day to the present

---

1   Letter to the *Daily News*, 28 February 1846, on capital punishment.

is well known and well documented throughout this volume. Alongside this question of anti-Semitism, however, there is also the aesthetic question of how Dickens manages to make such a stereotype – for Fagin is a stereotype – achieve almost mythic status. When so many other anti-Semitic stereotypes have disappeared, why is Fagin alive even in the twenty-first century cultural consciousness?

This passage also foregrounds Dickens's imaginative entwinement with the city, in particular with London (see **pp. 15–16**). It is well established that Dickens is one of the first and best writers to capture the realities of modern city living, and in his description of the fetid streets of London, Dickens demonstrates both his detailed knowledge of the city and the hold the city had on his imagination. It is a critical commonplace that Dickens and other writers of the city such as T. S. Eliot were appalled and depressed by modern urban living. But if this is true, it is also true that Dickens (like Eliot) was inspired by the city, and – we are back to the 'attraction of repulsion' again – by a landscape that left so many 'wallowing in filth'.

CHAPTER VIII
OLIVER WALKS TO LONDON. HE ENCOUNTERS ON THE ROAD, A STRANGE SORT OF YOUNG GENTLEMAN

[. . .]

The stone by which he was seated, bore, in large characters, an intimation that it was just seventy miles from that spot to London. The name awakened a new train of ideas in the boy's mind. London!—that great large place!—nobody—not even Mr. Bumble—could ever find him there! He had often heard the old men in the workhouse, too, say that no lad of spirit need want in London; and that there were ways of living in that vast city, which those who had been bred up in country parts had no idea of. It was the very place for a homeless boy, who must die in the streets, unless some one helped him. As these things passed through his thoughts, he jumped upon his feet, and again walked forward.

[. . .]

[. . .] Upon this, the boy crossed over; and, walking close up to Oliver, said, 'Hullo! my covey, what's the row?'[2]

The boy who addressed this inquiry to the young wayfarer, was about his own age: but one of the queerest-looking boys that Oliver had ever seen. He was a snub-nosed, flat-browed, common-faced boy enough; and as dirty a juvenile as one would wish to see; but he had about him all the airs and manners of a man. He was short of his age: with rather bow-legs: and little, sharp, ugly eyes. His hat was stuck on the top of his head so lightly, that it threatened to fall off every moment; and would have done so, very often, if the wearer had not had a knack of every now and then giving his head a sudden twitch: which brought it back to

---

2   Street slang for, 'Hello! My fellow, what's the matter?' Slang or flash 'terms' were not uncommon in texts about criminal, low and/or metropolitan life. Gay's *The Beggar's Opera*, which Dickens mentions in his 1841 Preface, employs slang.

its old place again. He wore a man's coat, which reached nearly to his heels. He had turned the cuffs back, halfway up his arm, to get his hands out of the sleeves: apparently with the ultimate view of thrusting them into the pockets of his corduroy trousers; for there he kept them. He was, altogether, as roystering and swaggering a young gentleman as ever stood four feet and six, or something less, in his bluchers.[3]

[. . .]

'My eyes, how green!' exclaimed the young gentleman. 'Why, a beak's a madgst'rate; and when you walk by a beak's order, it's not straight forerd, but always a going up, and nivir a-coming down agin. Was you never on the mill?'[4]

'What mill?' inquired Oliver.

'What mill!—why, *the* mill—the mill as takes up so little room that it'll work inside a Stone Jug; and always goes better when the wind's low with people, than when it's high: acos then they can't get workmen. But come,' said the young gentleman; 'you want grub, and you shall have it. I'm at low-water-mark myself— only one bob and a magpie; but, *as* far *as* it goes, I'll fork out and stump. Up with you on your pins. There! Now then! Morrice!'[5]

Assisting Oliver to rise, the young gentleman took him to an adjacent chandler's shop:[6] where he purchased a sufficiency of ready-dressed ham and a half-quartern loaf: or, as he himself expressed it, 'a fourpenny bran;' the ham being kept clean and preserved from dust, by the ingenious expedient of making a hole in the loaf by pulling out a portion of the crumb, and stuffing it therein. Taking the bread under his arm, the young gentleman turned into a small public-house: and led the way to a tap-room in the rear of the premises. Here, a pot of beer was brought in, by direction of the mysterious youth; and Oliver: falling to, at his new friend's bidding: made a long and hearty meal; during the progress of which, the strange boy eyed him from time to time with great attention.

'Going to London?' said the strange boy, when Oliver had at length concluded.

'Yes.'

'Got any lodgings?'

'No.'

[. . .]

This unexpected offer of shelter, was too tempting to be resisted: especially as it was immediately followed up, by the assurance that the old gentleman already referred to, would doubtless provide Oliver with a comfortable place, without loss of time. This led to a more friendly and confidential dialogue; from which Oliver discovered that his friend's name was Jack Dawkins: and that he was a peculiar pet and *protégé* of the elderly gentleman before mentioned.

Mr. Dawkins's appearance did not say a vast deal in favour of the comforts

---

3   Half-boots or high shoes, named after the Prussian commander Field-Marshal von Blucher (1742–1819), who wore them.

4   Green: innocent; beak's order: order from a magistrate to leave an area; the mill: the treadmill, a device used for hard labour in prisons until 1898.

5   Slang terms for 'a prison' or 'Newgate gaol'; 'when the money is short'; 'thieves'; 'one shilling and a halfpenny'; 'produce the money and pay'; 'legs'; and 'Make haste!'

6   Originally the makers and sellers of candles, by the early nineteenth century, chandlers sold basic foodstuffs as well.

which his patron's interest obtained for those whom he took under his protection; but as he had a rather flighty and dissolute mode of conversing: and furthermore avowed that among his intimate friends he was better known by the *sobriquet*[7] of 'The Artful Dodger:' Oliver concluded that, being of a dissipated and careless turn, the moral precepts of his benefactor had hitherto been thrown away upon him. Under this impression, he secretly resolved to cultivate the good opinion of the old gentleman as quickly as possible; and, if he found the Dodger incorrigible, as he more than half suspected he should, to decline the honour of his farther acquaintance.

As John Dawkins objected to their entering London before nightfall, it was nearly eleven o'clock when they reached the turnpike at Islington. They crossed from the Angel into St. John's-road; struck down the small street which terminates at Sadler's Wells Theatre; through Exmouth-street and Coppice-row; down the little court by the side of the workhouse; across the classic ground which once bore the name of Hockley-in-the-Hole; thence into Little Saffron-hill; and so into Saffron-hill the Great[8]: along which, the Dodger scudded at a rapid pace: directing Oliver to follow close at his heels.

Although Oliver had enough to occupy his attention in keeping sight of his leader, he could not help bestowing a few hasty glances on either side of the way, as he passed along. A dirtier or more wretched place he had never seen. The street was very narrow and muddy; and the air was impregnated with filthy odours. There were a good many small shops; but the only stock in trade appeared to be heaps of children, who, even at that time of night, were crawling in and out at the doors, or screaming from the inside. The sole places that seemed to prosper, amid the general blight of the place, were the public-houses; and in them, the lowest orders of Irish[9] were wrangling with might and main. Covered ways and yards, which here and there diverged from the main street, disclosed little knots of houses, where drunken men and women were positively wallowing in filth; and from several of the doorways, great ill-looking fellows were cautiously emerging: bound, to all appearance, on no very well-disposed or harmless errands.

[. . .]

The walls and ceiling of the room were perfectly black, with age and dirt. There was a deal table before the fire: upon which were a candle, stuck in a ginger-beer bottle: two or three pewter pots: a loaf and butter: and a plate. In a frying-pan, which was on fire, and which was secured to the mantelshelf by a string, some sausages were cooking; and standing over them, with a toasting-fork in his hand, was a very old shrivelled Jew, whose villainous-looking and repulsive face was obscured by a quantity of matted red hair. He was dressed in a greasy flannel gown, with his throat bare; and seemed to be dividing his attention between the frying-pan and a clothes-horse, over which a great number of silk handkerchiefs

---

7   Nickname.
8   Islington was the last village to the north of London before it merged with London in the 1830s. At the coaching-inn, the Angel, Oliver and the Dodger travel past Sadler's Wells theatre (built 1683) towards Clerkenwell Green, past Clerkenwell workhouse (built 1790) and then on to the slum area of Saffron Hill. Hockley-in-the-Hole was near the north-west of Clerkenwell Green, and was used in the seventeenth and early eighteenth centuries for bull-baiting, boxing and cock-fighting.
9   The reading in *Bentley's* up to and including 1841, is, 'Irish (who are generally the lowest orders of anything'.

were hanging.[10] Several rough beds made of old sacks, were huddled side by side on the floor; and seated round the table were four or five boys: none older than the Dodger: smoking long clay pipes, and drinking spirits, with the air of middle-aged men. These all crowded about their associate as he whispered a few words to the Jew; and then turned round and grinned at Oliver; as did the Jew himself, toasting-fork in hand.

[...]

Figure 7 **George Cruikshank, 'Oliver Introduced to the Respectable Old Gentleman', Dickens House Museum.**

---

10 Handkerchiefs were both practical and fashionable, and there was a flourishing trade in them in the nineteenth century. See Jordan, **pp. 79–84**, for a reading of their symbolic significance in the novel.

Oliver 'Between Sleeping and Waking'; Oliver is Given a Lesson in Pickpocketing

The 'drowsy state, between sleeping and waking' described in this section is one of two passages in *Oliver Twist* where Dickens explores a state of semi-consciousness (see also 'Oliver Half Asleep', **pp. 161–3**). These passages are unusual in Dickens's writings because he characteristically avoids the kind of overt analysis of psychological processes favoured by George Eliot, preferring to dramatize rather than analyse. The *Oliver Twist* speculations prove that Dickens had an interest in theories of the mind, however. In his *Companion to Oliver Twist*, David Paroissien links this passage, for example, with the psychological research and phrenological interests of Robert Macnish (1802–37), who believed that 'sleep exists in two states'.[1] Dickens owned some of Macnish's works and had a lifelong interest in dreams, sleep and hypnotism.[2] His own works have been likened to hallucinations by Hippolyte Taine.[3]

The main business of this chapter is the attempts of Fagin and his gang to train Oliver as a pickpocket. Before the light-hearted 'game' (or pickpocketing demonstration) which the 'merry old gentleman' stages with his pupils, we are reminded of the sinister nature of the man who corrupts young children when Fagin thinks that Oliver has seen him inspecting his jewels. When Fagin seizes the bread knife, Oliver's life is clearly in danger. Indeed, from Fagin's ironic mutterings about his support for capital punishment to his enquiries about the crowd at the public execution, the passage is laced with reminders that crime leads to punishment and that the merriness on show is in fact a front for violence. Contemporary criticisms of the novel as a 'Newgate novel' miss the self-reflexive critique in the novel of the glamorization of crime in life and in novels (see John, **pp. 89–91**). Thus, though the Artful Dodger and Charley Bates are endearing fictional characters, they are also indoctrinated with the romantic myth (upheld in some Newgate novels) that crime leads to heroic greatness. It is not difficult to see why some critics have seen Fagin as a representation of the kind of Newgate artist that Dickens was accused of being. For the significance of handkerchiefs in the novel, see Jordan, **pp. 79–84**.

CHAPTER IX

CONTAINING FURTHER PARTICULARS CONCERNING THE
PLEASANT OLD GENTLEMAN, AND HIS HOPEFUL PUPILS

[. . .]

Although Oliver had roused himself from sleep, he was not thoroughly awake. There is a drowsy state, between sleeping and waking, when you dream more in five minutes with your eyes half open, and yourself half conscious of everything

---

1   Paroissien, *Companion*, p. 101.
2   See Fred Kaplan, *Dickens and Mesmerism: The Hidden Springs of Fiction* (Princeton, NJ: Princeton University Press, 1975).
3   Hippolyte Taine, 'Charles Dickens, son talent et ses oeuvres', *Revue des deux mondes*, 1 (1 February 1856).

that is passing around you, than you would in five nights with your eyes fast closed, and your senses wrapt in perfect unconsciousness. At such times, a mortal knows just enough of what his mind is doing, to form some glimmering conception of its mighty powers: its bounding from earth and spurning time and space: when freed from the restraint of its corporeal associate.

[. . .]

'What a fine thing capital punishment is![4] Dead men never repent; dead men never bring awkward stories to light. Ah, it's a fine thing for the trade! Five of 'em strung up in a row; and none left to play booty,[5] or turn white-livered!'

As the Jew uttered these words, his bright dark eyes, which had been staring vacantly before him, fell on Oliver's face; the boy's eyes were fixed on his in mute curiosity; and, although the recognition was only for an instant – for the briefest space of time that can possibly be conceived – it was enough to shew the old man that he had been observed. He closed the lid of the box with a loud crash; and, laying his hand on a bread knife which was on the table, started furiously up. He trembled very much though; for, even in his terror, Oliver could see that the knife quivered in the air.

'What's that?' said the Jew. 'What do you watch me for? Why are you awake? What have you seen? Speak out, boy! Quick – quick! for your life!'

'I wasn't able to sleep any longer, sir,' replied Oliver, meekly. 'I am very sorry if I have disturbed you, sir.'

[. . .]

The Dodger said nothing, but he smoothed Oliver's hair over his eyes, and said he'd know better by and by; upon which the old gentleman, observing Oliver's colour mounting, changed the subject by asking whether there had been much of a crowd at the execution[6] that morning. This made him wonder more and more; for it was plain from the replies of the two boys that they had both been there; and Oliver naturally wondered how they could possibly have found time to be so very industrious.

When the breakfast was cleared away, the merry old gentleman and the two boys played at a very curious and uncommon game, which was performed in this way: The merry old gentleman: placing a snuff-box in one pocket of his trousers, a note-case[7] in the other, and a watch in his waistcoat-pocket: with a guard-chain[8] round his neck: and sticking a mock diamond pin in his shirt: buttoned his coat tight round him, and putting his spectacle-case and handkerchief in his pockets, trotted up and down the room with a stick, in imitation of the manner in which old gentlemen walk about the streets any hour in the day. Sometimes he stopped at the fire-place, and sometimes at the door; making belief that he was staring with all his might into shop-windows. At such times, he would look constantly

---

4 Before the early nineteenth century, capital punishment had been the main instrument of the criminal law, and although reformers had replaced hanging with prison for many offences by the 1830s, Fagin uses the idea of hanging to frighten and control others.
5 To betray or inform.
6 Public executions attracted large crowds who frequently regarded the spectacle as entertainment. Dickens deplored public executions. (See Philip Collins, *Dickens and Crime*, 2nd edn (London: Macmillan, 1965).)
7 Now called a wallet.
8 Gentlemen's watches were attached to their clothes by a chain and carried in the pocket.

round him, for fear of thieves; and would keep slapping all his pockets in turn, to see that he hadn't lost anything; in such a very funny and natural manner, that Oliver laughed till the tears ran down his face. All this time, the two boys followed him closely about: getting out of his sight, so nimbly, every time he turned round, that it was impossible to follow their motions At last, the Dodger trod upon his toes, or ran upon his boot accidentally, while Charley Bates stumbled up against him behind; and in that one moment they took from him, with the most extraordinary rapidity, snuff-box, note-case, watch, guard-chain, shirt-pin, pocket-handkerchief; even the spectacle-case. If the old gentleman felt a hand in any one of his pockets, he cried out where it was; and then the game began all over again.

[. . .]

'There, my dear,' said Fagin. 'That's a pleasant life, isn't it? They have gone out for the day.'

'Have they done work, sir?' inquired Oliver.

'Yes,' said the Jew; 'that is, unless they should unexpectedly come across any, when they are out; and they won't neglect it, if they do, my dear: depend upon it.

'Make 'em your models, my dear. Make 'em your models,' said the Jew, tapping the fire-shovel on the hearth to add force to his words; 'do everything they bid you, and take their advice in all matters: especially the Dodger's, my dear. He'll be a great man himself, and will make you one too, if you take pattern by him. [. . .]'

[. . .]

Bill Sikes

Everything about Bill Sikes's appearance announces his character. In the tradition of melodrama and caricature, Dickens uses external detail symbolically. Though Cruikshank claims to have invented Sikes,[1] the ruffian he epitomizes is a generic type seen on the contemporary stage and no doubt on the streets of London. Dickens hesitated over his age (he was originally forty-five) and the spelling of his name (sometimes Sykes), but there is nothing uncertain about Sikes. Like Fagin, however, he teaches us to understand the term 'stereotype' anew. At their best, Dickens's stereotypes have a luminosity, a hyper-reality rather than an unreality. This is partly to do with the detail with which Dickens depicts them – Sikes's 'large swelling calves', for example, 'which look in an unfinished and incomplete state without a set of fetters to garnish them' – and with the symbolism of that detail. Sikes's relationship with his canine clone, Bull's-eye, for example, is an obvious yet effective means of conveying his animalism, violence, thirst for power and, arguably, need for companionship.

1   Paroissien, *Companion to OT*, pp. 131–2.

CHAPTER XIII

SOME NEW ACQUAINTANCES ARE INTRODUCED TO THE
INTELLIGENT READER; CONNECTED WITH WHOM, VARIOUS PLEASANT
MATTERS ARE RELATED, APPERTAINING TO THIS HISTORY

[. . .]

The man who growled out these words, was a stoutly-built fellow of about five-and-thirty, in a black velveteen coat, very soiled drab breeches, lace-up half boots, and grey cotton stockings, which inclosed a very bulky pair of legs, with large swelling calves;—the kind of legs, that in such costume, always look in an unfinished and incomplete state without a set of fetters to garnish them. He had a brown hat on his head, and a dirty belcher handkerchief[2] round his neck: with the long frayed ends of which, he smeared the beer from his face as he spoke; disclosing, when he had done so, a broad heavy countenance with a beard of three days' growth: and two scowling eyes; one of which, displayed various parti-coloured symptoms of having been recently damaged by a blow.

'Come in, d'ye hear?' growled this engaging ruffian.

Figure 8 **Fagin (Ron Moody) and Sikes (Oliver Reed) from Carol Reed (dir.),** *Oliver!* **(Warwick-Romulus, 1968).**

2   See p. 81, n. 3.

A white shaggy dog,[3] with his face scratched and torn in twenty different places, skulked into the room.

'Why didn't you come in afore?' said the man. 'You're getting too proud to own me afore company, are you? Lie down!'

This command was accompanied with a kick, which sent the animal to the other end of the room. He appeared well used to it, however; for he coiled himself up in a corner very quietly, without uttering a sound; and winking his very ill-looking eyes twenty times in a minute, appeared to occupy himself in taking a survey of the apartment.

[. . .]

Oliver, Mr Brownlow and Books; Mr Grimwig

After Oliver is wrongly accused of stealing from Mr Brownlow, Brownlow takes pity on him and takes him into his home. Oliver's conversation with Mr Brownlow forms part of the self-reflexive layer of the novel through which Dickens discusses the social role of books, authorship, narratives and drama. At one level, books represent culture and respectability throughout the novel, but Dickens also implies that culture is the creature of an economically driven, materialist society and not something that can completely transcend it. Mr Brownlow has books because he can read them and he can afford them. Books represent economic and cultural capital. Oliver's preference to be a bookseller rather than an author is an in-joke through which Dickens no doubt released some of the resentment he felt about those who made money from his works (including Bentley; see **pp. 28–31**), but it also shows Oliver to be more aware of the power of money than his distaste for criminal profits may have implied.

Mr Grimwig is one of Dickens's 'grotesque' characters – that is, his characterization is deliberately and comically distorted. His 'manner of screwing his head on one side as he spoke' is both peculiar/eccentric and peculiar to him. His obsession with orange peel and his constant threats to 'eat his own head' foreshadow the comic genius of characters such as Mrs Nickleby, Mrs Gamp and Mr Dick in later Dickens novels, and the surreal strain in modern British comedy from Monty Python onwards. Dickens's characters frequently announce themselves with a catchphrase, a technique for which he was heavily criticized by, among others, G. H. Lewes, who argued that Dickens's characters were like 'frogs whose brains had been taken out for physiological purposes' (see **p. 44** and n. 2). Grimwig's ongoing debate with Brownlow about whether Oliver is good or bad contributes to the novel's ongoing debate about whether human beings are inherently good or bad, or indeed *inherently* anything.

---

3 Sikes's dog, Bull's-eye, is not shaggy in later appearances but, in Cruikshank's illustrations, more like a bulldog or bull-terrier.

CHAPTER XIV

COMPRISING FURTHER PARTICULARS OF OLIVER'S STAY AT MR. BROWNLOW'S. WITH THE REMARKABLE PREDICTION WHICH ONE MR. GRIMWIG UTTERED CONCERNING HIM, WHEN HE WENT OUT ON AN ERRAND

[. . .]

Thus encouraged, Oliver tapped at the study-door. On Mr. Brownlow calling to him to come in, he found himself in a little back room, quite full of books: with a window, looking into some pleasant little gardens. There was a table drawn up before the window, at which Mr. Brownlow was seated reading. When he saw Oliver, he pushed the book away from him, and told him to come near the table, and sit down. Oliver complied; marvelling where the people could be found to read such a great number of books as seemed to be written to make the world wiser. Which is still a marvel to more experienced people than Oliver Twist, every day of their lives.

'There are a good many books, are there not, my boy?' said Mr. Brownlow: observing the curiosity with which Oliver surveyed the shelves that reached from the floor to the ceiling.

'A great number, sir,' replied Oliver. 'I never saw so many.'

'You shall read them, if you behave well,' said the old gentleman kindly; 'and you will like that, better than looking at the outsides,—that is, in some cases; because there *are* books of which the backs and covers are by far the best parts.'

'I suppose they are those heavy ones, sir,' said Oliver, pointing to some large quartos, with a good deal of gilding about the binding.

'Not always those,' said the old gentleman, patting Oliver on the head, and smiling as he did so; 'there are other equally heavy ones, though of a much smaller size. How should you like to grow up a clever man, and write books, eh?'

'I think I would rather read them, sir,' replied Oliver.

'What! wouldn't you like to be a book-writer?' said the old gentleman.

Oliver considered a little while; and at last said, he should think it would be a much better thing to be a bookseller; upon which the old gentleman laughed heartily, and declared he had said a very good thing. Which Oliver felt glad to have done, though he by no means knew what it was.

'Well, well,' said the old gentleman, composing his features. 'Don't be afraid! We won't make an author of you, while there's an honest trade to be learnt, or brick-making[1] to turn to.'

[. . .]

At this moment, there walked into the room: supporting himself by a thick stick: a stout old gentleman, rather lame in one leg, who was dressed in a blue coat, striped waistcoat, nankeen breeches and gaiters, and a broad-brimmed white hat, with the sides turned up with green.[2] A very small-plaited shirt-frill, stuck out from his waistcoat; and a very long steel watch-chain, with nothing but a key at the end, dangled loosely below it. The ends of his white neckerchief were

---

1   Brick-making was seasonal labour, usually performed by Irish immigrants.
2   Nankeen is a buff-coloured cotton. Paroissien states that 'Grimwig's overall appearance suggests a country style appropriate to the early part of the nineteenth century' (*Companion to OT*, p. 140).

twisted into a ball about the size of an orange; the variety of shapes into which his countenance was twisted, defy description. He had a manner of screwing his head on one side when he spoke: and of looking out of the corners of his eyes at the same time: which irresistibly reminded the beholder of a parrot. In this attitude, he fixed himself, the moment he made his appearance; and, holding out a small piece of orange-peel at arm's length, exclaimed in a growling, discontented voice,

'Look here! do you see this? Isn't it a most wonderful and extraordinary thing that I can't call at a man's house but I find a piece of this poor-surgeon's-friend on the staircase? I've been lamed with orange-peel once, and I know orange-peel will be my death at last. It will, sir; orange-peel will be my death, or I'll be content to eat my own head, sir!'

This was the handsome offer with which Mr. Grimwig backed and confirmed nearly every assertion he made [. . .].

[. . .]

Now, the fact was, that, in the inmost recesses of his own heart, Mr. Grimwig was strongly disposed to admit that Oliver's appearance and manner were unusually prepossessing; but he had a strong appetite for contradiction: sharpened on this occasion by the finding of the orange-peel; and inwardly determining that no man should dictate to him whether a boy was well-looking or not, he had resolved, from the first, to oppose his friend. When Mr. Brownlow admitted that on no one point of inquiry could he yet return a satisfactory answer; and that he had postponed any investigation into Oliver's previous history until he thought the boy was strong enough to bear it; Mr. Grimwig chuckled maliciously. And he demanded, with a sneer, whether the housekeeper was in the habit of counting the plate at night; because, if she didn't find a table-spoon or two missing some sunshiny morning, why, he would be content to—and so forth.

Nancy Argues with Fagin

In this scene, Oliver is back in the thieves' den, having been recaptured by the prostitute Nancy (who pretended that Oliver was her prodigal brother) with the help of Bill Sikes. Oliver claims not to 'belong' to her, but the people who watch the scene believe Nancy, partly because Sikes supports her story and partly because the idea of a female child abductor would have run so contrary to Victorian ideas about women as naturally maternal and caring. In Chapter 16, however, Nancy appears to feel some regret for her actions, though she no doubt realizes that they were necessary: Oliver could have betrayed the whole gang to the law if he was not recaptured. In this scene, we begin to understand why Wilkie Collins regarded Nancy as the most accomplished of Dickens's female characters: she demonstrates the resignation and fatalism of a woman who has been abused and victimized her whole life at the same time that she shows glimmers of a better nature and the strength of character to rebel against her abusers. Dickens's representation of a prostitute as 'the soul of goodness in things evil', as he calls her in one of the 1867 running titles to the novel, was in obvious ways radical. But Dickens's affection for Nancy is also based on her maternal feelings for Oliver, which in part reposition her as a conventional 'womanly woman'. These maternal, protective feelings announce themselves dramatically in this chapter as Nancy sees the similarities between the attempted corruption of Oliver, in which she is largely implicated, and Fagin's corruption of her as a child. It is through her protectiveness towards Oliver that Dickens manages to make Nancy, to borrow one of Patricia Ingham's categories, a 'true Mother' (Ingham, *Dickens, Women, and Language*). As Ingham points out in **pp. 84–7**, Nancy is a 'fallen girl', a 'nubile girl' and a 'womanly woman'. Nancy is indeed one of the few morally mixed characters in a novel that takes its oppositional moral structure (by which characters are good or bad) from melodrama and allegory rather than from realist fiction. There is undoubtedly ambition and complexity in Dickens's conception of Nancy (see Bowen, **pp. 87–9**, and Michie, **p. 77**): in the violent passion she directs at Fagin, for example, Nancy is demonstrating the kind of intense passion which Dickens and mainstream Victorian values regarded as unacceptable and dangerous in women (though she faints and becomes 'feminine' again). Despite Fagin's use of other negative stereotypes about women to claim that Nancy is 'clever' and 'acting beautifully' in her displays of anger, she is clearly as sincere as she was insincere when she recaptures Oliver. Indeed, the leap between Nancy's clever acting when she reclaims Oliver and her remorse and passion here is a stark one that can be accounted for either as an example of artistic unevenness from a young, serial novelist, or as a deliberate 'abrupt change' in characterization, an anti-realist technique which Dickens's narrator explains and defends in Chapter 17 of the novel (see **pp. 151–3**).

CHAPTER XVI
RELATES WHAT BECAME OF OLIVER TWIST, AFTER HE HAD
BEEN CLAIMED BY NANCY

[. . .]

The girl stamped her foot violently on the floor as she vented this threat; and with her lips compressed, and her hands clenched, looked alternately at the Jew and the other robber: her face quite colourless from the passion of rage into which she had gradually worked herself.

'Why, Nancy!' said the Jew, in a soothing tone; after a pause, during which he and Mr. Sikes had stared at one another in a disconcerted manner; 'you—you're more clever than ever to-night. Ha! ha! my dear, you are acting beautifully.'

'Am I!' said the girl. 'Take care I don't overdo it. You will be the worse for it, Fagin, if I do; and so I tell you in good time to keep clear of me.'

There is something about a roused woman: especially if she add to all her other strong passions, the fierce impulses of recklessness and despair: which few men like to provoke. The Jew saw that it would be hopeless to affect any further mistake regarding the reality of Miss Nancy's rage; and, shrinking involuntarily back a few paces, cast a glance, half imploring and half cowardly, at Sikes: as if to hint that he was the fittest person to pursue the dialogue.

[. . .]

'God Almighty help me, I am!' cried the girl passionately; 'and I wish I had been struck dead in the street, or had changed places with them we passed so near to-night, before I had lent a hand in bringing him here. He's a thief, a liar, a devil: all that's bad, from this night forth. Isn't that enough for the old wretch without blows?'

'Come, come, Sikes,' said the Jew, appealing to him in a remonstratory tone, and motioning towards the boys, who were eagerly attentive to all that passed; 'we must have civil words; civil words, Bill.'

'Civil words!' cried the girl, whose passion was frightful to see. 'Civil words, you villain! Yes, you deserve 'em from me. I thieved for you when I was a child not half as old as this!' pointing to Oliver. 'I have been in the same trade, and in the same service, for twelve years since. Don't you know it? Speak out! don't you know it?'

'Well, well,' replied the Jew, with an attempt at pacification; 'and, if you have, it's your living!'

'Aye, it is!' returned the girl; not speaking, but pouring out the words in one continuous and vehement scream. 'It is my living; and the cold, wet, dirty streets are my home; and you're the wretch that drove me to them long ago; and that'll keep me there, day and night, day and night, till I die!'

'I shall do you a mischief!' interposed the Jew, goaded by these reproaches; 'a mischief worse than that, if you say much more!'

The girl said nothing more; but, tearing her hair and dress in a transport of frenzy, made such a rush at the Jew as would probably have left signal marks of her revenge upon him, had not her wrists been seized by Sikes at the right moment; upon which, she made a few ineffectual struggles: and fainted.

'She's all right now,' said Sikes, laying her down in a corner. 'She's uncommon strong in the arms, when she's up in this way.'

The Jew wiped his forehead: and smiled, as if it were a relief to have the disturbance over; but neither he, nor Sikes, nor the dog, nor the boys, seemed to consider it in any other light than a common occurrence incidental to business.

'It's the worst of having to do with women,' said the Jew, replacing his club; 'but they're clever, and we can't get on, in our line, without 'em. Charley, show Oliver to bed.

[. . .]'

The Narrator on the Novel: The 'streaky bacon' Passage

Chapter 17 of *Oliver Twist* begins with one of the few critical interjections in all of Dickens's works as the narrator goes to great lengths to define and to defend his novelistic practice. In the famous 'streaky bacon' passage, as it is known, Dickens cites 'good, murderous melodramas' as the model for his own 'craft'. (He specifically does not use the term 'narrative'.) Popular melodrama was characterized by starkly oppositional scenes and characters. Dickens's conception of novelistic progression is evidently quite different from that of a linear chain of events or, for that matter, the evolutionary *Bildungsroman* (novel of self-development) that is often assumed to be Oliver's story; neither does this passage suggest a sophisticated play with narratives. Oliver is an allegorical pawn in a novel whose anti-narrative principle is as strong as its narrative impulse. As this passage makes clear, 'alternation', 'changes', 'violent transitions' and 'sudden shiftings', all potentially disruptive of narrative flow coexist with that very desire to forge narratives (or, to echo Dickens's own terminology, histories). Crucial to Dickens's defence of his method here is an emphasis on 'abrupt impulses of passion and feeling', natural to those experiencing the emotion, anti-naturalistic to those observing. But what is interesting is the attempt to educate the reader into an understanding of the function of emotion in life, drama and, by implication, the novel, which has something in common with the playwright's Bertholt Brecht's (1898–1956) later engineering of alienation effects in his drama.[1]

To Dickens, emotion as an artistic and political tool can be used to disrupt narratives that reassure, to defamiliarize and to fragment stories. Alternatively or simultaneously, it can do just the opposite, satisfying primitive desires for emotional wholeness. All depends on our angle of vision, whether we are immersed in, or watching, the passions. Interestingly and characteristically, Dickens's example of those immersed in passionate experience is taken from the theatre: they are 'actors in the mimic life of the theatre', a slippage which complicates any temptation we may have to paraphrase this passage thus: 'narrative distances; drama immerses'. The passage seems to understand that in order for a text to affect the views of the reader, it must be experienced as all-encompassing emotion; if it is not experienced as such, it appears 'outrageous and preposterous'. Given Dickens's acknowledgement of the potentially alienating effects of extreme passion on audiences, however, perhaps his ideal reader like the ideal author, would maintain the ability to immerse him/herself in emotional experience and to detach him/herself from the experience simultaneously.

CHAPTER XVII
OLIVER'S DESTINY, CONTINUING UNPROPITIOUS, BRINGS A GREAT MAN TO LONDON TO INJURE HIS REPUTATION

IT is the custom on the stage: in all good, murderous melodramas: to present the tragic and the comic scenes, in as regular alternation, as the layers of red and white in a side of streaky, well-cured bacon. The hero sinks upon his straw bed, weighed down by fetters and misfortunes; and, in the next scene, his faithful but unconscious squire regales the audience with a comic song. We behold, with throbbing bosoms, the heroine in the grasp of a proud and ruthless baron: her

---

1   Alienation effects are anti-realist techniques designed to make the audience fully conscious that what they are watching is not real so that they maintain the ability to analyse the issues the play raises.

virtue and her life alike in danger; drawing forth her dagger to preserve the one at the cost of the other; and, just as our expectations are wrought up to the highest pitch, a whistle is heard: and we are straightway transported to the great hall of the castle: where a grey-headed seneschal[2] sings a funny chorus with a funnier body of vassals,[3] who are free of all sorts of places from church vaults to palaces, and roam about in company, carolling perpetually.

Such changes appear absurd; but they are not so unnatural as they would seem at first sight. The transitions in real life from well-spread boards to death-beds, and from mourning weeds to holiday garments, are not a whit less startling; only, there, we are busy actors, instead of passive lookers-on; which makes a vast difference. The actors in the mimic life of the theatre, are blind to violent transitions and abrupt impulses of passion or feeling, which, presented before the eyes of mere spectators, are at once condemned as outrageous and preposterous.

As sudden shiftings of the scene, and rapid changes of time and place, are not only sanctioned in books by long usage, but are by many considered as the great art of authorship: an author's skill in his craft being, by such critics, chiefly estimated with relation to the dilemmas in which he leaves his characters at the end of every chapter: this brief introduction to the present one may perhaps be deemed unnecessary. [. . .]

Oliver's Education in the Thieves' Den

In this passage, Fagin watches behind the scenes as the Artful Dodger, beer and tobacco in hand – believing himself to be the incarnation of 'romance and enthusiasm' – uses the capitalist vocabuary of self-help to persuade Oliver of the greatness of the life of the thief. The language used by the Artful Dodger and Charley Bates echoes that in the Utilitarian Poor Law Amendment Act (see **pp. 11–13**), which was meant to promote economic self-sufficiency. Throughout the passage, Dickens makes use of free indirect style to create irony. (Compare **pp. 143–5** and John, **pp. 89–91**.)

CHAPTER XVIII
HOW OLIVER PASSED HIS TIME, IN THE IMPROVING
SOCIETY OF HIS REPUTABLE FRIENDS

[. . .]

Whether it was the sense of freedom and independence which a rational animal may be supposed to feel when he sits on a table in an easy attitude, smoking a pipe, swinging one leg carelessly to and fro, and having his boots cleaned all the time, without even the past trouble of having taken them off, or the prospective misery of putting them on, to disturb his reflections; or whether it was the goodness of the tobacco that soothed the feelings of the Dodger, or the mildness of the

2 Steward.
3 Slave, humble dependant.

beer that mollified his thoughts, he was evidently tinctured, for the nonce,[1] with a spice of romance and enthusiasm, foreign to his general nature. He looked down on Oliver, with a thoughtful countenance, for a brief space; and then, raising his head, and heaving a gentle sigh, said, half in abstraction, and half to Master Bates:

'What a pity it is he isn't a prig!'[2]

'Ah!' said Master Charles Bates; 'he don't know what's good for him.'

The Dodger sighed again, and resumed his pipe: as did Charley Bates. They both smoked, for some seconds, in silence.

'I suppose you don't even know what a prig is?' said the Dodger mournfully.

'I think I know that,' replied Oliver, looking up. 'It's a th—; you're one, are you not?' inquired Oliver, checking himself.

'I am,' replied the Dodger. 'I'd scorn to be anythink else.' Mr. Dawkins gave his hat a ferocious cock, after delivering this sentiment; and looked at Master Bates, as if to denote that he would feel obliged by his saying anything to the contrary.

[. . .]

'No more it has,' said Charley. 'Why don't you put yourself under Fagin, Oliver?'

'And make your fortun' out of hand?' added the Dodger, with a grin.

'And so be able to retire on your property, and do the gen-teel: as I mean to, in the very next leap-year but four that ever comes, and the forty-second Tuesday in Trinity-week,'[3] said Charley Bates.

[. . .]

'Go!' exclaimed the Dodger. 'Why, where's your spirit? Don't you take any pride out of yourself? Would you go and be dependent on your friends?'

[. . .]

'Look here!' said the Dodger, drawing forth a handful of shillings and half-pence. 'Here's a jolly life! What's the odds where it comes from? Here, catch hold; there's plenty more where they were took from. You won't, won't you? Oh, you precious flat!'[4]

'It's naughty, ain't it, Oliver?' inquired Charley Bates. 'He'll come to be scragged, won't he?'[5]

'I don't know what that means,' replied Oliver.

'Something in this way, old feller,' said Charley. As he said it, Master Bates caught up an end of his neckerchief; and, holding it erect in the air, dropped his head on his shoulder, and jerked a curious sound through his teeth: thereby indicating, by a lively pantomimic representation, that scragging and hanging were one and the same thing.

[. . .]

'If you don't take pocket hankechers and watches,' said the Dodger, reducing his conversation to the level of Oliver's capacity, 'some other cove[6] will; so that

---

1   Coloured for the moment.
2   Slang for pickpocket.
3   Bates means that a fortune and retirement will never be achieved by working for Fagin. Bates's humorous scepticism about the life of crime (and Fagin's miserliness) is interesting in the light of his eventual reform.
4   Slang for simpleton or honest man.
5   Slang for hanged.
6   Slang for man, fellow.

the coves that lose 'em will be all the worse, and you'll be all the worse too, and nobody half a ha'p'orth the better, except the chaps wot gets them – and you've just as good a right to them as they have.'

'To be sure, to be sure!' said the Jew, who had entered, unseen by Oliver, 'It all lies in a nutshell, my dear; in a nutshell, take the Dodger's word for it. Ha! ha! He understands the catechism of his trade.'[7]

Oliver Reads a Book Resembling the
Newgate Calendar

Using Charley Bates and the Artful Dodger, Fagin is clearly orchestrating a campaign to indoctrinate Oliver with the idea that crime is glamorous, profitable and fun (see **pp. 143–5** and **pp. 153–5**). On the eve of a robbery in which Oliver is supposed to take part, Fagin's intended master stroke is to give him a book to read that bears no accidental resemblance to the *Newgate Calendar*, a popular volume of criminal biographies which is thought to have fed the market for 'Newgate' fiction. It is conspicuous, however, that the least visibly effective of all Fagin's attempts to corrupt using Newgate-style myths about crime is this very instance. When indoctrination is disguised as pleasure or entertainment, by contrast, and does not involve the cultural capital that the written word represents, Oliver is far more susceptible (see John, **pp. 89–91**).

CHAPTER XX
WHEREIN OLIVER IS DELIVERED OVER TO
MR. WILLIAM SIKES

[. . .]

[. . .] It was a history of the lives and trials of great criminals; and the pages were soiled and thumbed with use. Here, he read of dreadful crimes that made the blood run cold; of secret murders that had been committed by the lonely wayside: and bodies hidden from the eye of man in deep pits and wells: which would not keep them down, deep as they were, but had yielded them up at last, after many years, and so maddened the murderers with the sight, that in their horror they had confessed their guilt, and yelled for the gibbet[1] to end their agony. Here, too, he read of men who, lying in their beds at dead of night, had been tempted (as they said) and led on, by their own bad thoughts, to such dreadful bloodshed as it made the flesh creep, and the limbs quail, to think of. The terrible descriptions were so real and vivid, that the sallow pages seemed to turn red with gore; and the words upon them, to be sounded in his ears, as if they were whispered, in hollow murmurs, by the spirits of the dead.

7 He has a thorough understanding of his work. The catechism of the Church of England takes people through all the mysteries of faith by question and answer.

1 The gallows.

In a paroxysm of fear, the boy closed the book, and thrust it from him. Then, falling upon his knees, he prayed Heaven to spare him from such deeds; and rather to will that he should die at once, than be reserved for crimes, so fearful and appalling. [. . .]

Mr Bumble and Mrs Corney

After Oliver is shot in the attempted robbery, Dickens employs the 'streaky-bacon' technique of alternating scenes described in Chapter 17, by leaving readers in suspense about his fate while we are entertained by Mr Bumble's flirtation with Mrs Corney, who he will eventually marry. The scene is a brilliant set piece and shows Dickens as a skilled exponent of the comedy of manners. Both Bumble and Mrs Corney are playing roles and each cons the other into believing that they are wealthier and more respectable than they are. The narrator's feigned innocence parodies that of the two characters and adds to the sense of the ludicrous that attends the scene. The use of free, indirect style, the brilliance of the dialogue, and the comedy of manners set piece, are all reminiscent of Jane Austen (see **pp. 129–30**). Where Dickens differs from Austen is in the extravagance and excess of his characters and their behaviour which, stylistically if not conceptually, partakes more of pantomime than it does of realism. Bumble's 'extraordinary performance' at the end, where he takes a secret inventory of Mrs Corney's material possessions, is hilarious, coming as it does immediately after his performance as genteel suitor. Yet it also continues a more serious theme in the novel: that materialism pervades society[1] and that the legally sanctioned authority, which Bumble at this point represents, is as grasping and corrupt as the thieves that eventually look after Oliver. Indeed, it has often been remarked that Fagin's den provides an alternative (and in some ways better) environment for Oliver than the workhouse system with which Mr Bumble and Mrs Corney are bound up.

CHAPTER XXIII
WHICH CONTAINS THE SUBSTANCE OF A PLEASANT
CONVERSATION BETWEEN MR. BUMBLE AND A LADY; AND
SHEWS THAT EVEN A BEADLE MAY BE SUSCEPTIBLE ON
SOME POINTS

[. . .]

It was a round table; and as Mrs. Corney and Mr. Bumble had been sitting opposite each other: with no great space between them, and fronting the fire: it will be seen that Mr. Bumble, in receding from the fire, and still keeping at the table, increased the distance between himself and Mrs. Corney; which proceeding, some prudent readers will doubtless be disposed to admire, and to consider

---

1   See Stein, *Victoria's Year*, pp. 101–34.

an act of great heroism on Mr. Bumble's part: he being in some sort tempted by time, place, and opportunity, to give utterance to certain soft nothings, which, however well they may become the lips of the light and thoughtless, do seem immeasurably beneath the dignity of judges of the land, members of parliament, ministers of state, lord-mayors, and other great public functionaries, but more particularly beneath the stateliness and gravity of a beadle: who (as is well known) should be the sternest and most inflexible among them all.

Whatever were Mr. Bumble's intentions, however: and no doubt they were of the best: it unfortunately happened, as has been twice before remarked, that the table was a round one; consequently Mr. Bumble, moving his chair by little and little, soon began to diminish the distance between himself and the matron; and, continuing to travel round the outer edge of the circle, brought his chair, in time, close to that in which the matron was seated. Indeed, the two chairs touched; and when they did so, Mr. Bumble stopped.

Now, if the matron had moved her chair to the right, she would have been scorched by the fire; and if to the left, she must have fallen into Mr. Bumble's arms; so (being a discreet matron, and no doubt foreseeing these consequences at a glance) she remained where she was, and handed Mr. Bumble another cup of tea.

'Hard-hearted, Mrs. Corney?' said Mr. Bumble, stirring his tea, and looking up into the matron's face; 'are *you* hard-hearted, Mrs. Corney?'

'Dear me!' exclaimed the matron, 'what a very curious question from a single man. What can you want to know for, Mr. Bumble?'

The beadle drank his tea to the last drop; finished a piece of toast; whisked the crumbs off his knees; wiped his lips; and deliberately kissed the matron.

'Mr. Bumble!' cried that discreet lady in a whisper; for the fright was so great, that she had quite lost her voice, 'Mr. Bumble, I shall scream!' Mr. Bumble made no reply; but, in a slow and dignified manner, put his arm round the matron's waist.

As the lady had stated her intention of screaming, of course she would have screamed at this additional boldness, but that the exertion was rendered unnecessary by a hasty knocking at the door: which was no sooner heard, than Mr. Bumble darted [. . .].

[. . .]

Mr. Bumble's conduct on being left to himself, was rather inexplicable. He opened the closet, counted the tea-spoons, weighed the sugar-tongs, closely inspected a silver milk-pot to ascertain that it was of the genuine metal; and, having satisfied his curiosity on these points, put on his cocked hat corner-wise, and danced with much gravity four distinct times round the table. Having gone through this very extraordinary performance, he took off the cocked hat again; and, spreading himself before the fire with his back towards it, seemed to be mentally engaged in taking an exact inventory of the furniture.

Rose Maylie

After Oliver is wounded in the failed robbery attempt, he is cared for by the people whose house he was attemping to burgle, the orphan Rose Maylie and her aunt, Mrs Maylie. The Maylie sections of the novel, in which goodness and conventional middle-class values appear to go hand in hand, have long been criticized as 'dull' and unimaginative in comparison with the low-life scenes. Rose Maylie, like many other Dickens heroines, has not been seen as one of his successes. Many critics have observed the similarity between Dickens's representation of Rose Maylie and his descriptions of his sister-in-law, Mary Hogarth, whose death while he was writing *Oliver Twist* profoundly affected Dickens (see **pp. 11, 27–9**). Indeed, David Paroissien notes that the pairing of adjectives in the extract – 'Cast in so slight and exquisite a mould; so mild and gentle; so pure and beautiful [. . .] sweetness and good humour' – also appears in several of the letters Dickens wrote on Mary's death.[1] The idea that Rose's attributes 'were made for Home' also appears in the Letters about Mary.[2] The idea of the perfect woman as an 'angel' who combined moral and spiritual purity with domestic dedication is also a cultural stereotype, however, with which the Victorian period has become synonymous. These characters are often referred to as examples of 'the angel in the house', a label taken from the title of a popular poem by Coventry Patmore (1854–62). While there are far more exceptions to this ideal in Victorian literature than there are examples, there is no doubt that Dickens played a large part in consolidating the importance of this cultural stereotype even before Patmore published his work. There are many angelic child-women in Dickens's novels who are not past seventeen years of age, a fact which some commentators have attributed to Mary's influence on Dickens's imagination but which can more convincingly be ascribed to Dickens's idealization of a certain kind of femininity that Mary happened to appear to embody.

The case for the latter interpretation of Dickens's relationship with Mary and indeed with his fictional female characters can be made by paying close attention to the detail of Dickens's language. The language in which Rose is described is utterly abstract, stereotypical and lacking in detail. It is language that is repeated again to describe many of Dickens's 'good' women. If we compare the opening description of Rose with the opening description of Fagin, the Artful Dodger or Sikes, for example, the difference is stark. In the case of the latter, stereotypes are animated with use of idiosyncratic detail, whereas in the description of Rose, there is nothing to individualize her. As Rose is allegedly based on a real woman with whom Dickens was obsessed, this lack of specificity is somewhat strange. Patricia Ingham has rightly revised crude biographical notions of Dickens's relationship with Mary Hogarth and his attitudes to women more generally.[3]

---

1   Paroissien, *Companion to OT*, p. 197.
2   Ibid.
3   See also Claire Tomalin, *The Invisible Woman: The Story of Nelly Ternan and Charles Dickens* (Harmondsworth: Penguin, 1991).

CHAPTER XXIX

HAS AN INTRODUCTORY ACCOUNT OF THE INMATES OF
THE HOUSE, TO WHICH OLIVER RESORTED

[. . .]

The younger lady was in the lovely bloom and spring-time of womanhood; at that age, when, if ever angels be for God's good purposes enthroned in mortal forms, they may be, without impiety, supposed to abide in such as hers.

She was not past seventeen. Cast in so slight and exquisite a mould; so mild and gentle; so pure and beautiful; that earth seemed not her element,[4] nor its rough creatures her fit companions. The very intelligence that shone in her deep blue eye, and was stamped upon her noble head, seemed scarcely of her age or of the world; and yet the changing expression of sweetness and good humour; the thousand lights that played about the face, and left no shadow there; above all, the smile; the cheerful, happy smile; were made for Home; for fireside peace and happiness.

Blathers and Duff; Conkey Chickweed

This chapter introduces Blathers and Duff, the Bow Street runners, who attend the Maylie household in Chertsey to help the local law-enforcement officers investigate the attempted robbery. Though they only make a fleeting appearance in the novel, they are an intrinsic part of the text's interest in crime and punishment. Between the eighteenth and nineteenth centuries, the investigation and punishment of crime changed dramatically (see **pp. 15–17**). 'The Bow Street runners' was a colloquial term used from the eighteenth century onwards for a mobile patrol of plain-clothed officers who worked under the direction of the police court of London. The Metropolitan Police as such was not formed until 1829, but even before this, the Bow Street runners were very powerful, operating in parts of the Home Counties as well as in London. Dickens was a supporter of the Metropolitan Police but made several unfavourable comments on the Bow Street runners. His main point in introducing the incompetent Blathers and Duff was to argue that a competent, professionally trained police service was needed in areas other than London to ensure that victims of crime would not be exposed to both local and outside incompetence as happens in the novel. The word 'blathers' usually refers to someone who talks too much or talks about nothing, while the word 'Duff' comes from the word 'duffer' which means someone who is inept; David Paroissien points out that 'in nineteenth-century underworld usage a "duffer" was a metropolitan cheat who sold pretended stolen or smuggled goods to country people entering London'.[1]

---

4   c.f. *Twelfth Night*, 3.4.117, 'Go, hang yourselves all! You are idle shallow things; I am not of your element [. . .]'.

1   Paroissien, *Companion to OT*, p. 204.

The willingness of Blathers and Duff to tell the story of 'Conkey Chickweed' (a man who robbed himself) and to become distracted from the crime in hand reinforces the idea of their incompetence. Until relatively recently, the presence and length of their interpolated tale had been attributed to Dickens's need to fulfill his word-length requirement, as the tale seemed an irrelevant distraction from the main narrative. As an awareness of Dickens's self-conscious interest in narrative (or self-reflexivity) and in crime fiction has developed, however, several critics have tried to make sense of the interpolation in terms of Dickens's larger interests. For D. A. Miller in *The Novel and the Police*, the story 'nicely illustrates the unity of both sides of the law in the delinquent context [. . .]. Police and offenders are conjoined in a single system for the formation and re-formation of delinquents.'[2] For Stephen Connor, it is 'a meta-narrative about the imprudence of inventing false narratives',[3] while Robert Tracy regards the tale as 'a minature Newgate novel'.[4] As Blathers directly compares the story to a novel, the assumption that the interpolation is self-reflexive has some credence. Restrictions on length prevents the full reprinting of the story here, but an analysis of its function in the novel may prove a useful classroom exercise.

CHAPTER XXXI
INVOLVES A CRITICAL POSITION

[. . .]

The man who had knocked at the door, was a stout personage of middle height: aged about fifty: with shiny black hair, cropped pretty close; half-whiskers; a round face; and sharp eyes. The other was a red-headed, bony man, in top-boots: with a rather ill-favoured countenance: and a turned-up, sinister-looking, nose.

[. . .]

'Get out!' retorted Mr. Blathers; 'I know better. Do you mind that time when Conkey was robbed of his money, though? What a start that was! Better than any novel-book *I* ever see!'

'What was that?' inquired Rose: anxious to encourage any symptoms of good humour in the unwelcome visitors.

'It was a robbery, miss, that hardly anybody would have been down upon,' said Blathers. 'This here Conkey Chickweed –'

'Conkey means Nosey, ma'am,' interposed Duff.

'Of course the lady knows that, don't she?' demanded Mr. Blathers. 'Always interrupting, you are, partner! This here Conkey Chickweed, miss, kept a public-house over Battle-bridge[5] way; [. . .]'.

[. . .]

---

2 D. A. Miller, *The Novel and the Police* (Berkeley, Calif.: University of California Press, 1988), p. 5.
3 Stephen Connor, ' "They're All in One Story": Public and Private Narratives in *Oliver Twist*', *Dickensian*, 85 (1989), 3–16 (p. 12).
4 Robert Tracy, ' "The Old Story" and Inside Stories: Modish Fiction and Fictional Modes in *Oliver Twist*', *Dicken Studies Annual*, 17 (1988), 1–33 (p. 21.) See 'Further Reading'.
5 An area in London now known as King's Cross.

A Rural Idyll; Oliver Half Asleep

Chapter 34 charts Oliver's continued recovery in the countryside and its brief interruption when he becomes dimly conscious of Monks and Fagin, who want to recapture him, watching him sleeping at a window. His representation of place draws on well-known oppositions, in particular, of the country and the city (see Lucas, **pp. 72–3**). The very purity of the country scenes has struck readers as lacking in imaginative vitality, however, especially in relation to Dickens's descriptions of London, which enable us to almost see, touch and smell the place. Like Dickens's description of Rose, his rendering of the country she inhabits is lacking in detail and reliant on abstract stereotypes – the leaves are 'green' and the flowers are 'wild'. In this extract, however, Dickens does at least comment on the idea that beauty is in the eye of the beholder, a hackneyed enough sentiment, but one that reinforces the self-conscious fictionality which so often attends Dickens's representations of goodness. Paroissien comments interestingly that for part of the passage – 'Men who look on nature [. . .] clearer vision' – Dickens seems to refute a comment from Thomas Malthus that 'dark hints [. . .] are really in the picture, and not from a jaundiced eye or an inherent spleen of disposition'.[1] The extract also seems influenced by Romantic representations of nature, in which nature is seen as a spiritualizing force and on prominent philosophical debates in the eighteenth century and Romantic period about whether the world shaped the mind (Empiricism) or the mind shaped the world (Idealism).

The kind of passage in which Oliver is described in a kind of waking sleep is highly unusual in Dickens novels; like the related passage in Chapter 9, (**pp. 143–5**) it is one of the few times that Dickens's narrator openly analyses the processes of the mind in the whole Dickens canon. (See his evasive letter to Lewes, **pp. 29–30**). Paroissien has related the passage to the Victorian authority on dreams, Robert Macnish, who argued that favourable conditions such as warm weather could induce the kind of state described by Dickens (see **pp. 143–5**).[2] In his book *Dickens and Mesmerism*, Fred Kaplan outlines Dickens's interest in the demonstrations of mesmerism (or hypnotism) of John Elliotson, a physician and academic. In mesmeric trance, Kaplan explains, 'the order of human experience is distinctly different from that of ordinary consciousness',[3] but there are various different kinds of trance; the trance described in this chapter is different, for example, from that described in Chapter 9. Like Oliver, the mesmerized subject in Elliotson's experiments could see with his/her eyes shut.[4] Though Dickens characteristically chose to dramatize rather than analyse psychological states in his fiction, these early *Twist* passages are evidence that he was not disinterested in the mind but chose to reflect on its processes by implication. (See John, *Dicken's Villains*, for suggestions about Dickens's reasons for so doing.)

1   Paroissien, *Companion*, p. 216.
2   *ibid.*, p. 217.
3   Kaplan, *Dickens and Mesmerism*, p. 151.
4   *ibid.*, p. 152.

CHAPTER XXXIV
CONTAINS SOME INTRODUCTORY PARTICULARS
RELATIVE TO A YOUNG GENTLEMAN WHO NOW ARRIVES
UPON THE SCENE; AND A NEW ADVENTURE WHICH
HAPPENED TO OLIVER

[. . .]

Oliver rose next morning, in better heart; and went about his usual early occupations, with more hope and pleasure than he had known for many days. The birds were once more hung out, to sing, in their old places; and the sweetest wild flowers that could be found, were once more gathered to gladden Rose with their beauty and fragrance. The melancholy which had seemed to the sad eyes of the anxious boy to hang, for days past, over every object: beautiful as all were: was dispelled by magic. The dew seemed to sparkle more brightly on the green leaves; the air to rustle among them with a sweeter music; and the sky itself to look more blue and bright. Such is the influence which the condition of our own thoughts, exercises, even over the appearance of external objects. Men who look on nature, and their fellow-men, and cry that all is dark and gloomy, are in the right; but the sombre colours are reflections from their own jaundiced eyes and hearts. The real hues are delicate, and need a clearer vision.

[. . .]

The little room in which he was accustomed to sit, when busy at his books, was on the ground-floor, at the back of the house. It was quite a cottage-room, with a lattice-window: around which were clusters of jessamine and honeysuckle, that crept over the casement, and filled the place with their delicious perfume. It looked into a garden, whence a wicket-gate opened into a small paddock; all beyond, was fine meadow-land and wood. There was no other dwelling near, in that direction; and the prospect it commanded was very extensive.

One beautiful evening, when the first shades of twilight were beginning to settle upon the earth, Oliver sat at this window, intent upon his books. He had been poring over them for some time; and as the day had been uncommonly sultry, and he had exerted himself a great deal; it is no disparagement to the authors: whoever they may have been: to say, that gradually and by slow degrees, he fell asleep.

There is a kind of sleep that steals upon us sometimes, which, while it holds the body prisoner, does not free the mind from a sense of things about it, and enable it to ramble at its pleasure. So far as an overpowering heaviness, a prostration of strength, and an utter inability to control our thoughts or power of motion, can be called sleep, this is it; and yet we have a consciousness of all that is going on about us; and if we dream at such a time, words which are really spoken, or sounds which really exist at the moment, accommodate them-selves with surprising readiness to our visions, until reality and imagination become so strangely blended that it is afterwards almost a matter of impossibil-ity to separate the two. Nor is this, the most striking phenomenon incidental to such a state. It is an undoubted fact, that although our senses of touch and sight be for the time dead, yet our sleeping thoughts, and the visionary scenes that pass before us, will be influenced, and materially influenced, by the *mere silent presence* of some external object: which may not have been near us when we closed our eyes: and of whose vicinity we have had no waking consciousness.

[. . .]

Nancy's Interview with Rose

After drugging Sikes with laudanum, Nancy seeks out Rose to tell her of the danger Oliver is in. Despite her obvious guilt and shame about the principal part she played in the recapture of Oliver and about the life of crime she has led, Nancy will not agree to leave her life or betray her associates. The sense of conscience which has led her to risk her life by working secretly on Oliver's behalf is the same as that which will not allow her to betray the man she loves. In the extract, Dickens emphasizes both her 'better feelings' and the feelings which are the inevitable result of abuse. Though Dickens has often been criticized for his patriarchal views on women (and in his emphasis on Nancy's 'feeble gleam of [. . .] one womanly feeling' these can indeed be seen here), this passage also shows a startling insight into the feelings of low self-esteem, fatalism and misguided loyalty which are so often experienced by those in violent and abusive relationships. Dickens's active involvement with Urania Cottage, a home for fallen women, gives some evidence that his insight into deviant women was more sophisticated than is often thought (see also **pp. 31–3**). Indeed, his fictional deviant women are often more interesting than their angelic counterparts. Paroissien has noted, for example, that when Nancy calls Rose, 'young, and good, and beautiful', her language (unimaginatively) echoes Dickens's earlier description of Rose (Chapter 35), as well as the words he used for the inscription on Mary Hogarth's headstone.[1] Nancy's ultimate fate suggests that Rose's religiously inflected pleas to Nancy to start a new life are more unrealistic than Nancy's feelings of entrapment. However, Dickens's early mention of 'woman's original nature left in her still', demonstrates his idealized views of women and renders the novel's representation of the relationship between nature and nurture even more confused. (See also Michie, Ingham and Bowen on Nancy, **p. 77, pp. 84–7** and **pp. 87–9**.)

CHAPTER XL

A STRANGE INTERVIEW, WHICH IS A SEQUEL TO
THE LAST CHAPTER

THE girl's life had been squandered in the streets, and among the most noisome of the stews[2] and dens of London, but there was something of the woman's original nature left in her still; and when she heard a light step approaching the door opposite to that by which she had entered, and thought of the wide contrast which the small room would in another moment contain, she felt burdened with

---

1 Paroissien, *Companion to OT*, p. 240.
2 Brothels.

the sense of her own deep shame: and shrunk as though she could scarcely bear the presence of her with whom she had sought this interview.

But struggling with these better feelings was pride,—the vice of the lowest and most debased creatures no less than of the high and self-assured. The miserable companion of thieves and ruffians, the fallen outcast of low haunts, the associate of the scourings of the jails and hulks,[3] living within the shadow of the gallows itself,—even this degraded being felt too proud to betray a feeble gleam of the womanly feeling which she thought a weakness, but which alone connected her with that humanity, of which her wasting life had obliterated so many, many traces when a very child.

She raised her eyes sufficiently to observe that the figure which presented itself was that of a slight and beautiful girl; and then, bending them on the ground, she tossed her head with affected carelessness [. . .].

[. . .]

'Is it possible,' cried Rose, 'that for such a man as this, you can resign every future hope, and the certainty of immediate rescue? It is madness.'

'I don't know what it is,' answered the girl; 'I only know that it is so, and not with me alone, but with hundreds of others as bad and wretched as myself. I must go back. Whether it is God's wrath for the wrong I have done, I do not know; but I am drawn back to him through every suffering and ill-usage: and should be, I believe, if I knew that I was to die by his hand at last.'

'What am I to do?' said Rose. 'I should not let you depart from me thus.'

[. . .]

'When ladies as young, and good, and beautiful as you are,' replied the girl steadily, 'give away your hearts, love will carry you all lengths—even such as you, who have home, friends, other admirers, everything to fill them. When such as I, who have no certain roof but the coffin-lid, and no friend in sickness or death but the hospital nurse, set our rotten hearts on any man, and let him fill the place that has been a blank through all our wretched lives, who can hope to cure us? Pity us, lady—pity us for having only one feeling of the woman left, and for having that turned, by a heavy judgment, from a comfort and a pride, into a new means of violence and suffering.'

[. . .]

Fagin Consoles Charley Bates over the Capture of the Artful Dodger; The Trial of the Artful Dodger

Perhaps the most striking illustration of Fagin's manipulation of the myth of romantic criminality comes when the Artful Dodger is captured by the police for stealing a snuff-box. Charley Bates is so distraught that his friend has been

---

3   Old sailing ships converted into prisons.

caught for stealing a snuff-box and not for something glamorous like robbing an old gentleman of his 'walables' that he comes very close to realizing that fame is rarely the lot of juvenile delinquents. The passage brilliantly dramatizes Fagin's ability to infect Charley Bates's understanding through his imagination, using the current obsession with *The Newgate Calendar* and its criminals, as well as with the popular contemporary newspaper accounts of the trials of villains, to convince Charley that the Artful Dodger's career will be notorious (see John, **pp. 89–91**). Tellingly, however, before Fagin learns of the Dodger's fate, he has been putting quite a different spin on things, threatening Noah Claypole with the gallows and the halter and reminding him of the utilitarian philosophy that pervades the thieves' den, that 'a regard for number one holds us all together'.

The intriguing aspect of the Artful Dodger's trial – deliberately positioned in the same chapter – is that he does indeed behave like a comic actor. The deliberately warped image of Jack Dawkins's end, presented to Charley Bates by Fagin, appears to be mirrored by the trial itself. There are several points to be made and questions to be asked about the trial scene. First, it is important to remember that the episode is seen through the eyes of Noah Claypole (alias Morris Bolter) and Dickens's narrator simultaneously. This means that there are two narrative voices in play, that of Claypole already indoctrinated to believe in the myth of the romance of crime, and that of the narrator, using terms like 'glorious reputation' ironically. Claypole sees the Dodger as Fagin would like him to be seen, as a heroic actor-villain, whereas it is possible to see him as a young boy who has just lost his freedom. There is a problem here, however, because there is no disputing the fact that Fagin's projected vision of the Dodger as a hero is the stronger in this scene. Though the Dodger's surface charms in the novel are organically involved with, and hence metamorphosed by, the overall moral scheme of the novel, it is not difficult to see why the apparently carnivaleque mood of this scene has given some adapters a festive idea of the Dodger. In fact, however, the way in which the Dodger confirms Fagin's vision of his trial is disturbing, revealing as it does the way in which the boy is Fagin's creature, a controlled role-player who revels in his own power and in the myth of criminality which he thinks will give him that power. It is in keeping with the more open, spontaneous character of Charley Bates that he is the one who eventually reforms. See also Kettle, *An Introduction to the English Novel*,[1] and Lucas, *The Melancholy Man*,[2] for discussions of the trial scene.

1   Arnold Kettle, *An Introduction to the English Novel (1951)*, 2 vols, 2nd edn (London: Hutchinson, 1967; repr. 1981), Vol. I, p. 121.
2   John Lucas, *The Melancholy Man: A Study of Dicken's Novels* (London: Methuen, 1970).

CHAPTER XLIII
WHEREIN IS SHOWN HOW THE ARTFUL DODGER
GOT INTO TROUBLE

[. . .]

'Only think,' said the Jew, shrugging his shoulders, and stretching out his hands; 'only consider. You've done what's a very pretty thing, and what I love you for doing; but what at the same time would put the cravat round your throat, that's so very easily tied and so very difficult to unloose – in plain English, the halter!'

[. . .]

'The gallows,' continued Fagin, 'the gallows, my dear, is an ugly finger-post,[3] which points out a very short and sharp turning that has stopped many a bold fellow's career on the broad highway. To keep in the easy road, and keep it at a distance, is object number one with you.'

[. . .]

'[. . .] The more you value your number one, the more careful you must be of mine; so we come at last to what I told you at first—that a regard for number one holds us all together, and must do so, unless we would all go to pieces in company.'

[. . .]

'It's all up, Fagin,' said Charley, when he and his new companion had been made known to each other.

'What do you mean?' asked the Jew with trembling lips.

'They've found the gentleman as owns the box; two or three more's a-coming to 'dentify him; and the Artful's booked for a passage out,'[4] replied Master Bates. 'I must have a full suit of mourning, Fagin, and a hatband,[5] to wisit him in, afore he sets out upon his travels. To think of Jack Dawkins—lummy[6] Jack—the Dodger—the Artful Dodger—going abroad for a common twopenny-halfpenny sneeze-box![7] I never thought he'd a done it under a gold watch, chain, and seals, at the lowest. Oh, why didn't he rob some rich old gentleman of all his walables, and go out *as* a gentleman, and not like a common prig,[8] without no honour nor glory!'

With this expression of feeling for his unfortunate friend, Master Bates sat himself on the nearest chair with an aspect of chagrin and despondency.

'What do you talk about his having neither honour nor glory for!' exclaimed Fagin, darting an angry look at his pupil. 'Wasn't he always top-sawyer[9] among you all! Is there one of you that could touch him or come near him on any scent! Eh?'

---

3 Finger-shaped signpost.
4 Due to be transported. See n. 7 below.
5 Hat-bands were made from silk or black crape, long pieces of which were wrapped around the hat and left to hang down the back. Pallbearers and others involved in the funeral procession wore such bands.
6 First-rate.
7 Transportation of juveniles was common at the time even for minor misdemeanours. A sneeze-box was a snuff box.
8 Thief or pickpocket.
9 The best or top dog.

'Not one,' replied Master Bates, in a voice rendered husky by regret; 'not one.'

'Then what do you talk of?' replied the Jew angrily; 'what are you blubbering for?'

' 'Cause it isn't on the rec-ord, is it?' said Charley, chafed into perfect defiance of his venerable friend by the current of his regrets; ' 'cause it can't come out in the 'dictment; 'cause nobody will never know half of what he was. How will he stand in the Newgate Calendar? P'raps not be there at all. Oh, my eye, my eye, wot a blow it is!'

'Ha! ha!' cried the Jew extending his right hand, and turning to Mr. Bolter in a fit of chuckling which shook him as though he had the palsy; 'see what a pride they take in their profession, my dear. Ain't it beautiful?'

Mr. Bolter nodded assent; and the Jew, after contemplating the grief of Charley Bates for some seconds with evident satisfaction, stepped up to that young gentleman and patted him on the shoulder.

'Never mind, Charley,' said Fagin soothingly; 'it'll come out, it'll be sure to come out. They'll all know what a clever fellow he was; he'll shew it himself, and not disgrace his old pals and teachers. Think how young he is too! What a distinction, Charley, to be lagged[10] at his time of life!'

'Well, it is a honour that is!' said Charley, a little consoled.

'He shall have all he wants,' continued the Jew. 'He shall be kept in the Stone Jug,[11] Charley, like a gentleman. Like a gentleman! With his beer every day, and money in his pocket to pitch and toss with, if he can't spend it.'

'No, shall he though?' cried Charley Bates.

'Aye, that he shall,' replied the Jew, 'and we'll have a big-wig,[12] Charley: one that's got the greatest gift of the gab: to carry on his defence; and he shall make a speech for himself too, if he likes; and we'll read it all in the papers—"Artful Dodger—shrieks of laughter—here the court was convulsed"—eh, Charley, eh?'

'Ha! ha!' laughed Master Bates, 'what a lark that would be, wouldn't it, Fagin? I say, how the Artful would bother 'em, wouldn't he?'

'Would!' cried the Jew. 'He shall—he will!'

'Ah, to be sure, so he will,' repeated Charley, rubbing his hands.

'I think I see him now,' cried the Jew, bending his eyes upon his pupil.

'So do I,' cried Charley Bates. 'Ha! ha! ha! so do I. I see it all afore me, upon my soul I do, Fagin. What a game! What a regular game! All the big-wigs trying to look solemn, and Jack Dawkins addressing of 'em as intimate and comfortable as if he was the judge's own son making a speech arter dinner—ha! ha! ha!'

In fact, the Jew had so well humoured his young friend's eccentric disposition, that Master Bates, who had at first been disposed to consider the imprisoned Dodger rather in the light of a victim, now looked upon him as the chief actor in a scene of most uncommon and exquisite humour, and felt quite impatient for the arrival of the time when his old companion should have so favourable an opportunity of displaying his abilities.

[. . .]

---

10 To be transported or sent abroad for penal servitude.
11 The Stone Jug is Newgate prison. Fagin is alluding to the fact that lax internal procedures made it possible to smuggle in comforts to prisoners.
12 Underworld slang for magistrate or lawyer.

It was indeed Mr. Dawkins, who, shuffling into the office with the big coat sleeves tucked up as usual, his left hand in his pocket, and his hat in his right hand, preceded the jailer, with a rolling gait altogether indescribable, and, taking his place in the dock, requested in an audible voice to know what he was placed in that 'ere disgraceful sitivation for.

'Hold your tongue, will you?' said the jailer.

'I'm an Englishman, ain't I?' rejoined the Dodger. 'Where are my priwileges?'

'You'll get your privileges soon enough,' retorted the jailer, 'and pepper with 'em.'

'We'll see wot the Secretary of State for the Home Affairs has got to say to the beaks,[13] if I don't,' replied Mr. Dawkins. 'Now then! Wot is this here business? I shall thank the madg'strates to dispose of this here little affair, and not to keep me while they read the paper, for I've got an appointment with a genelman in the city, and as I'm a man of my word and wery punctual in business matters, he'll go away if I ain't there to my time, and then pr'aps there won't be an action for damage against them as kep me away. Oh no, certainly not!'

At this point, the Dodger, with a show of being very particular with a view to proceedings to be had thereafter, desired the jailer to communicate 'the names of them two files[14] as was on the bench,' which so tickled the spectators, that they laughed almost as heartily as Master Bates could have done if he had heard the request.

'Silence there!' cried the jailer.

'What is this?' inquired one of the magistrates.

'A pick-pocketing case, your worship.'

[. . .]

'No,' replied the Dodger, 'not here, for this ain't the shop for justice; besides which, my attorney is a-breakfasting this morning with the Wice President of the House of Commons;[15] but I shall have something to say elsewhere, and so will he, and so will a wery numerous and 'spectable circle of acquaintance as'll make them beaks wish they'd never been born, or that they'd got their footmen to hang 'em up to their own hat-pegs, afore they let 'em come out this morning to try it on upon me. I'll—'

[. . .]

Sikes's Murder of Nancy

After Fagin hears of Nancy's meeting with Brownlow and Rose, he skilfully manipulates Sikes into believing that Nancy has betrayed him while advising that Sikes is 'not too violent for safety'. The brutal Sikes is unlikely to be restrained and bludgeons Nancy to death, despite her pleas for mercy. The scene is highly melodramatic and the symbolism of its ending is in the style of the Victorian

13 Underworld slang for magistrate.
14 Slang term for man or fellow (old file: an experienced criminal).
15 This office has never existed.

theatre's *tableaux vivants* (see **p. 100**). These tableaux were often employed at the end of a scene in the same way that Dickens employs the technique at the end of a chapter (a particularly effective device for the serial novelist, who needs to keep readers interested). As indicated in the 'Work in Performance' section, the 'Sikes and Nancy' reading (**pp. 96–8, 105–6**) was Dickens's favourite reading from his own novels. The passage combines the melodramatic with the understated: there is, for example, no description of the final clubbing. The melodramatic dialogue which precedes this does work in the context of the novel: the reader has become absorbed in the intensity of the situation and the characters' emotions and, at this point, excess is the natural medium. The scene has always proved difficult for adapters, however; particularly in the Victorian period and in the context of the 'Newgate' debate, it was difficult to reconcile it with conventional standards of taste and decency. Even a century later, David Lean's classic film adaptation does not dramatize the scene directly, a decision which can be justified on both aesthetic and moral grounds.

CHAPTER XLVII
FATAL CONSEQUENCES

[. . .]

'Get up!' said the man.

'It *is* you, Bill!' said the girl, with an expression of pleasure at his return.

'It is,' was the reply. 'Get up.'

There was a candle burning, but the man hastily drew it from the candlestick, and hurled it under the grate. Seeing the faint light of early day, without, the girl rose to undraw the curtain.

'Let it be,' said Sikes, thrusting his hand before her. 'There's light enough for wot I've got to do.'

'Bill,' said the girl, in the low voice of alarm, 'why do you look like that at me!'

The robber sat regarding her, for a few seconds, with dilated nostrils and heaving breast; and then, grasping her by the head and throat, dragged her into the middle of the room, and looking once towards the door, placed his heavy hand upon her mouth.

'Bill, Bill!' gasped the girl, wrestling with the strength of mortal fear,—'I—I—won't scream or cry—not once—hear me—speak to me—tell me what I have done!'

'You know, you she devil!' returned the robber, suppressing his breath. 'You were watched to-night; every word you said was heard.'

'Then spare my life for the love of Heaven, as I spared yours,' rejoined the girl, clinging to him. 'Bill, dear Bill, you cannot have the heart to kill me. Oh! think of all I have given up, only this one night, for you. You *shall* have time to think, and save yourself this crime; I will not loose my hold, you cannot throw me off. Bill, Bill, for dear God's sake, for your own, for mine, stop before you spill my blood! I have been true to you, upon my guilty soul I have!'

The man struggled, violently, to release his arms; but those of the girl were clasped round his, and tear her as he would, he could not tear them away.

'Bill,' cried the girl, striving to lay her head upon his breast, 'the gentleman, and that dear lady, told me to-night of a home in some foreign country where I could end my days in solitude and peace. Let me see them again, and beg them, on my knees, to shew the same mercy and goodness to you; and let us both leave this dreadful place, and far apart lead better lives, and forget how we have lived, except in prayers, and never see each other more. It is never too late to repent. They told me so—I feel it now—but we must have time—a little, little time!'

The housebreaker freed one arm, and grasped his pistol. The certainty of immediate detection if he fired, flashed across his mind even in the midst of his fury; and he beat it twice with all the force he could summon, upon the upturned face that almost touched his own.

She staggered and fell: nearly blinded with the blood that rained down from a deep gash in her forehead; but raising herself, with difficulty, on her knees, drew from her bosom a white handkerchief—Rose Maylie's own—and holding it up, in her folded hands, as high towards Heaven as her feeble strength would allow, breathed one prayer for mercy to her Maker.

It was a ghastly figure to look upon. The murderer staggering backward to the wall, and shutting out the sight with his hand, seized a heavy club and struck her down.

The Flight of Sikes

Dickens's evocation of Sikes's state of mind after the murder of Nancy must be one of the most stunning passages in all Dickens's works. It pre-empts the darker mood and the interest in complex psychological states that is often associated with Dickens's later works. In the case of Sikes, he is obsessed with the blood stains he is unable to remove, his obsession echoing that of Shakespeare's Lady Macbeth who cannot cope with the aftermath of murders she encouraged her husband to commit. The symbolism of the blood stains is reinforced by the appearance in this chapter of a mountebank selling potions for stains who could have been drawn straight from Shakespeare. More striking and complexly rendered, however, is the image of Nancy's lifeless eyes that brands itself on Sikes's consciousness. There are many ways in which we could read Sikes's reaction to the murder, and this is one of the advantages of Dickens's implicit, dramatic technique: his response could suggest a guilty conscience, fear, a realization of his love for Nancy, a realization of Nancy's love for him (and his consequent isolation), and a consciousness of his barbarism. The idea of Sikes as worse than animalistic is reinforced at the end of the chapter when even his dog double, Bull's-eye, abandons him, after Sikes tries to murder him. However we read Sikes's motivation, what is interesting in the passage is that, paradoxically, murder has humanized him in the eyes of the reader, even if the human we see is a violent murderer. Whereas Fagin seems to feel nothing in the dock, Sikes's emotions take over when he has taken Nancy's life. The incident when Sikes helps to put out a fire shows him desperately trying to escape from himself as much as it shows any compassion; he wants to lose his individuality by merging with the group. The recklessness with which he does so has something self-destructive about it, just as his attempt to kill his double, Bull's-eye, is symbolically in keeping with the self-hanging that eventually takes his life. In the emotional economy of Dickens's novels, excess always doubles back on itself.

In this passage, Dickens employs one of his characteristic techniques: he animates the inanimate and vice versa (see **p. 135**). The 'uncanny' use of eye imagery is crucial to this exchange in this passage. For Dickens, eyes are ideally the mirrors of the soul; hence, one of his most disturbing yet frequent images is that of eyes that betray surface but no depth. This image suggests a severing of outward expression from inner life: Nancy is 'a corpse endowed with the mere machinery of life'. Lifeless eyes are also, of course, used to describe corpses, or to hint at death. More complexly, Dickens's eye imagery foregrounds the ambivalence that attends the idea of interiority in his novels (see my comments on the related use of eye imagery in Fagin's trial scene, **pp. 177–8**). Sikes is strangely humanized when haunted by Nancy's 'glassy' eyes because it is only then that he values what he has lost: emotional connectedness with other human beings. The image of Nancy's eyes, for example, frightens Sikes, partly because they turn him into an object. Lack of sympathy from an audience or companion turns the person under scrutiny into an object – from the outside if not the inside – and this feeling of intense isolation turns Sikes, paradoxically, into a subject from the perspective of the reader.

Dickens is rightly renowned for his powerful dramatizations of the deviant psyche. What is partly at stake in Dickens's remarkable dramatizations of the emotional life of villains at moments of crisis is indeed the moral and social function of the imagination. The established explanation of the unrivalled power of such passages derives from the biographical, psychoanalytic work of Wilson and House (see **pp. 64–7**): the artist, that is, psychologically identifies with the alienation of the outsider or the criminal. Anti-social alienation as well as guilt are preconditions of imagination. Another way of explaining the imaginativeness of the murderer, however, foregrounds the notion of sympathy and connectedness. Characters such as Sikes seem, after all, by common assent, most human (and least villainous) when they are most imaginative. It is only when socially sanctioned emotional connections are severed that their value is realized. Consciousness of the self in an emotional relation to others is thus a precondition of imagination. The fact that this consciousness occurs after violent, anti-social acts is of course in keeping with the House/Wilson theory of imagination. But the idea that imagination is associated solely with criminality in Dickens is too simple. Dickens's ambivalent attitudes to imagination, as they express themselves in the Dickens canon as a whole (including, of course, *Hard Times*), are as much about the role of the imagination in forging socially constructive, emotional connections between people as they are about the anti-social properties of the imagination.

CHAPTER XLVIII
THE FLIGHT OF SIKES

[. . .]

[. . .] He had plucked it off again. And there was the body—mere flesh and blood, no more – but such flesh, and so much blood!

He struck a light, kindled a fire, and thrust the club into it. There was hair upon the end, which blazed and shrunk into a light cinder, and, caught by the air, whirled up the chimney. Even that frightened him, sturdy as he was; but he held the weapon till it broke, and then piled it on the coals to burn away, and smoulder into ashes. He washed himself, and rubbed his clothes; there were spots that would not be removed, but he cut the pieces out, and burnt them. How those stains were dispersed about the room! The very feet of the dog were bloody.

All this time he had, never once, turned his back upon the corpse; no, not for a moment. Such preparations completed, he moved, backward, towards the door: dragging the dog with him, lest he should soil his feet anew and carry out new evidences of the crime into the streets. He shut the door softly, locked it, took the key, and left the house.

[. . .]

He went on doggedly; but as he left the town behind him, and plunged into the solitude and darkness of the road, he felt a dread and awe creeping upon him which shook him to the core. Every object before him, substance or shadow, still or moving, took the semblance of some fearful thing; but these fears were nothing compared to the sense that haunted him of that morning's ghastly figure following at his heels. He could trace its shadow in the gloom, supply the smallest item of the outline, and note how stiff and solemn it seemed to stalk along. He could hear its garments rustling in the leaves; and every breath of wind came laden with that last low cry. If he stopped it did the same. If he ran, it followed—not running too: that would have been a relief: but like a corpse endowed with the mere machinery of life, and borne on one slow melancholy wind that never rose or fell.

At times, he turned, with desperate determination, resolved to beat this phantom off, though it should look him dead; but the hair rose on his head, and his blood stood still, for it had turned with him and was behind him then. He had kept it before him that morning, but it was behind now—always. He leaned his back against a bank, and felt that it stood above him, visibly out against the cold night-sky. He threw himself upon the road—on his back upon the road. At his head it stood, silent, erect, and still—a living grave-stone, with its epitaph in blood.

Let no man talk of murderers escaping justice, and hint that Providence must sleep. There were twenty score of violent deaths in one long minute of that agony of fear.

There was a shed in a field he passed, that offered shelter for the night. Before the door, were three tall poplar trees, which made it very dark within; and the wind moaned through them with a dismal wail. He *could not* walk on, till daylight came again; and here he stretched himself close to the wall—to undergo new torture.

For now, a vision came before him, as constant and more terrible than that from which he had escaped. Those widely staring eyes, so lustreless and so glassy, that he had better borne to see them than think upon them, appeared in the midst of the darkness; light in themselves, but giving light to nothing. There were but two, but they were everywhere. If he shut out the sight, there came the room with every well-known object—some, indeed, that he would have forgotten, if he had gone over its contents from memory—each in its accustomed place. The body was in *its* place, and its eyes were as he saw them when he stole away. He got up, and rushed into the field without. The figure was behind him. He re-entered the shed, and shrunk down once more. The eyes were there, before he had lain himself along.

[. . .]

The Pursuit of Sikes at Jacob's Island and his Death

The episode in which Sikes flees to Jacob's Island and the pursuit of him to his death exhibit two kinds of writing for which Dickens has rightly become renowned: descriptions of the city, (especially 'low-life' scenes), and of the mob mentality. In many ways, these descriptions should speak for themselves. In both, detail upon detail is piled up to excess until we feel that we are in the 'maze of close, narrow, and muddy streets', baying for the blood of the murderer. Dickens was making a didactic point in the description of the poor sanitary conditions in the once-thriving Jacob's Island. The intensity with which Dickens argues for improvements in the sanitary conditions for the poor is made explicit in the 1850 Preface to the novel (see **pp. 124–7**), though the pleas made in a Preface surely cannot be as effective an instrument of reform as an artistic representation such as this. As so often in Dickens's works, visual detail argues a point. The mob scene – reminiscent of the lynch mobs that were not uncommon before reform of the criminal law – foreshadows similar scenes in *Barnaby Rudge* and *A Tale of Two Cities*: people lose their sense of individual identity as they become swept up by something larger than themselves, in this instance, a 'current' and a 'field of corn moved by an angry wind'. These images suggest a natural force and in Dickens's mob scene, there is the sense that people's behaviour transforms beyond recognition in a passionate group. Even when the impulse behind the mob is moral, as it is in this scene, there is something violent and disturbing about mob behaviour. The effect in this scene is that paradoxically, the mob takes on something of Sikes's aggressive energies while Sikes becomes their victim. He is not a victim we feel sorry for, however – his defiance resembles that of the villains of stage melodrama, and Charley Bates's uncharacteristic passionate attack on Sikes (not reprinted here) aligns the reader's feelings on the 'side of good'. Do readers thus become part of the lynch mob and experience 'the universal eagerness for [his] capture'? Sikes's eventual death by hanging is symbolically fitting and the ambiguity surrounding its depiction is in keeping with both Sikes's character and the moral pattern of the novel. His murder of Nancy literally comes back to haunt and destroy him, the image of Nancy's eyes prompting a death which is both accidental and self-directed (in the sense that the image of the eyes is created by his imagination). The dog's death contains a similar mixture of obvious and ambiguous symbolism. Taken in isolation it could seem corny and it is undoubtedly stylized, but in the context of the reading experience, it is a satisfying full stop to the scene. To use the terms Dickens's narrator uses to describe melodramatic art in Chapter 17, during this scene we are 'busy actors, instead of passive lookers-on [. . .] blind to violent transitions and abrupt impulses of passion or feeling, which, presented before the eyes of mere spectators, are at once described as outrageous and preposterous' (see **p. 153**).

CHAPTER L

THE PURSUIT AND ESCAPE

NEAR to that part of the Thames on which the church at Rotherhithe[1] abuts, where the buildings on the banks are dirtiest and the vessels on the river blackest with the dust of colliers[2] and the smoke of close-built low-roofed houses, there exists, at the present day, the filthiest, the strangest, the most extraordinary of the many localities that are hidden in London, wholly unknown, even by name, to the great mass of its inhabitants.

To reach this place, the visitor has to penetrate through a maze of close, narrow, and muddy streets, thronged by the roughest and poorest of water-side people, and devoted to the traffic they may be supposed to occasion. The cheapest and least delicate provisions are heaped in the shops; the coarsest and commonest articles of wearing apparel dangle at the salesman's door, and stream from the house-parapet and windows. Jostling with unemployed labourers of the lowest class, ballast-heavers, coal-whippers,[3] brazen women, ragged children, and the very raff and refuse of the river, he makes his way with difficulty along, assailed by offensive sights and smells from the narrow alleys which branch off on the right and left, and deafened by the clash of ponderous waggons that bear great piles of merchandise from the stacks of warehouses that rise from every corner. Arriving, at length, in streets remoter and less-frequented than those through which he has passed, he walks beneath tottering house-fronts projecting over the pavement, dismantled walls that seem to totter as he passes, chimneys half crushed half hesitating to fall, windows guarded by rusty iron bars that time and dirt have almost eaten away, and every imaginable sign of desolation and neglect.

In such a neighbourhood, beyond Dockhead in the Borough of Southwark, stands Jacob's Island, surrounded by a muddy ditch, six or eight feet deep and fifteen or twenty wide when the tide is in, once called Mill Pond, but known in these days as Folly Ditch. It is a creek or inlet from the Thames, and can always be filled at high water by opening the sluices[4] at the Lead Mills from which it took its old name. At such times, a stranger, looking from one of the wooden bridges

---

1 St Mary's at Rotherhithe, next to Bermondsey on the south bank of the river.
2 Coal-ships bringing coal from northern coalfields.
3 Ballast-heavers shoveled sand and gravel ballast from dredgers into empty vessels which needed ballast. Coal-whippers transferred coal into barges from the collier.
4 Sliding gates or mechanisms for controlling the flow or volume of water.

thrown across it at Mill-lane, will see the inhabitants of the houses on either side lowering from their back-doors and windows, buckets, pails, domestic utensils of all kinds, in which to haul the water up; and when his eye is turned from these operations to the houses themselves, his utmost astonishment will be excited by the scene before him. Crazy wooden galleries common to the backs of half a dozen houses, with holes from which to look upon the slime beneath; windows, broken and patched: with poles thrust out, on which to dry the linen that is never there; rooms so small, so filthy, so confined, that the air would seem too tainted even for the dirt and squalor which they shelter; wooden chambers thrusting themselves out above the mud, and threatening to fall into it—as some have done; dirt-besmeared walls and decaying foundations; every repulsive lineament of poverty, every loathsome indication of filth, rot, and garbage; all these ornament the banks of Folly Ditch.[5]

In Jacob's Island, the warehouses are roofless and empty; the walls are crumbling down; the windows are windows no more; the doors are falling into the streets; the chimneys are blackened, but they yield no smoke. Thirty or forty years ago, before losses and chancery suits[6] came upon it, it was a thriving place; but now it is a desolate island indeed. The houses have no owners; they are broken open, and entered upon by those who have the courage; and there they live, and there they die. They must have powerful motives for a secret residence, or be reduced to a destitute condition indeed, who seek a refuge in Jacob's Island.

[. . .]

'Damn you!' cried the desperate ruffian, throwing up the sash and menacing the crowd. 'Do your worst! I'll cheat you yet!'

Of all the terrific yells that ever fell on mortal ears, none could exceed the cry of the infuriated throng. Some shouted to those who were nearest, to set the house on fire; others roared to the officers to shoot him dead. Among them all, none showed such fury as the man on horseback, who, throwing himself out of the saddle, and bursting through the crowd as if he were parting water, cried, beneath the window, in a voice that rose above all others, 'Twenty guineas to the man who brings a ladder!'

The nearest voices took up the cry, and hundreds echoed it. Some called for ladders, some for sledge-hammers; some ran with torches to and fro as if to seek them, and still came back and roared again; some spent their breath in impotent curses and execrations; some pressed forward with the ecstasy of madmen, and thus impeded the progress of those below; some among the boldest attempted to climb up by the water-spout and crevices in the wall; and all waved to and fro, in the darkness beneath, like a field of corn moved by an angry wind: and joined from time to time in one loud furious roar.

[. . .]

On pressed the people from the front—on, on, on, in a strong struggling current of angry faces, with here and there a glaring torch to light them up, and shew them

---

5 The specificity of the location implies that Dickens believed that this low-life setting would be unknown to many readers. Dockhead was at the head of St Saviour's in Bermondsey, a tidal creek. Folly Ditch, originally Mill Pond, served the mill of Bermondsey Abbey.

6 Legal disputes about wills and property that ended up in the Court of Chancery. Dickens satirized Chancery's notorious slowness in *Bleak House* (1852–3).

out in all their wrath and passion. The houses on the opposite side of the ditch had been entered by the mob; sashes were thrown up, or torn bodily out; there were tiers and tiers of faces in every window; cluster upon cluster of people clinging to every house-top. Each little bridge (and there were three in sight) bent beneath the weight of the crowd upon it. Still the current poured on, to find some nook or hole from which to vent their shouts, and only for an instant see the wretch.

[. . .]

There was another roar. At this moment the word was passed among the crowd that the door was forced at last, and that he who had first called for the ladder had mounted into the room. The stream abruptly turned, as this intelligence ran from mouth to mouth; and the people at the windows, seeing those upon the bridges pouring back, quitted their stations, and, running into the street, joined the concourse that now thronged pell-mell to the spot they had left: each man crushing and striving with his neighbour, and all panting with impatience to get near the door, and look upon the criminal as the officers brought him out. The cries and shrieks of those who were pressed almost to suffocation, or trampled down and trodden under foot in the confusion, were dreadful; the narrow ways were completely blocked up; and at this time, between the rush of some to regain the space in front of the house, and the unavailing struggles of others to extricate themselves from the mass, the immediate attention was distracted from the murderer, although the universal eagerness for his capture was, if possible, increased.

[. . .]

Roused into new strength and energy, and stimulated by the noise within the house which announced that an entrance had really been effected, he set his foot against the stack of chimneys, fastened one end of the rope tightly and firmly round it, and with the other made a strong running noose by the aid of his hands and teeth almost in a second. He could let himself down by the cord to within a less distance of the ground than his own height, and had his knife ready in his hand to cut it then and drop.

At the very instant when he brought the loop over his head previous to slipping it beneath his arm-pits, and when the old gentleman before-mentioned (who had clung so tight to the railing of the bridge as to resist the force of the crowd, and retain his position) earnestly warned those about him that the man was about to lower himself down—at that very instant the murderer, looking behind him on the roof, threw his arms above his head, and uttered a yell of terror.

'The eyes again!' he cried in an unearthly screech.

Staggering as if struck by lightning, he lost his balance and tumbled over the parapet. The noose was on his neck. It ran up with his weight, tight as a bowstring, and swift as the arrow it speeds. He fell for five-and-thirty feet. There was a sudden jerk, a terrific convulsion of the limbs; and there he hung, with the open knife clenched in his stiffening hand.

The old chimney quivered with the shock, but stood it bravely. The murderer swung lifeless against the wall; and the boy,[7] thrusting aside the dangling body which obscured his view, called to the people to come and take him out, for God's sake.

---

7   Charley Bates.

A dog, which had lain concealed till now,[8] ran backwards and forwards on the parapet with a dismal howl, and collecting himself for a spring, jumped for the dead man's shoulders. Missing his aim, he fell into the ditch, turning completely over as he went; and striking his head against a stone, dashed out his brains.

Fagin's Trial and Fagin in the Condemned Cell

Fagin's trial scene is a brilliant set-piece scene. The exact nature of the charges levelled against him is not specified, and some critics have argued that in reality, Fagin would not have been hanged (see, for example, **pp. 60–1**). Paroissien argues that Fagin would have been hanged for being 'an accessory before the fact' (Chapter 50) to murder but not to theft.[1] Dickens was never overly concerned with factual detail, however, and hanging is clearly the poetic justice required for a villain who has made fear of hanging a tool of intimidation in his abuse of others. What is interesting, however, is that Dickens chooses not to represent Fagin's execution. This is possibly because of the anti-capital punishment stance Dickens adopted vociferously in the 1840s. Even when Dickens became more ambivalent about the issue in later years, however, he remained consistent about the degrading effects of watching public executions on the crowd observing.[2]

His trial would have taken place in the Old Bailey, and the way in which 'the Jew' is isolated and scrutinized by the viewing public is reminiscent of Shakespeare's representation of Shylock in court in The Merchant of Venice. The scene is also in some ways reminiscent of modern trials of those whom society has deemed incomparably evil – war criminals or serial killers, for example. The eeriness of the scene is evoked by the complete emotional dislocation between Fagin and those watching in the courtroom. Justice for the passionless villain is itself passionless, whereas in Sikes's case, it was fittingly passionate. The lack of any emotional connection between Fagin and others is relayed here through the same eye imagery that seemed to transform Sikes. Fagin is 'surrounded by a firmament, all bright with gleaming eyes' but 'in no one face could he read the faintest sympathy with himself'. The objectification of 'the Jew' tells us something about the way racism works as well as the way in which society dehumanizes criminals that are seen as beyond the pale.[3] What is shocking about this scene, however, is the way in which Fagin is emotionless in response. His dislocated responses to his arrest indeed foreshadow Albert Camus's existentialist rendering of the mind of the prisoner in L'Étranger (1946). What is striking about the invisible life of a passionless villain such as Fagin is the

---

8   Cruikshank's plate appears to contradict the text. It shows Sikes's dog on top of the roof, near the chimney.

1   Paroissien, Companion to OT, p. 274.
2   See Philip Collins, Dickens and Crime, 2nd edn (London: Macmillan, 1965).
3   See Stein, Victoria's Year, pp. 168–9.

lack of imagination that informs the view of the courtroom. He itemizes his audience as they objectify him: factually and unimaginatively. It is in fact the sense of superficiality and materiality that attends his vision which makes it so startling: surfaces are meaningless beyond themselves. The relationship between 'objects' and 'life and animation' is indeed under scrutiny throughout the passage (see my comments on the relationship between the inanimate and the inanimate in the Sikes scenes earlier, **p. 171**).

Also embedded in this scene is a complex symbolic analysis of the relationship between subjectivity and objectivity and of the role of the artist in representing subjectivity, objectivity and, indeed, criminality. Fagin sees an artist in the court 'sketching his face in a little note-book' and 'he wondered whether it was like'. After his sentence is pronounced, Fagin seems transformed from an artist's object into an artistic object: '[H]e stood, like a marble figure, without the motion of a nerve'. When Sikes is on the run, by contrast, he is humanized by his heightened awareness of his surroundings. His surroundings and his imaginings are, in fact, the objective correlative of his guilt and fear. In the case of Sikes, he becomes imaginative after the murder of Nancy in a way he was not before.

Cruikshank's role in the creation of Fagin is interesting here. Cruikshank is said to have told George Hodder that he discovered the pose for the startling illustration of Fagin in the condemned cell accidentally when 'he sat up in bed one morning with his hand covering his chin and the tips of his fingers between his lips' and saw himself in the mirror.[4] Though he later denied the story, the idea of Fagin as a wicked artist haunts the text.[5] The illustration has also been seen as anti-Semitic, Fagin resembling a frightened rodent, and it no doubt intensified the insights of the text here, and vice versa. Oliver's visit to Fagin in the cell is especially effective. Although Paroissien relates Brownlow's justification for the visit to the evangelical fervour for inculcating virtue,[6] the visit is also an aesthetic opportunity for a last showdown between 'good' and 'evil'. Having refused religious support, Fagin's denial of reality in Oliver's presence suggests a breakdown unexpected in a villain of such detachment; yet it is also brilliantly in keeping with his creation of fictions throughout the text. What is unexpectedly moving and disturbing is the fact that he has now become detached from the reality of his situation and not simply from emotions. A moral ending ('crime doesn't pay') coexists with a scene of great psychological power and complexity.

CHAPTER LII
THE JEW'S LAST NIGHT ALIVE

THE court was paved, from floor to roof, with human faces. Inquisitive and eager eyes peered from every inch of space. From the rail before the dock, away into the sharpest angle of the smallest corner in the galleries, all looks were fixed upon one

---

4 Paroissien, *Companion to OT*, p. 289.
5 See Hillis Miller, **pp. 73–5** and Stein, *Victoria's Year*, pp. 168–9.
6 Paroissien, *Companion to OT*, p. 288.

man—the Jew. Before him and behind: above, below, on the right and on the left: he seemed to stand surrounded by a firmament, all bright with gleaming eyes.

He stood there, in all this glare of living light, with one hand resting on the wooden slab before him, the other held to his ear, and his head thrust forward to enable him to catch with greater distinctness every word that fell from the presiding judge, who was delivering his charge to the jury. At times, he turned his eyes sharply upon them to observe the effect of the slightest featherweight in his favour; and when the points against him were stated with terrible distinctness, looked towards his counsel, in mute appeal that he would, even then, urge something in his behalf. Beyond these manifestations of anxiety, he stirred not hand or foot. He had scarcely moved since the trial began; and now that the judge ceased to speak, he still remained in the same strained attitude of close attention, with his gaze bent on him, as though he listened still.

A slight bustle in the court, recalled him to himself. Looking round, he saw that the jurymen had turned together, to consider of their verdict. As his eyes wandered to the gallery, he could see the people rising above each other to see his face: some hastily applying their glasses to their eyes: and others whispering their neighbours with looks expressive of abhorrence. A few there were, who seemed unmindful of him, and looked only to the jury, in impatient wonder how they could delay. But in no one face—not even among the women, of whom there were many there—could he read the faintest sympathy with himself, or any feeling but one of all-absorbing interest that he should be condemned.

As he saw all this in one bewildered glance, the death-like stillness came again, and looking back, he saw that the jurymen had turned towards the judge. Hush!

They only sought permission to retire.

He looked, wistfully, into their faces, one by one, when they passed out, as though to see which way the greater number leant; but that was fruitless. The jailer touched him on the shoulder. He followed mechanically to the end of the dock, and sat down on a chair. The man pointed it out, or he would not have seen it.

He looked up into the gallery again. Some of the people were eating, and some fanning themselves with handkerchiefs; for the crowded place was very hot. There was one young man sketching his face in a little note-book. He wondered whether it was like, and looked on when the artist broke his pencil-point, and made another with his knife, as any idle spectator might have done.

In the same way, when he turned his eyes towards the judge, his mind began to busy itself with the fashion of his dress, and what it cost, and how he put it on. There was an old fat gentleman on the bench, too, who had gone out, some half an hour before, and now come back. He wondered within himself whether this man had been to get his dinner, what he had had, and where he had had it; and pursued this train of careless thought until some new object caught his eye and roused another.

Not that, all this time, his mind was, for an instant, free from one oppressive overwhelming sense of the grave that opened at his feet; it was ever present to him, but in a vague and general way, and he could not fix his thoughts upon it. Thus, even while he trembled, and turned burning hot at the idea of speedy death, he fell to counting the iron spikes[7] before him, and wondering how the head of one had been broken off, and whether they would mend it, or leave it as it was. Then, he thought of all the horrors of the gallows and the scaffold—and stopped to watch a man sprinkling the floor to cool it—and then went on to think again.

At length there was a cry of silence, and a breathless look from all towards the door. The jury returned, and passed him close. He could glean nothing from their faces; they might as well have been of stone. Perfect stillness ensued—not a rustle—not a breath—Guilty.

The building rang with a tremendous shout, and another, and another, and then it echoed loud groans that gathered strength as they swelled out, like angry thunder. It was a peal of joy from the populace outside, greeting the news that he would die on Monday.

[. . .]

He sat down on a stone bench opposite the door, which served for seat and bedstead; and casting his blood-shot eyes upon the ground, tried to collect his thoughts. After a while, he began to remember a few disjointed fragments of what the judge had said: though it had seemed to him, at the time, that he could not hear a word. These gradually fell into their proper places, and by degrees suggested more: so that in a little time he had the whole, almost as it was delivered. To be hanged by the neck, till he was dead—that was the end. To be hanged by the neck till he was dead.

As it came on very dark, he began to think of all the men he had known who had died upon the scaffold; some of them through his means. They rose up, in such quick succession, that he could hardly count them. He had seen some of them die,—and had joked too, because they died with prayers upon their lips. With what a rattling noise the drop went down; and how suddenly they changed, from strong and vigorous men to dangling heaps of clothes!

Some of them might have inhabited that very cell—sat upon that very spot. It was very dark; why didn't they bring a light? The cell had been built for many years. Scores of men must have passed their last hours there. It was like sitting in a vault strewn with dead bodies—the cap,[8] the noose, the pinioned arms,[9] the faces that he knew, even beneath that hideous veil—Light, light!

[. . .]

'Outside, outside,' replied the Jew, pushing the boy before him towards the door, and looking vacantly over his head. 'Say I've gone to sleep—they'll believe *you*. You can get me out, if you take me so. Now then, now then!'

'Oh! God forgive this wretched man!' cried the boy with a burst of tears.

'That's right, that's right,' said the Jew. 'That'll help us on. This door first. If I shake and tremble, as we pass the gallows, don't you mind, but hurry on. Now, now, now!'

'Have you nothing else to ask him, sir?' inquired the turnkey.

[. . .]

Day was dawning when they again emerged. A great multitude had already

---

7   On the corners of the railing around the dock.

8   A square black cap, known as the sentence cap, which a judge put on when he pronounced judgment.

9   Just before execution, the condemned prisoner's arms were bound.

Figure 9 **George Cruikshank, 'Fagin in the Condemned Cell', Dickens House Museum.**

assembled; the windows were filled with people, smoking and playing cards to beguile the time; the crowd were pushing, quarrelling, and joking. Everything told of life and animation, but one dark cluster of objects in the centre of all—the black stage, the cross-beam, the rope, and all the hideous apparatus of death.

The Happy Ending

The happy ending of the novel fulfils the generic expectations of melodrama or fairy tale: Virtue triumphs and Vice is punished. It is possible to criticise the ending for sentimentality and unreality. It is also true that goodness is the preserve of the middle classes at the end of the novel. The sole exception to the association between goodness and gentility is Charley Bates, who, 'appalled by Sikes's crime, fell into a train of reflection whether an honest life was not, after all, the best', and concluding that it was, became 'the merriest young grazier in all Northamptonshire'. However, the character of Monks (whose name was probably influenced by the villainous monk protagonist of Matthew Gregory Lewis's gothic novel, *The Monk* (1796)) complicates the ending: legit-imate but bad, he dies of the fits (probably epilepsy) to which he is prone, a fact which functions symbolically to suggest the link between degeneracy and legit-imacy rather than to evoke sympathy. It is furthermore worth remembering that the novel ends with a sympathetic reminder of Oliver's dead mother Agnes, who was 'weak and erring'. The final plate showing 'Rose Maylie and Oliver' looking at the inscription of Agnes's name on a tablet in church replaced the domestic 'Fireside' plate (see **p. 9**) and troubles the association between goodness and 'home' that in other respects the ending works to promote.

The matter of the sentimentality and unreality of the ending is also compli-cated. The ending is clearly sentimental and improbable, but this is only a prob-lem artistically if we regard the novel as a realist text. While the novel is a hybrid of the realist and the anti-realist, for this reader in any case, the novel is closer to fairy tale and allegory than to classic realism, and any ending other than the conventional 'happy ending' would have been artistically unsatisfying, lacking the sense of closure that the novel leads us to expect. While it is easy to criticize the ending, it is a useful classroom exercise to imagine the effect on the novel of another kind of ending.

CHAPTER LIII
AND LAST

THE fortunes of those who have figured in this tale, are nearly closed. The little that remains to their historian to relate, is told in a few and simple words.

Before three months had passed, Rose Fleming and Harry Maylie were mar-ried, in the village church which was henceforth to be the scene of the young clergyman's labours; on the same day they entered into possession of their new and happy home.

Mrs. Maylie took up her abode with her son and daughter-in-law, to enjoy, during the tranquil remainder of her days, the greatest felicity that age and worth can know—the contemplation of the happiness of those on whom the warmest affections and tenderest cares of a well-spent life, have been unceasingly bestowed.

[. . .]

Monks, still bearing that assumed name, retired, with his portion, to a distant part of the New World; where, having quickly squandered it, he once more fell into his old courses, and, after undergoing a long confinement for some fresh act of fraud and knavery, at length sunk under an attack of his old disorder, and died in prison. As far from home, died the chief remaining members of his friend Fagin's gang.

Mr. Brownlow adopted Oliver as his own son. [. . .]

5

Further Reading

Further Reading

Recommended Editions of *Oliver Twist*

Various editions of the novel were produced during Dickens's lifetime and there are many different editions of the novel available today.

Kathleen Tillotson (ed.), *Oliver Twist* (Oxford: Clarendon Press, 1966). Based on the 1846 edition of the novel, the 'Clarendon edition' is the definitive scholarly edition. It was prohibitively expensive and is now out of print, but is available in many university libraries.

Stephen Gill (ed.), *Oliver Twist*, Oxford World's Classics (Oxford: Oxford University Press, 1999). The Oxford World's Classics edition of *Oliver Twist* reprints the text used by the Clarendon edition and also makes available some of its scholarly apparatus. The World's Classics edition is not much more expensive than the very cheapest editions and, unlike some cheap editions, it includes indispensable background information on the novel in appendices, notes and a bibliography, as well as the 1841 Preface to the novel in full.

Recommended Critical Works

There are many good critical works on Dickens and *Oliver Twist*, and students should exercise their own judgment when exploring the texts available. The critical works listed here have all helped me to rethink the text and Dickens's work in new and productive ways. They were not included in the extracts above either for reasons of copyright or because they demand to be read in their entirety (rather than in extract form) to do their arguments justice.

Kathryn Chittick, *Dickens and the 1830s* (Cambridge: Cambridge University Press, 1990). This is a fascinating literary historical study which interweaves a study of Dickens's career until 1841 with an analysis of various 'contexts', demonstrating that Dickens's works were very much of their time and not autonomous 'novels' in the sense that they have often been seen since. Among many areas covered, Chittick looks at reviews of Dickens's work, his editorship, the historical and political context, publishing and literary history, genre, high/low art, and the Newgate debate.

Stephen Connor, ' "They're All in One Story": Public and Private Narratives in *Oliver Twist*', *Dickensian*, 85 (1989), pp. 3–16. Using post-structuralist theory, Connor analyses the novel's self-reflexive interest in narrative. He applies his insights into origins and narrative to both specific textual examples and to the larger cultural concern with the same issues.

Sergei Eisenstein, 'Dickens, Griffith, and Ourselves' (1942) *Selected Works*, edited by Richard Taylor and William Powell, 4 vols (London: British Film Institute, 1996), Vol. III, 193–238 (p. 212). In this seminal analysis of the relationship between film and literature, the Soviet director Sergei Eisenstein positions Dickens as one of the 'ancestors' of film and, interestingly, uses Dickens's name to enhance the prestige of film: 'our cinema is not entirely without an ancestry and a pedigree, a past and traditions, or a rich cultural heritage from earlier epochs' (see **p. 99**). He traces the influence of Dickens's fiction on the work of early film-maker, D. W. Griffith, focusing on the optical qualities they share. He uses *Oliver Twist* to demonstrate Dickens's filmic uses of a technique called 'montage'.

John Kucich, 'Repression and Representation: Dickens's General Economy', *Nineteenth Century Fiction*, 38 (1983), pp. 62–77. Kucich offers a sophisticated way of understanding Dickens's characters not as one-dimensional, psychological representations of real people, but as figural representations, that function in clusters, of drives such as violence and repression. Kucich argues that Dickens abandons 'an essentialist, subject-centred economy of violence and repression for one based on a more transpersonal symbolic order' (p. 67). Between violence and repression, he sees 'a metonymic relation between terms usually seen as oppositional' (p. 69), which is a particularly interesting insight with regard to the relationship between Sikes and Fagin in *Oliver Twist*.

Robert L. Patten, *Charles Dickens and his Publishers* (Oxford: Clarendon Press, 1978). A superbly detailed and scholarly account of the relationship between Dickens and his publishers.

Richard Stein's *Victoria's Year: English Literature and Culture, 1837–38* (Oxford: Oxford University Press, 1987). Genuinely interdisciplinary, on *Oliver Twist* it effortlessly analyses the novel and its illustrations in the context of various discourses of the time (for example, science, political economy, materialism and bestiality).

Robert Tracy, ' "The Old Story" and Inside Stories: Modish Fiction and Fictional Modes in *Oliver Twist*', *Dickens Studies Annual*, 17 (1988), pp. 1–33. A good account of the way in which Dickens makes self-conscious use of different contemporary fictional modes in *Oliver Twist*, including the Newgate novel.

Burton M. Wheeler, 'The Text and Plan of *Oliver Twist*', *Dickens Studies Annual*, 12 (1983), pp. 41–61. In the Clarendon edition of the novel, Kathleen Tillotson claims that Dickens had conceived of the novel *Oliver Twist* as early as 1833. Wheeler's persuasive, scholarly article argues that the novel was begun as a short serial, that four instalments had been published before Dickens decided to make it a novel, and that 'its plot did not take shape even in general form' (p. 41) until seven instalments had been issued.

Reference Works

David Paroissien (ed.), *The Companion to Oliver Twist* (Edinburgh: Edinburgh University Press, 1992). This indispensable companion takes its place in a series which provides, in the words of the series editors, 'the most comprehensive annotation of the works of Dickens ever undertaken'. The annotation is factual rather than critical, elucidating overt and covert allusions and references.

David Paroissien (ed.), *Oliver Twist: An Annotated Bibliography* (New York: Garland, 1986). An excellent bibliography which lists works on areas relating to the novel (for example, Dickens's relevant writings, the Poor Laws, historical background and stage, film and television adaptations), as well as on the novel itself. The first of two planned supplements to this has been published in *Dickens Studies Annual*, 35 (2005), 397, 514.

Paul Schlicke (ed.), *The Oxford Reader's Companion to Dickens* (Oxford: Oxford University Press, 1999). An indispensable guide to Dickens's works and their cultural context. Paul Schlicke's *Oliver Twist* section is extremely helpful and well informed.

INDEX

Note: Page references in italics indicate illustrations

adaptations 1, 95–113, 169
advertising 106–7
Ainsworth, William Harrison 36, 43, 44
alienation 18, 45, 66, 67, 171
alienation effects 152
All Year Round 22, 23
Almar, George 1, 103–5
American Notes 21
'Amusements of the People, The' 96–7
animation 135, 171, 178
Annual Register 24, 26
anti-Semitism 1, 2, 17, 23, 33, 49, 68–70,
    82–84, 108–11, 138–9
'Appeal to Fallen Women, An' 21, 31–3
Artful Dodger 16, 90, 137–8, 143, 164–5
Austen, Jane 19, 130, 156

baby-farming 129, 131 n.3
Balzac, Honoré de 120
Barnaby Rudge 14, 21, 173
Barney 83
Bart, Lionel 1, 95
Barthes, Roland 90
Bates, Charley 16, 90, 143, 164–5, 166–8,
    173, 182
Battle of Life, The 21
Bayley, John 46, 70–1
BBC 95–6, 100
Beadnell, Maria 20
Beard, Thomas 27
Beggar's Opera (Gay) 121–2
Belsey, Catherine 45
Bentham, Jeremy 13, 128, 131 n.5
Bentley, Richard 8–9, 28, 29, 31
Bentley's Miscellany 2, 7, 20, 44, 127;
    Dicken's resigns as editor of 8, 28
Bildungsroman (novel of self-development)
    152
'biographical' critical approach 10–11,
    45–6, 49, 66–7, 71–2
Blathers 159–60
Bleak House 22, 120
Bleasdale, Alan 100, 109, 111–13
body, denial of the 77

books: access to 16; social role of 147
Bow Street runners 159–60
Bowen, John 49, 87–9, 109
Brecht, Bertolt 152
Brontë, Charlotte 21
Brontë, Emily 21
Brownlow, Mr 71, 117, 147, 168, 178, 183
Buller, Charles 51–2
Bulwer Lytton, Sir Edward 38–9, 43, 44,
    119, 122
Bumble, Mr 13, 76, 80, 156
Bunyan, John 48
Burdett Coutts, Angela 21, 31
bureaucracy 17
Burke, Edmund 24

Camus, Albert 177
capital punishment 144 n.4
capitalism 117, 153
carceral institutions 17, 79
caricature 9, 48, 74–5, 137, 145
Carlyle, Thomas 20, 21
castration anxiety 79, 81
catchphrases 147
Cervantes, Miguel de 123
Chadwick, Edwin 13, 15, 17
Chapman and Hall 8
characterization 17–18, 47–8, 54–5, 56, 64,
    102; of the Artful Dodger 137–9; of
    Fagin 18, 49, 69, 83, 90, 137–9; of Sikes
    145–6; of women 17–18, 49, 158, 163
Chartist movement 16
Chesterton, G. K. 47, 63–4, 128
Chickweed, Conkey 159–160
children 12–13, 15, 26, 27, 129, 131 n.3
Child's History of England, A 22
Chimes, The 21
Chittick, Kathryn 16, 187–8
Christmas books 21
Christmas Carol, A 1, 21, 22, 64, 96
chronology 19–23
Chuzzlewit, Jonas 67
city, descriptions of 15, 139, 161, 173
Clarendon edition 2, 10, 187

class 14–18, 43, 44, 46, 49, 62, 65–6, 77–8, 84–7; and language 85–6
Claypole, Noah 136, 165
Collins, Philip 96
Collins, Wilkie 149
commercialism 102, 106–7
connectedness, emotional 171
Connor, Stephen 160
contrasts, use of 71, 72
Cooke, Alistair 96
copyright law 21, 29
Corney, Mrs 156
countryside/nature 58, 72–3, 161
Cowen, William 106–7
Cricket on the Hearth, The 21
crime 15–16, 38–9; glamorization of 16, 43, 90, 120, 143, 155, 164–5
Cruikshank, George 2, 8, 9–10, 30, 44, 70, 71, 74–5, 100; claim as originator of idea for *Oliver Twist* 35–7; and creation of Fagin 36, 178; 'Fagin in the Condemned Cell' *181*; 'Oliver Asking for More' *135*; 'Oliver Introduced to the Respectable Old Gentleman' *142*
cultural background 11–18
culture industry 102
culture-text 1–2

Daily News 21
Daily Telegraph 109, 110–11
Darwin, Charles 22
David Copperfield 20, 21, 22, 23
Davis, Mrs Eliza 17, 33–4
Davis, Paul 1
delinquency 77, 78
Derrida, Jacques 79
Dickens, Charles: on adaptations of his novels 102–3; autobiography 21; biographical and literary background 7–11, 19–23, 49; letters 27–34, 102–3; preface to third edition (1841) 21, 43, 119–24; preface to cheap edition (1850) 17, 124–7
Dickens, Dora 22
Dickens, John 22
dietaries 24–5
'Dinner at Poplar Walk, A' 20
Disney 102
Dombey and Son 21
Dostoevsky, Fyodor 65
dreams 143, 161
Duff 159–60

Edinburgh Review 54–5
education 16
Eisenstein, Sergei 99, 100, 188
Eliot, George 22, 29, 44–5, 87, 137, 143
Eliot, T. S. 139
Elliotson, John 161
emotion 91, 152, 171, 177
Empiricism 161
Engel, Elliott 16
Étranger, L' (Camus) 177
Evangelical religion 75–6
Evening Standard 109
Examiner 14, 51, 52
experimental philosopher, idea of 131 n.5
eye imagery 171, 177

Factory Act (1833) 15
Fagin 13, 15, 18, 30, 48, 57, 82–4, 91, 108–13, 143, 164–5; anti-Semitism and representation of 2, 17, 33, 68–70, 83, 84, 108–13, 138–9; biographical approach to character 45, 71–2; characterization 18, 49, 69, 83, 90, 137–9, 178; Cruikshank's illustrations 74, 83, 100, *142, 181*; origin of character 15, 36, 45, 71–2, 90; stage and screen portrayals 49, 100, *101*, 108–9, 111–13, *146*; trial of 177
Fagin, Bob 34, 45, 71
Fairclough, Peter 11
Fang, Mr 27, 56
fiction market 16
Fielding, Henry 43, 119, 120, 126, 127
film adaptations 1, 95, 96, 99, 100–2, 106–12, 169
Ford, Richard 57–60
Forster, E. M. 47
Forster, John 9; biography of Dickens 21, 23, 34–5, 105; Dickens first meets 20; *Examiner* review 51, 52; letters from Dickens 30–1; and public readings 98
Foucault, Michel 16–17
Fox, W. J. 91
franchise 14, 23
Fraser's Magazine 43, 51, 57, 60–1, 119
freedom, limits on 17, 77
Freud, Sigmund 63 n.1, 87
Froude, Richard Hurrell 58
Furst, Lilian 45

Gill, Stephen 10, 11
Gilmour, Robin 14

Gissing, George 49, 62
Gombrich, E. H. 74
good and evil 13–14, 67, 75–6, 86, 117, 178
Gothic mode 134, 182
Great Expectations 23, 66, 100
Greene, Graham 67, 75
Griffith, D. W. 99, 188
Grimwig, Mr 80, 147
Guardian 109
Guinness, Alec 100, *101*

Haines, Thomas 27
handkerchiefs, symbolic significance of 79–82
Hard Times 13, 22
Haunted Man, The 21
Hayward, Abraham 8
Heller, Deborah 49, 82–4
Hexam, Lizzie 85
Hillis Miller, J. 46–7, 73–5, 79
historical background 11–18, 19–23
Hobsbawm, Eric 73
Hogarth, Catherine 20
Hogarth, Mrs George 28
Hogarth, Mary 7, 11, 20, 27, 28–9, 49, 158
Hogarth, William 9, 54, 123
homosocial relations 48
House, Humphry 10, 34, 45, 46, 66–7, 138, 171
Household Words 22
Hughes, Thomas 22

Idealism 161
identity politics 49
illustrations 2, 9–10, 30, 73–5; *see also* Cruikshank, George
imagination, theory of 171
Independent Review 111
Ingham, Patricia 49, 84–7, 150, 158
irony 130, 136, 153
ITV 100

Jack Sheppard (Ainsworth) 44
Jacob's Island 15, 17, 124–6, 173
James, Henry 10, 45, 70, 73
Jews 1, 2, 17, 33, 66, 68–70, 82–4, 108–13, 138–9
John, Juliet 89–91
Johnson, Barbara 79
Johnson, Edgar 72

Johnson, Samuel 122
Jordan, John O. 79–82

Kaplan, Fred 161
Kettle, Arnold 46, 72
King, Margaret F. 16
Koenig, Rhoda 111
Kucich, John 47–8

Lacan, Jacques 79
Laing, Allan Stewart 27, 28
language and class 85–6
Laurie, Sir Peter 124–5, 126–7
Lean, David 1, 95, 100–1, 107–8, 169
Leavis, F. R. 45
legal system 15
Lesser, Sol 99
Lewes, G. H. 10, 29, 44–5, 53, 130, 147
Lewis, Matthew Gregory 182
Lindsay, Robert 109, 111, 112, 113
Lister, Thomas Henry 54–5
literacy 16
Literary Gazette 56
Little Dorrit 22
Lloyd, Frank 99
London Labour and the London Poor (Mayhew) 15–16
London and Westminster Review 51–2
Lucas, John 72–3

Macheath (*Beggar's Opera*) 122
Macnish, Robert 143, 161
Macready, William 97, 98, 105
Macrone, John 8
Malthus, Thomas 13, 161
Manichaeism 67
Mann, Mrs 129, 130
Marcus, Steven 34, 45–6, 71–2
Martin Chuzzlewit 21
Master Humphrey's Clock 21
Mayhew, Henry 15–16
Maylie, Rose 11, 27, 71, 78, 158–9, 163–4
Meisel, Martin 100
Melbourne, Lord 15, 16, 37, 44
melodrama 48, 91, 145, 151, 152–3
men, relations between 48
Merchant of Venice, The (Shakespeare) 177
mesmerism 161
Metropolitan Sanitary Association 125
Micawber, Mr 22
Michie, Helena 77
Miller, D. A. 49, 77–9, 160

Minerva Press 16
Mirror of Parliament 8
mob mentality 173
Monks 80, 117, 182
montage 99
Monthly Repository 91
morals 43–4, 64, 65, 85, 86
Morning Chronicle 8, 14, 20, 51
Municipal Reform Act (1835) 15
musical adaptations 1, 95, 100
Mystery of Edwin Drood, The 23

Nancy 18, 49, 59, 84–7, 120, 123–4, 149–
    50, 151, 163–4; and denial of the body
    77; form of language 85–6; goodness of
    13–14, 78; as idenitified with truth 87–9;
    murder of 1, 86–7, 95, 97–8, 105–6,
    168–70
National Magazine and Monthly Critic 53,
    130
nature/countryside 58, 72–3, 161
nature/nurture debate 120, 128, 136,
    163
New Criticism 47
the New Poor Law *see* Poor Law
    Amendment Act
Newgate Calendar, The 43, 155, 165, 167
'Newgate' novels 15, 16, 38, 43–4, 89,
    90–1, 119–20, 138, 155
newspapers 16, 109–11
Nicholas Nickleby 20, 21

objectivity 178
Oedipal fantasies 79, 81
Old Curiosity Shop, The 21
Oliver 1, 46, 48, 59, 72–3
Oliver and Company (cartoon film) 102
Oliver! (musical) 1, 95, 100
Orwell, George 65–6
Othello (Shakespeare) 82
Our Mutual Friend 23, 33, 48, 66

paedophilia 48, 112
parody 130
Paroissien, David 12 n.15, 14 n.17, 24, 132
    n.11, 143, 158, 159, 161, 163, 177, 178,
    189
Patmore, Coventry 158
Patten, Robert 9, 188
Paul Clifford (Bulwer Lytton) 38, 119, 122
Peel, Sir Robert 15, 68
People's Charter and National Petition 20

Pickwick Papers, The 8, 9, 20
Pictures from Italy 21
Pilgrim's Progress, The (Bunyan) 48
plagiarism 29
pleasure 91
Poe, Edgar Allan 79
police 15, 77, 78, 159–60
political correctness 100, 111
Poor Law Amendment Act (1834)(the New
    Poor Law) 11, 12–13, 14, 24, 26–7, 46,
    51, 75, 76, 127, 128, 129, 153
Poor Law Commission 12, 24, 25
poor relief 11–14, 76, 127
Pope, Alexander 126
post-structuralism 46–7, 73, 79, 87
press, expansion of the 16
prostitutes/prostitution 15, 31–3, 77, 85
psychoanalytic approach 45, 71–2, 79, 87,
    171
psychological realism 45, 46, 66–7, 137
psychological states 29, 143, 161, 170–1
psychology 29, 45, 48
public executions 144 n.6
public health 15, 17, 124
Public Health Act (1848) 125
'Public Life of Mr Tulrumble, Once Mayor
    of Mudfog' 7, 127
public readings 1, 22, 23, 97–8, 105–6
publishing industry 16
Punch 61–2

Quarterly Review 8, 14, 51, 57–60
queer theory 48

race 49; *see also* Jews, anti-Semitism
racism 17, 177; *see also* anti-Semitism
Rampton, James 111
realism 44–7, 64, 73–5, 120, 182;
    psychological 45–6, 66–7, 137; social 46
Reed, Carol 95
Reform Act (1832) 14
Reform Bill (1867) 23
religion 75–6, 178
repression 48
Riah (the Jew in *Our Mutual Friend*) 33
romance 91, 119–20, 123
Rose, Jacqueline 87
Rosenberg, Brian 47
Rousseau, Jean-Jacques 128

Sadoff, Dianne 81
sanitation 15, 124, 125, 173

satire 9, 48, 53, 130
Schlicke, Paul 8, 189
Scott, George C. 109
Scott, Sir Walter 19, 126
Scrooge 64–5
Sedgwick, Eve 48–9
self-interest 13, 128, 129
Senior, Nassau 13
serialization 2, 7, 16, 127
Seymour, Robert 9
Shakespeare, William 82, 126, 138, 177
Shelley, Percy Bysshe 9
Shylock 111, 138, 177
Sikes, Bill 30, 48, 120, 124;
    characterization of 145–6; flight and
    death of 170–7; and murder of Nancy 67,
    95–6, 104, 105–6, 168–70
Sketches by Boz 8, 20, 73
sleep 143, 144, 161, 162–3
Smiles, Samuel 22
Smollett, Tobias 123, 126
social background 11–18
social realism 46
social reform 14–15, 46
Solomons, Ikey 15, 68, 90
Spectator 55–6
Spenlow, Dora 20
stage adaptations 1, 95–7, 98, 102–5
Stein, Richard 49–50, 188
stereotypes 69, 83, 138–9, 145
Stone, Harry 17, 49, 68–70
'streaky bacon' passage 151–2
style 44, 45
subjectivity 178
surveillance 17, 77
Sutherland, John 43
sympathy 171

tableaux vivants 100, 169
Taine, Hippolyte 143
Tale of Two Cities, A 14, 22, 173
television adaptations 95–6, 100, 109,
    111–13
Tennyson, Alfred Lord 22
Ternan, Ellen 23
Thackeray, William Makepeace 21, 43, 44,
    51, 57, 60, 138
Tillotson, Kathleen 2, 10, 11, 14, 35, 187,
    188
Times Literary Supplement 109
Tracy, Robert 91–138, 160, 188
True Sun 14, 91
truth, Nancy as identified with 87–9

Urania Cottage 18, 31, 163
urbanization 14, 15
Utilitarianism 13–14, 76, 127, 128

Victoria, Queen 37–8
violence 48, 95–6

Walder, Dennis 75–6, 128
Walkowitz, Judith R. 85
Wheeler, Burton M. 10, 188
Wilson, Edmund 10, 34, 45, 64–5, 138,
    171
women 12–13, 84–9; 'An Appeal to Fallen
    Women' 31–3; characterization of 17–18,
    49, 158, 163; and denial of the body 77;
    hysterical 87–9; *see also* Nancy; Mary
    Hogarth
Wordsworth, William 22
workhouse system 11, 12–13, 24–7, 127

Yates, Frederick 102–3